K·I·S·S

DK

The Only Guides You'll Ever Need!

THIS SERIES IS YOUR TRUSTED GUIDE through all of life's stages and situations. Want to learn how to surf the Internet or care for your new dog? Or maybe you'd like to become a wine connoisseur or an expert gardener? The solution is simple: Just pick up a K.I.S.S. Guide and turn to the first page.

Expert authors will walk you through the subject from start to finish, using simple blocks of knowledge to build your skills one step at a time. Build upon these learning blocks and by the end of the book, you'll be an expert yourself! Or, if you are familiar with the topic but want to learn more, it's easy to dive in and pick up where you left off.

The K.I.S.S. Guides deliver what they promise: simple access to all the information you'll need on one subject. Other titles you might want to check out include: Playing Golf, Managing Your Career, the Internet, Microsoft Windows, Astrology, Sex, and many more.

K.I.S.S

GUIDE TO

Sailing

STEVE SLEIGHT

Foreword by Dennis Conner

America's Cup Champion

A Dorling Kindersley Book

LONDON, NEW YORK, SYDNEY, DELHI, PARIS,
MUNICH, AND JOHANNESBURG

DK Publishing, Inc.

Senior Editor Jennifer Williams
US Consultant Richard Hazelton
Category Publisher LaVonne Carlson

Dorling Kindersley Limited

Project Editor David Tombesi-Walton
Project Art Editor Simon Murrell

Managing Editor Maxine Lewis
Managing Art Editor Heather McCarry

Production Heather Hughes
Category Publisher Mary Thompson

Produced for Dorling Kindersley by

13 SOUTHGATE STREET WINCHESTER HAMPSHIRE SO23 9DZ

Senior Editor Jane Baldock
Senior Art Editor Sharon Moore
Project Editor Kate Hayward
Project Art Editor Laura Watson

Copyright © 2001
DK Publishing, Inc.
Text copyright © 2001 Steve Sleight

2 4 6 8 10 9 7 5 3 1

Published in the United States by DK Publishing, Inc.
95 Madison Avenue, New York, New York 10016

A CIP catalog record for this book is available from the Library of Congress

ISBN 0-7894-8052-2

DK Publishing, Inc. offers special discounts for bulk purchases for sales promotions or premiums. Specific, large-quantity needs can be met with special editions, including personalized covers, excerpts of existing guides, and corporate imprints. For more information, contact Special Markets Department, DK Publishing, Inc., 95 Madison Avenue, New York, NY 10016 Fax: 800-600-9098.

Color reproduction by Colourscan
Printed and bound by Printer Industria Grafica, S.A., Barcelona, Spain

For our complete catalog visit

www.dk.com

Contents at a Glance

CONTENTS

PART FOUR Cruiser Sailing Skills

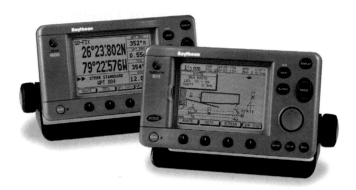

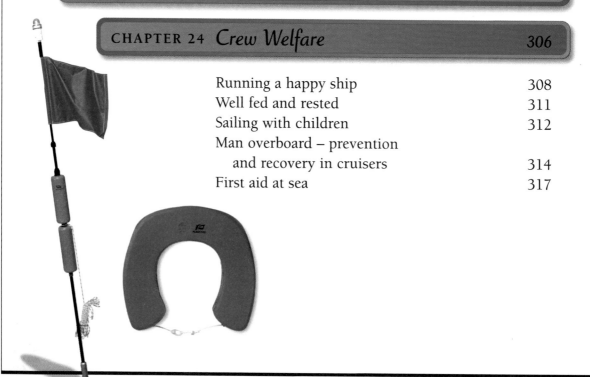

Foreword

NOTHING EVOKES THOUGHTS *of freedom and adventure more than the sight of a sailboat gliding across shimmering waters. No other sport offers so many different ways to enjoy it: from poking around a pond in an El toro or racing dinghies in your local waters, to competing in the Olympics. Little did I know, when I was learning to sail, that it would take me all around the world to four America's Cup Championships.*

But sailing isn't just for those who get a kick from competition. For many, learning to sail is all about the simple pleasure of just sailing around for the day alone or with good friends, while others use their sailing skills to take them from local gunk holes to exotic adventures on the high seas. Sailing has something for everyone – from the beginner right up to the accomplished sailor.

Author Steve Sleight starts with a brief history of sailing, and how it has shaped the world, to give you a sense of the heritage you're about to share when you go afloat. Throughout the book, he encourages would-be sailors to take lessons from a certified sailing school, while using the book as a tool before, during, and after lessons to make sailing safer and more fun.

After going over the basics to get you acquainted with boats and some of the specialized language of sailing, he begins with dinghies – the smallest and simplest of sailboats and, for many, the most fun. It's in these little boats that you learn the skills that will carry through to every kind of sailing you want to do, from the family cruiser to an America's Cup Yacht. In short, if you can sail a dinghy you can sail anything.

After you've gotten a few tacks under your belt, and some proficiency and confidence in your sailing, the book moves onto larger boats. Although they may be bigger and more complicated, you'll soon realize that everything you need to know is rooted in the basics you've already learned. Some of these larger boats are built for competition, while others offer more comfort. In any case, their size enables you to go cruising, sail further, and explore new waters with greater comfort and safety.

If racing is your passion, a larger boat will give you opportunities to enjoy the challenge of handling bigger sails, as well as developing teamwork with a bigger crew. Cruising enthusiasts will need to develop anchoring, reefing, and passage-making skills, not the least of which is navigation. The K.I.S.S. Guide to Sailing shows you how to use a chart for plotting courses and positions, using the tried and true methods that have been used by voyagers for decades. Crucially, this book also covers sailing at night and the international rules and regulations that will prepare you to safely assess and handle situations at sea.

In short, the K.I.S.S. Guide to Sailing provides an excellent foundation in a sport that, after mastering a few basic skills, can be enjoyed for a lifetime. So, whatever course you choose to take, you're off to a good start. Enjoy, and I look forward to crossing tacks with you.

DENNIS CONNER

Introduction

TAKING UP ANY NEW SPORT OR ACTIVITY *can be daunting,
especially if you don't know anyone who can guide you through your first
faltering steps. I hope that this K.I.S.S. Guide to Sailing will be the friend you
need to help you get started in the wonderful sport of sailing.*

*When I started sailing, longer ago than I care to contemplate, it could be quite
difficult to get into the sport if you did not have family or friends who sailed.
Although there were lots of books on the subject, most were fairly technical
and some gave the impression that you had to learn the skills of the Ancient
Mariner before you went afloat!*

STEVE SLEIGHT ABOARD A STARLIGHT 35

*Today, you have many more
opportunities for learning to sail —
and for having lots of fun while you
do so. This book has been written to
get you started on what I hope will
be a life-long involvement with
sailing, and to help you learn the
basic skills and avoid picking up bad
habits along the way. I would not
pretend that you can, or should,
learn to sail solely by reading this or
any book, but by working your way
through the sections that follow, you
will be very well prepared for some
practical, on-the-water training.*

*I hope you will choose to take some
training courses at a good club or
sailing school, where you will be
taught by qualified instructors who*

can ensure that you learn quickly and safely in controlled conditions. As you develop your skill, you can refer back to this guide to reinforce the instruction you receive, and to prepare yourself for learning more advanced skills as you progress through different boats and types of sailing.

Above all, I hope you enjoy your sailing and discover the immense pleasures that are to be had from spending time afloat, whatever type of boat you sail.

Good sailing!

Steve

STEVE SLEIGHT
Cowes
www.stevesleight.com
www.silverpetrel.com

Symbols used in this book		
WIND DIRECTION	TIDE DIRECTION	BOAT DIRECTION

What's Inside?

THE INFORMATION in the K.I.S.S. Guide to Sailing *is arranged from the simple to the more advanced, making it most effective if you start from the beginning and slowly work your way to the more involved chapters.*

PART ONE

In Part One I'll introduce you to the sport of sailing, from its history, to the many types of sailing available today. I'll also tell you how to go about looking for a sailing course.

PART TWO

In Part Two I'll tell you about the principles of handling a small boat and how to start, stop, and steer the boat to change direction. I'll also introduce you to the safety issues.

PART THREE

In Part Three I'll explain what you need to know about weather and water conditions. I will then teach you how to increase your speed with a view to learning to race.

PART FOUR

Part Four builds on your experience, taking you up a level to larger boats. There are specialist skills that you'll need to acquire to maneuver a cruising boat.

PART FIVE

Part Five looks at what you need to know in order to become a competent navigator – from understanding how to use a chart, to becoming proficient in using modern technological navigation tools.

PART SIX

Part Six discusses the issues you'll need to address as skipper of your boat. You need to take steps to ensure your crew are safe and happy and that everyone aboard is fully aware of what to do in the event of an emergency.

The Extras

THROUGHOUT THE BOOK, *you will notice a number of boxes and symbols. They are there to emphasize certain points I want you to pay special attention to, because they are important to your understanding and improvement. You'll find:*

Very Important Point

This symbol points out a topic I believe deserves careful attention. You really need to know this information before continuing.

Complete No-No

This is a warning, something I want to advise you not to do or to be aware of.

Getting Technical

When the information is about to get a bit technical, I'll let you know so that you can read carefully.

Inside Scoop

These are special suggestions that come from my own personal experience. I want to share them with you because they helped me when I was learning to sail.

You'll also find some little boxes that include information I think is important, useful, or just plain fun.

Trivia...

These are simply fun and interesting facts that will give you an extra insight into various aspects of the sport of sailing.

DEFINITION

Here I'll define words and terms for you in an easy-to-understand style. You'll also find a glossary at the back of the book that explains sailing terms.

INTERNET
www.dk.com

The Internet is a great resource for sailors. I've researched several sailing-related web sites to add to your enjoyment and understanding of the sport.

PART ONE

Getting Started

SAILING IS A RICHLY VARIED SPORT with a long history born out of exploration, trade, and more recently, *recreation* and *competition*. Today, there are so many ways to enjoy the sport that you are bound to find a type of sailing that suits your ambitions and abilities.

Let's start by investigating the types of sailing available to you and deciding on the type of boat that will be best for you to learn on. Consider joining a club if there is a suitable one in your area, and explore the options for taking a *sailing course* to get you started. I'll tell you about the basic clothing and safety equipment you will need to keep you warm, dry, and safe, and you'll need to learn the basic language of sailing in preparation for your *first time afloat.*

Chapter 1

Why Go Sailing?

WHAT IS IT ABOUT SAILING that hooks millions of otherwise sane and rational people and causes many of the symptoms of a love affair? Why do so many of us willingly submit to the possibility of getting cold and wet, tired and seasick, or even scared on occasion? The answers are as varied as the sailors you ask, but it's only fair that I try to give you some idea of the background and addictive properties this wonderful sport before you risk permanent infection by the sailing bug.

In this chapter...

✓ A timeless experience

✓ Tasting freedom

✓ A thirst for competition

✓ Something for everyone

FEW PLEASURES CAN EQUAL THE PEACEFUL SIMPLICITY OF BEING AFLOAT

A timeless experience

ONE OF THE MOST POWERFUL *attractions of sailing is its timelessness. Another is its simplicity. By learning the art of handling a boat under sail, you are continuing a practice that dates back thousands of years. The skills are essentially the same as those our ancestors used to explore the world. Yes, today's boats are faster, safer, and more comfortable than those of our predecessors, and life afloat need not be a physical hardship, but the challenge of traveling under sail and the rewards of a safe arrival are little changed and still have few equals.*

An ancient skill

Our seafaring ancestors would probably be astonished at the idea of sailing solely for pleasure. For them it was simply the only way to explore, conquer, and trade with the rest of the world. For thousands of years, up until the invention of the steam engine, the use of sails was the only alternative to rowing and paddling. Now, while rowing and paddling are still essential skills and can be great fun in small doses, it's easy to see why a very enlightened (or lazy) person had the idea of using a sail. In fact, lots of people seem to have had the same idea. All over the world, different types of sailing boats evolved to meet particular local needs. Whether the requirement was to carry cargo or people along rivers, across shallow seas or rough oceans, or to carry troops to invade the neighbors, individual solutions were devised. The successful ones proved their worth at sea and the rest showed where there was room for improvement. The builders and sailors who created and manned these craft developed the skills of design, seamanship, and navigation that stretch in an unbroken line to us today.

■ **The** *Mayflower*, *which carried the Pilgrim Fathers in 1620, epitomizes the importance of sailing in the history of man's exploration and settlement of new lands.*

A sport was born

In the 16th and 17th centuries, Holland was the most powerful seafaring nation in the world, with a huge fleet of sailing ships that maintained the country's trade links with Africa, India, and Southeast Asia. A particular type of small, light, and fast ship was known as a *jaght*, from the Dutch word *jaghen*, which means to pursue or chase. These ships were normally used for transportation and communication in Holland's sheltered waters but, sometimes, their wealthy owners used them for pleasure sailing. In 1660, the English king, Charles II, was given a Dutch *jaght* and the words *yacht* and *yachting* entered the English language. A year later, English shipbuilders had taken up the challenge of improving the Dutch design. The Pett brothers presented the *Catherine* to King Charles and the *Anne* to his brother, the Duke of York. Then, as now, boys and their new toys meant a race. In this case, a race down the River Thames from Greenwich to Gravesend and back. The King won this first recorded competition between two yachts, which was perhaps fortunate or he may have banned the sport before it began.

By the early 19th century, the practice of yachting for pleasure and competition was established among English gentlemen led by the Prince Regent, later to become George IV. From small, if royal, beginnings the idea of sailing for pleasure quickly spread overseas. Today, the International Sailing Federation has 121 member countries, each with their own national organization for the management and development of the sport.

DEFINITION

Because sailing for pleasure started in yachts the sport became known as yachting. Today, the term sailing is more commonly used since it covers all types and sizes of boats, while yachting is specific to sailing larger boats, which usually have some accommodation. Yachting also carries connotations of wealth and social standing as exemplified by the status afforded the various Royal and other "senior" (old) yacht clubs.

Trivia...

The Water Club of Cork in Ireland was the world's first yacht club. It was formed around 1720 but records disappear in the late 18th century. It was reestablished as The Cork Yacht Club in 1828 and became The Royal Cork Yacht Club in 1830.

EQUALITY IN SAILING

Sailing is an equal opportunity sport and there are no skills that a woman cannot master at least as well as a man. In fact, I have often found it easier to teach women since they tend to be more intuitive to changes in boat, wind, and water than men. That said, the demands of political correctness can wreak havoc when trying to write about a sport that developed as a predominantly male activity. Throughout this book, I have used words like "yachtsman" because they are the common terms. Alternatives, such as "yachtsperson," seem to me to be both ugly and unnecessary.

Tasting freedom

CENTRAL TO THE JOY of sailing is the sense of personal freedom that it creates. Each of us who travels under sail, whether over the horizon or across the local pond, experiences the severing, however briefly, of a few of the normal ties with land and society. Accompanied only by the people we choose to sail with, we can explore, relax, or pit our wits and our skill against the elements or other sailors.

■ **Once you are out** *on the water, during the length of your sail, you can enjoy a brief respite from the hassles of life ashore.*

Rules and regulations

Sailing for pleasure is traditionally very lightly regulated, and it is generally possible to sail with minimum, if any, certification or official interference. The requirements that do apply are usually sensible and not onerous. They seek to protect the inexperienced without diminishing the right to enjoy the freedom of the sea. Once we are afloat, we are free to sail how and where we like, with minimal restrictions. Most importantly, we are able to regain the sense of having some direct control over our destiny. We are in charge of the boat and we must rely solely on our knowledge, skills, and effort to get us safely to our destination.

An increasing number of states requires people in charge of larger pleasure boats to hold a certificate of competency, and to conform to specific United States Coast Guard requirements.

Accepting responsibility

If you break down you cannot just pull over to the side and wait for a tow-truck. Sure, rescue services do cover the inland and coastal waters of the US, but they may be unable to reach or find you quickly, if at all. So, with freedom comes responsibility: to your boat, your crew, and yourself. Thousands of years of sailing and modern materials and equipment have not changed the fact that you are exploring an untamed environment and must deal with wind and water on the same terms as sailors always have done.

Ultimately, you are in charge and you must be self-reliant.

Cruising for pleasure

Back in the middle of the 19th century, a few intrepid sailors became the pioneers of *cruising* in small sailing boats. At the time, yachting involved quite large yachts, many of which were used for racing with occasional pleasure voyages for friends and family. Few of the gentlemen or professional sailors of the time would have ever considered actually cruising offshore or making a *passage* in a small boat, but a small number of individualists started to do just that. Those early devotees discovered that cruising out of sight of land, and being solely responsible for your own welfare, brings enormous pleasure. Today, cruising yachts are immensely popular as more and more people are discovering the joys of cruising.

An antidote to modern life

Sailing is often used as an effective way of escaping for a time from the stresses of modern life. Life afloat always seems more relaxed than it does ashore (well, usually!). The world suddenly becomes simpler as the straightforward demands of your boat, the wind, and the tide replace the complex cares of ordinary life. There is little need or room afloat for posturing or arrogance, and the elements will quickly expose these traits. Sailors do well to learn some humility since wind and water, however placid and benign they may seem, are always capable of teaching a harsh lesson. Sailing is a good reminder of the power and scale of nature, and of the insignificance of many of our cares and worries.

Increasing affluence and greater access to sailing has meant that larger numbers of people than ever before are going afloat. Inevitably, a few people bring the aggressions of life ashore with them. These people have little time for learning and expect to be able to sail their boats as easily as they drive their car. They do not appreciate the subtleties of sailing or the strong traditions of a sea-faring heritage that still have relevance whenever we expose ourselves to the vagaries of elementary forces.

Do not be an ignorant sailor. Take the time and make the effort to learn how and why things are done, and respect the rights of other sailors to space, peace, and safe passage. Above all, leave road rage ashore and be prepared to slow down to the natural pace of life afloat.

Choosing the cruising lifestyle

For some sailors the ultimate freedom is to be found living aboard their boats and voyaging to near or distant lands. Ever since the early cruising sailors showed that small sailing boats could make long, transoceanic passages, countless others have elected to join the wandering band of live-aboard cruisers. Most go for a few months or a year or two, and plan to return home once the cruise is over. Others sell-all and sail, hoping to make cruising a permanent lifestyle. A few of these achieve their dreams and spend their time exploring under sail, perhaps staying in favorite places for several months before moving on as the fancy takes them.

However, by far the majority of would-be voyagers never set sail. They dream about the boat they will sail, the places they will visit, and the ocean passages that lie ahead. Many never even learn to sail! Some buy boats that are then left looking sad and unloved in a corner of the boatyard, waiting for their owners to have the time and money to prepare them for the voyage that never comes. The dreams sustain these armchair sailors but they never get to taste the real pleasures of cruising under sail. Do not let yourself miss out on the dream if you are drawn towards the cruising lifestyle. Remember that many successful, long-distance sailors live aboard yachts that are less than 35 ft (11 m) long.

Learn to sail first, then try cruising on other people's boats or charter a yacht for a couple of weeks. Don't wait until you can afford your ideal yacht; start with a small one and go sailing.

■ **Some yachts** are specially designed to be suitable for both comfortable cruising and competitive racing.

A thirst for competition

EVER SINCE KING CHARLES II *and his brother staged the first yacht race on the River Thames, yachtsmen have been ready to challenge each other. From its beginnings until the middle of the 20th century, yacht racing was the realm of the wealthy and well connected. The pinnacle of gentlemen's yachting was probably reached in the 1930s, when the enormous J-Class yachts that were built in the United States and Britain competed for the prestigious America's Cup – the oldest trophy in sport. But that style of racing yacht had become hugely expensive and World War II brought an end to the golden era. Although the war brought a hiatus in yacht racing, it had the side effect of encouraging the development of plywood and new techniques for laminating wood. These proved vitally important in helping the sport of sailing to emerge again in a form that was far more accessible to the general public.*

Small boat racing

The development of plywood also brought about the boom in *dinghy* racing in the 1960s and 1970s. Dozens of new, cheap, and exciting dinghy designs appeared as boatbuilders used the material to build lighter craft. Dinghy racing provided an accessible entry to competitive sailing for a generation of new sailors with increasing leisure time and money. Then, as now, sailing clubs organized racing events to suit all abilities. Today, you can enjoy dinghy racing at any level to match your aspirations. From simple club racing to National, World, and Olympic championships there really is something for everyone who likes the thrill of competition.

DEFINITION

A dinghy *is a small, open boat. Sailing dinghies are powered by sails, while other types of dinghies use oars or an outboard motor. Some general-purpose dinghies can be rowed, sailed, or used with an outboard. Most modern dinghies designed for racing have no provision for oars or an engine.*

■ **Many boat clubs** *stage races for dinghies. Some are for dinghies of the same type – called one-design racing – while others, as here, are for a mixed fleet of different designs.*

Fiberglass appeared as a convenient material for mass-production boatbuilding in the late 1960s and helped fuel the dinghy-racing boom. More recently, the invention of higher-performance materials and new building techniques has led to the development of lighter and more powerful dinghies that are very fast, exciting, and challenging to race.

Big boat racing

Yacht racing reappeared after World War II but in a new form. The yachts were smaller, more affordable, and were sailed by amateur crews. Many racing yachts were also designed to be good cruising yachts, and this dual-purpose nature of the yachts led to the heyday of cruiser racing in the 1970s. Since then, the design of racing yachts has diverged from the needs of cruising as designers have sought to decrease weight to achieve better performance. Today, big boat racing is alive and well with a number of dedicated racing classes of various sizes, complexity, and costs.

Owners of cruising boats or older racing boats can enjoy good local competition, while the dedicated racer can choose between many types of boats and events ranging from around-the-world races to the one-boat-versus-another match racing competition of the America's Cup.

■ **Ellen MacArthur** *is one of the world's leading solo, long-distance racers. She has proved conclusively that age and gender are less important than determination in achieving success at the highest level. Her yacht, Kingfisher, is an Open 60 Class boat designed to be raced singlehanded around the world.*

Something for everyone

YACHTING STARTED AS AN EXCLUSIVE, *expensive sport, accessible only to the rich or privileged. Today, most of the barriers have crumbled, and there are now so many ways of going sailing that you can take part whatever your age or ability. There are still a few stuffy yacht clubs full of "blue blazers" fondly recalling an earlier, more exclusive age, but for those of us who prefer to be less formal, there are plenty of alternatives.*

Young or old

The best time to learn to sail is when you are young, but do not despair if you already count several decades! There is no reason why you cannot start late in life. Sailing is almost unique among sports in that it can be enjoyed, even in competitive racing, at virtually any age – all that is needed is the desire.

■ **Learning to sail** *is an exciting and adventurous activity that many children love.*

Children learn to sail easily as long as they choose to do it and are not pushed into it by their parents. From a young age, children learn rapidly by doing and can be put into simple, stable dinghies on sheltered water and allowed to learn by experimenting to find out what works (and what doesn't).

Learning life skills

Sailing is often used in adventure-training schemes to help under-privileged or antisocial young people learn about themselves and find new ways of relating to others. Sailing aboard larger boats as part of a crew builds teamwork skills and teaches the importance of being able to rely on others and contribute to a team. If your children show an interest in going afloat, encourage their desire as much as possible because nothing develops confidence, independence, and self-reliance as effectively as sailing.

INTERNET

www.sailing.org

This is the site of the International Sailing Federation (ISAF). It has information on the organization of world sailing (mostly racing) and has links to national authorities for sailing.

SAILING FOR THE DISABLED

Unlike some other sports, sailing offers many opportunities to people with disabilities. Individuals with physical, visual, hearing, or learning impairments can all participate in sailing aboard a wide variety of boats. Organizations promoting sailing for the disabled exist in many countries, and international events such as the Paralympics and the Blind Sailing World Championships provide competition to the highest level.

■ **The Paralympics** *bring together the world's best disabled sailors in top-level competition. Watching these sailors in action is awe-inspiring.*

Fitness is not compulsory!

Fortunately for many of us, sailing does not demand much in the way of physical fitness, unless you want to sail high-performance dinghies or race at top level. The rest of us can get away with average levels of fitness and rely on the physical exercise of sailing to help us get fitter. Because the sport of sailing offers such great variety, you can choose a type of sailing to suit both your inclination and your physical ability.

Sailing has the advantage of being an extremely healthy sport that helps develop fitness without requiring us to undertake a painful fitness regimen before we can enjoy going afloat.

Trivia...

In 1998, blind yachtsman Geoffrey Hilton-Barber sailed alone from Durban, South Africa, to Fremantle, Western Australia, and became the first blind sailor to cross an ocean singlehanded.

Even when it's not fun, it's fun!

I must be honest, there are times when even the most dedicated sailor asks the question, "Why am I doing this?" At its best, sailing is unbeatable. You have freedom, satisfaction, and a real feeling of a connection with nature. On the other hand, sailing sometimes involves getting wet and cold, occasionally scares the hell out of you, and usually costs more than you will admit to your loved ones. But you still come back for more, even when you've sworn that you will positively never, ever go back on the water. Why do we do it? Because sailing offers a quality of reward that, if it could be bottled, would be worth a fortune. So, be warned, once you have tasted the champagne experiences that sailing can deliver, the occasional taste of vinegar will not stop you coming back for more.

A simple summary

✔ Sailing is an ancient skill that dates back thousands of years.

✔ You do not need expensive boats or complicated equipment to sail – even across oceans.

✔ Sailing is almost unique in the freedom it offers. You can explore the seas and oceans of the world at your own pace.

✔ When you are in charge of a boat, you are responsible for your vessel and your crew.

✔ The responsibilities of sailing should not be taken lightly since the water can be a harsh environment.

✔ If you enjoy competition, you can choose to race in many types of sailing boats from small dinghies to large yachts.

✔ If you like the idea of sailing there is nothing to stop you from trying it. Sailing is accessible to virtually anyone and there are many forms to choose from.

Chapter 2

How to Start

BECAUSE SAILING IS SUCH A VARIED activity, it can be hard for beginners to know where and how to get afloat. In fact, there are many ways that you could start depending on where you live, how old you are, and whether any of your family or friends already sail. Sailing is an accessible sport if you're lucky enough to live in the right place and know the right people, but it can seem daunting if you have no handy contacts. Fortunately, there are more opportunities today than ever before to learn how to handle a boat, whatever your age or background.

In this chapter...
✓ Where can you sail?

✓ What type of boat?

✓ Ways to learn

✓ Extending your skills

SIMPLE DINGHIES, LIKE THESE ENTERPRISES, CAN BE USED FOR LEARNING AND RACING

Where can you sail?

IF YOU ARE LUCKY ENOUGH to live in a popular sailing area, you should have little problem in finding somewhere to learn to sail. However, the desire to sail is not limited to people who live near the sea and, fortunately, neither are the opportunities to get afloat. Sailing takes place at a remarkable variety of venues. Lakes, rivers, and reservoirs in many countries are used for sailing and it is not uncommon to find sailing clubs based hundreds or even thousands of miles from the sea. Even if you do not have a sailing venue of any sort close by, there are opportunities for learning to sail on holiday or through residential courses that are available in all the desirable sailing locations.

Humble beginnings

As a child I knew no one else who sailed but, inspired like so many by Arthur Ransome's books, I was determined to learn. The solution for me was to read as much as possible about sailing before renting a simple sailing dinghy for an hour at a time. I first sailed on a local boating lake that was so small I had to change course every minute or two in order to avoid hitting the bank. From that simple beginning, I progressed to sailing on the nearby river, in the harbor, and finally on the sea. The same method is still possible today but, luckily, there are now many easier ways to learn than by attempting to teach yourself.

■ **Sailing can be** *enjoyed in so many different ways: in small boats or large boats, on the sea or on inland waters. Wherever you live, you should be able to find a way of getting started in sailing.*

In today's safety-conscious world, and with more popular and crowded waters, it makes sense to take a good sailing course, where you can master the basic skills safely without learning bad habits or putting yourself and others at risk.

People learn to sail in the most unlikely of places but, if you have a choice, there are a few key features that make learning easier. Choosing a quiet stretch of water reduces the risk of getting into difficulty with other boats. If you are really lucky, your choice of location will also be warm. It is so much nicer to sail in warm winds and water, but this is not essential from a learning point of view.

The ideal location is an uncongested area that is free of obstructions and has plenty of room to sail. It should be sheltered so that you can sail in smooth water without having to deal with waves or swells, and the wind should be predominantly light to medium.

What type of boat?

THOSE OF US WHO WERE LUCKY

enough to start sailing when we were young usually did so in a dinghy, and I would always be the first to recommend starting with a small boat, whatever your age. But we also have to recognize that the sport has changed in recent years with more and more people taking up sailing later in life and many new sailors choosing quite large craft as their first choice of boat.

■ **Dinghy sailing** *teaches you the fundamental skills far more quickly than learning in a larger boat.*

The first question to ask yourself is what sort of sailing you imagine yourself doing. If you are attracted by the fast racing dinghies that whiz around your local bay then it's obvious that you need to learn in a dinghy. On the other hand, dinghies may leave you cold but the idea of cruising between tropical anchorages is what appeals to you. If you never plan to sail a dinghy, then it makes sense to consider the alternatives, but do remember that, if you want to learn to sail really well, a dinghy will always be the best introduction. Having learned the basics in a dinghy, you can always move on to the boat of your choice.

Learning in a dinghy

Sailing schools and clubs vary in the types of dinghy they use for instruction. Some use small, singlehanded (one-person) dinghies, typically between 10 ft (3 m) and 12 ft (4 m) in length, while others use larger dinghies that have room for two or three crew. Most dinghies that are used for instruction purposes have a relatively stable hull shape and a moderate sail area. They may not be the fastest dinghies on the water, but they are ideal for learning in.

> **DEFINITION**
>
> *The people sailing a boat are collectively called the* crew. *The body of the boat, known as the* hull, *is the part that sits in the water.*

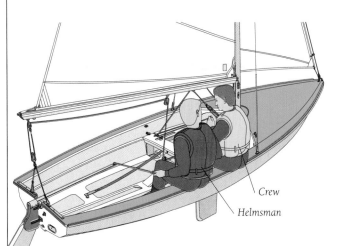

Crew

Helmsman

First the good news...

Learning in a singlehanded dinghy is the quickest method since you do not have to share the steering and you are solely responsible for how the boat sails so mistakes are obvious. Sailing with other beginners does offer camaraderie, however, and nervous beginners may prefer the safety-in-numbers approach.

■ **In a dinghy,** *the helmsman is usually the person who is in charge.*

Learning in a dinghy offers lots of benefits. The dinghy responds quickly to any changes you make such as moving your weight or altering the controls. This means that it is easy to see the effects of your actions and to feel the boat respond.

> **DEFINITION**
>
> *The person responsible for steering is the* helmsman. *He or she may refer to the other people sailing the boat as his or her crew.*

Dinghies are light and maneuvrable so you do not need great strength to adjust the sails. The loads on the equipment are not high enough to cause serious injury if you get things wrong. Dinghies can teach you the basics without complicated equipment. Also, the helmsman on a dinghy has a sail to adjust, whereas the helmsman on a larger boat only has to steer, so has less feedback to judge how things are working.

...Now the bad news

There are aspects to learning in a dinghy that some people would cite as disadvantages so it is only fair to point these out. For a start, you should expect to get wet! Dinghies are small and you sit close to the water. This should not be a problem as long as you have the correct clothing to keep you warm.

Also, you will capsize! How can I be so sure? Because any dinghy-sailing course should teach you how to right a capsized boat and, for that to happen, you have to capsize first. Again, there is no need to worry about this as it is a really important skill to learn and it will be taught in controlled circumstances.

You should be prepared for learning without an instructor on board. Some courses use dinghies that are large enough to accommodate an instructor along with the students, but many use smaller boats. In the latter case, the instructor usually shepherds his or her flock from a small motorboat. This system works very well but some beginners prefer to have an instructor next to them while they're getting to grips with the lesson.

Learning in a keelboat

Some sailing schools teach beginners in small *keelboats* designed for day sailing or racing. Suitable boats are usually between 20 ft (6 m) and 30 ft (9 m) long with a large, open *cockpit* that can accommodate three or four students along with an instructor.

Keelboat comfort

Learning to sail in a keelboat has the advantage of being more comfortable and drier than learning in a dinghy. Keelboats are much more stable than dinghies, making it less critical for you to move your weight to the right place at the right time. Also, you won't have to face a capsize-recovery drill and you won't capsize by accident. You will have the added benefit of having an instructor in the boat with you for at least the first stages of the course.

> **DEFINITION**
>
> *A boat that has a weighted keel underneath the hull is called a keelboat. The heavy keel helps to keep the boat upright and prevents a full capsize. A boat's cockpit is the space in which the helmsman and crew sit or stand to sail the boat.*

The disadvantages

The flip side of a keelboat's extra stability is reduced responsiveness, which makes it harder to gauge the differences made by moving your weight or altering the controls. Because the boat is heavier and larger than a dinghy, the sails, ropes, and equipment are also larger. This makes it a bit harder to adjust the controls.

■ **Keelboats** *are generally more stable than most dinghies.*

Learning in a cruiser

Another option available to you when you start sailing is to learn aboard a cruising boat. Cruisers used for teaching are typically at least 30 ft (9 m) long and many are larger still. Cruising courses are excellent for teaching all the skills associated with handling and running a cruising boat and for learning how to navigate, how to understand the weather, and the associated skills that sailors going offshore must learn.

Starting to sail aboard a cruiser is not the best way to learn. Do not assume that, because your eventual aim is to sail your own cruiser, you should learn to sail on one from the outset.

Cruisers are too big and too heavy to give much feedback to the inexperienced sailor. The loads on the equipment are high and it is possible to injure yourself if you mishandle the gear. Also, many cruisers are steered by a wheel, which provides far less feedback to the helmsman than the simple tiller found on all dinghies and most small keelboats.

■ **Cruiser sailing** *requires skills that are specific to boats of this size. Although skills acquired by sailing dinghies will stand you in good stead, you will need additional experience to be able to handle a cruiser.*

Ways to learn

YOU WILL CERTAINLY NOT be short of options when you set out to learn to sail. The boom in leisure activities has not left sailing behind. Today there are numerous books, magazines, and web sites devoted to sailing, clubs that cater to all aspects of the sport, and sailing schools and vacation centers that are vying for customers.

Doing it yourself

If you have friends or family who sail, you may be able to get afloat easily. This is a great way to sample the delights of sailing and to get an idea of what type of sailing attracts you most. But don't expect your friends to teach you to sail. Sure, you'll pick up some skills, but you may also pick up some bad habits. Unless you have a very experienced sailor in the family (preferably one with instructing experience and qualifications) who has the patience to teach family members to sail, you will be far better off learning in a more formal setting.

INTERNET

www.american-sailing.com

Check out the site of the American Sailing Association for their wide range of sail courses and locations.

Reading up

Another approach is to read lots of books and magazines and then attempt to put the information you have acquired into practice on a borrowed or hired boat. As someone who did exactly this, I am in a poor position to advise against it, but really it is much easier and far safer if you put theory into practice in the controlled setting of a good training course. Keep reading everything you can on the subject, however, because this is a great way to learn about a very varied and complex sport. There are vast numbers of books devoted to every aspect, and there is nothing nicer on a cold and windy winter's evening than losing yourself in a book about sailing. Join the author of a cruising book as he or she explores remote coral atols, or set about improving your racing results by studying the techniques of a top-class racing sailor. The choice is yours but, believe me, once you are hooked, your sailing library is likely to grow at an alarming rate!

Learn to sail in a dinghy or a keelboat so that you learn the basics properly and quickly. These basic skills will always apply to whatever type of boat you sail subsequently and are an essential part of your sailing repertoire.

Picking a training course

Finding a beginner's sailing course to suit your needs should not be difficult, especially if you happen to live near a center of sailing activity. Sailing magazines are a good place to start looking since most have dozens of adverts for sailing courses. You can also contact your national sailing authority, which is usually responsible for regulating approved training establishments and will be able to provide you with a list of officially recognized sailing schools. A visit to your local sailing club should result in useful information and advice. Many clubs run training courses for children and young people, and some also organize courses for adults. If all else fails, try asking sailors and marine businesses in your area for advice on the best places to learn.

Learning on vacation

An interesting alternative to learning in your own locality is to combine your sailing course with a vacation. Many companies offer watersport activities at holiday venues and some provide certified training courses that are worth considering. You can find details of these in sailing magazines, on the Internet, and through travel agents.

■ **Vacation sailing** *is a great way to learn and often has the added benefits of good weather conditions and calm waters.*

Before booking yourself on a sailing course, there are a few points you should check to make sure that the course you are considering is right for you:

- Ask about the curriculum and make sure it is intended for beginners
- Check that the school is recognized and approved by your national sailing authority
- Make sure that, if you pass the course, you gain a recognized certificate
- Find out what size boats are used and whether they are dinghies or keelboats
- Ask about the number of people in the class and how many people will sail on each boat
- Find out about the school's requirements for swimming ability
- Establish what clothing and safety equipment will be provided and what you need to take with you

A few sailing clubs are very snooty and more interested in social status than sailing, but most others welcome beginners and have a friendly and open atmosphere. Make sure that you pick one that is right for you before signing up for membership.

Extending your skills

ONCE YOU HAVE COMPLETED *your first course, you may be tempted to sign up immediately for the next level of certificate. Avoid this temptation and concentrate on practicing the skills you have just acquired and on gaining more experience afloat.*

Building on experience

Now is the time to seek out friends and family with boats and offer your services as crew. Keen crews are often in short supply so you should have no problem finding a boat on which to sail and increase your experience. This is also a good way to sample different boats and ways of sailing. Try to get as much experience on as wide a variety of boats as possible and concentrate on building your skills through time on the water.

If you do not know any boat owners, visit your local sailing club and ask if you can put a "crew-available" note on their notice board. Pick up details of their membership requirements and the facilities they provide. Joining a club is a good way to get to know other sailors and expand your opportunities for getting afloat. Take the time to check out local clubs to make sure that the atmosphere, facilities, and the type of sailing they support are suitable for you.

INTERNET

www.bostonsailing center.com

The Boston Sailing Center is one of the leading sailing schools in the United States.

A simple summary

✔ Sailing is popular in a wide variety of venues and you do not have to live by the sea in order to learn to sail.

✔ As a complete beginner, you have the choice of learning to sail in a dinghy or a small keelboat at a wide selection of sailing schools, clubs, and vacation venues.

✔ Learning to sail in a dinghy is the quickest and most effective way for most beginners to gain the basic skills.

✔ Once you have completed your first course, spend a year or so practicing the basic skills and gaining more experience afloat before taking further courses.

Chapter 3

Staying Warm and Safe

YOUR ENJOYMENT OF SAILING will be influenced greatly by how comfortable you are afloat. Fortunately, major advances in outdoor-sports clothing in recent years mean that there is highly effective clothing available for all types of sailing. The best gear is not cheap, so take your time to decide what type of sailing you will be doing before investing in the appropriate clothing. Personal safety equipment is just as important as your clothing, and here too you will find a wide choice of modern gear that is light, comfortable, and effective.

In this chapter...

✓ **Dress for comfort**

✓ **Picking the right clothing**

✓ **Personal safety gear**

✓ **Important accessories**

WITH THE RIGHT CLOTHING, YOU CAN STAY WARM AND DRY EVEN IN DIFFICULT CONDITIONS

Dress for comfort

YOUR CHOICE OF CLOTHING *will depend on what and where you sail. In particular, the weather, water temperature, and the type of boat will determine what you need to wear. If you are lucky enough to sail in warm wind and water, the occasional splash or even a soaking will not bother you, especially if you are sailing for only a short time and can come ashore to a hot shower and dry clothes. Once you head offshore in a larger boat or sail in colder waters, or in winter, you need to take your choice of clothing more seriously.*

■ **Make sure you choose** *clothing suitable for the type of sailing you do, and expect to get wet if you sail a fast dinghy.*

The smaller the boat you sail, the more likely you are to get wet, but even on a large boat there is always the chance that an unfriendly wave will choose to land on you. So, start off with the assumption that you are going to get wet and plan accordingly.

Go casual

When you start to sail, you do not need to invest in expensive specialist clothing. You probably already have some clothes that will be adequate until you decide that you are serious about sailing. If you learn to sail at a club or sailing school, they may provide you with a set of foul-weather gear. Normal casual or sports clothing will suffice under the foul-weather gear, and you can wear normal sneakers on your feet. Once you start to sail your own boat or crew for someone else, you'll want to invest in some specialist clothing to keep you warm and dry.

Staying warm

The key to comfort on the water is making sure you stay warm. The temperature is always lower afloat than ashore and it fluctuates much more widely, so don't go sailing dressed only in swimwear. It is never as hot afloat as you think unless there is no wind and baking sunshine, in which case you are better off on the beach! Remember that heat loss is one of the biggest dangers you can face afloat. Prolonged exposure to cold will quickly lead to exhaustion, and the speed with which this can happen always surprises the inexperienced.

A fit person, dressed normally and not exerting him- or herself, will lose consciousness 2–3 hours after immersion, even in calm water at 62° F (17° C). Even aboard the boat your energy levels will quickly deteriorate if you allow yourself to get wet and cold.

For your first few sailing trips, you can make do with comfortable trousers and sweaters but avoid cotton, since this material is cold once wet. Wool is the best natural fiber because it stays warm when wet. Best of all are the pile ("fleece") garments made of polypropylene or other synthetic fibers. These are light and comfortable to wear, dry quickly, and take water away from the skin by capillary action to keep you dry and comfortable. Air is trapped between the layers of clothing to create an insulating effect. Garments made from these fabrics make it easy to adjust your temperature by removing or adding a layer.

Several thin layers of clothing are far better than a single heavy one.

Staying dry

There is a wide variety of waterproof outerwear available, but you probably already have a suitable windbreaker or nylon shell jacket that will suffice for your first few trips.

One of the main problems with foul-weather or raingear has always been the amount of condensation that builds up inside. The more active you are, the more you perspire, and the perspiration collects on the inside of jackets and trousers, dampening your inner layer of clothing, and leaving you cold and damp as soon as you are less active.

Trivia...

Foul-weather gear is sometimes called oilskins. This is a reference to the days when seamen used canvas and leather waterproofed with fish oil – literally "oiled skin" – for their outer clothing.

No sweat!

Fortunately, this age-old problem has now been solved. The latest waterproof clothing is breathable, which means that although it will not let water in it will allow the passage of water vapour from the inside out. When you perspire, the water vapor escapes to the outside air, leaving you dry and comfortable. For the outer layer to work, you must wear a modern, synthetic inner layer that takes perspiration away from your skin and passes it outwards through the breathable layer. This layered system is very light, supple, and comfortable to wear.

Getting wet to stay warm

In most circumstances it is normal to concentrate on keeping dry so that you stay warm. When you are dinghy sailing, that is easier said than done, especially if you are sailing a high-performance dinghy. To avoid the problem of staying dry, many dinghy sailors choose to wear a wetsuit (sometimes called a steamer), which is a close-fitting garment made of a material called neoprene. The wetsuit traps a thin layer of water between the neoprene and your skin, which is warmed by your body heat. Because it is tight fitting, the wetsuit prevents water from circulating easily inside and the trapped water insulates you from the colder air or water beyond the neoprene. This only works effectively once you have gotten wet and created a layer of water inside the suit.

Picking the right clothing

VISIT ANY MARINE STORE and you are likely to find an enormous and confusing range of sailing clothing, much of it expensive! Do not rush off to buy the most colorful or fashionable gear you can find; instead, take your time to choose clothing that is really suitable for the type of sailing you intend to do.

Take advice

If you are not sure about the type of gear that will best suit your needs ask a few experienced sailors for advice, or take a look at what your local club members wear when they go sailing.

Clothing for dinghies

The type of dinghy you sail will help to determine your choice of clothing. You are likely to learn in a fairly stable dinghy in light or moderate conditions, so a simple waterproof smock and trousers will be quite adequate. If you later move on to sail high-performance dinghies, in which the chances of capsizing or getting wet from spray are much higher, you will want to look at more efficient clothing.

When the wind and water are warm, you'll probably be comfortable in shorts and a T-shirt with a lightweight waterproof smock for use if there is a lot of spray flying. In colder or wetter conditions, you can choose between a waterproof top and trousers, a wetsuit, or a drysuit.

Foul-weather gear

Foul-weather gear is available as a one-piece suit or as separate jacket and trousers. A one-piece suit offers fewer water entry points and is a good choice for active dinghy sailing, but separate items allow you to wear just the jacket or trousers as required.

Full arms for extra warmth

Wetsuits

Sailors of high-performance dinghies often choose wetsuits. Different weights of neoprene are used for summer and winter sailing and various styles are available. You can choose between suits without arms, with short legs, or full arms and legs. Your choice will depend mainly on the temperature of the water where you sail. Ask experienced sailors at your club for advice before you buy and remember that a very close fit is necessary for the wetsuit to work efficiently. Make sure that you are measured properly so that the suit can be tailored to fit you exactly.

Close-fitting collar with latex seal

WETSUIT

Drysuits

A drysuit is another popular option. This is a waterproof suit with neoprene or latex seals at the neck, ankles, and wrists. Drysuits made from breathable fabric are much more comfortable than the nonbreathable types because of the amount of perspiration that builds up inside the suit when you are very active. You need to select the garments you wear under the drysuit carefully, as it is easy to overheat when you are very active. The best choice is a thin, light, thermal layer that takes perspiration away from the skin.

Wide suspenders for comfort

High collar

Reinforced knees

Integral latex socks

DRYSUIT

Keelboat and cruiser clothing

There are several types of waterproof clothing suitable for keelboat and cruiser sailors. Most manufacturers offer conventional foul-weather gear alongside those made from the more expensive breathable materials. If you can afford the breathable gear then you'll appreciate the benefits, but if not, the conventional gear will be perfectly adequate.

Reinforced knees

BREATHABLE FOUL-WEATHER GEAR

Wetsuits are not appropriate on board larger boats, where it is usually much easier to stay dry than on a dinghy. The same is true of drysuits, unless you are working on deck aboard a fast racing yacht in rough conditions, in which case they will keep you dry when even the best foul-weather gear starts to let in water.

The main difference between foul-weather suits designed for coastal sailing and those intended for offshore or ocean passages is the weight and strength of the materials. Ocean gear will probably have a better hood arrangement and more storm seals on the cuffs, ankles, neck, and zip openings, but it will also be heavier to wear and more expensive.

Protecting the extremities

Good footwear will protect your feet and provide the grip you need to stay on your feet and on the boat. Shoes and boots for sailing should have flat, nonslip soles without a heel. Don't sail in bare feet or you risk stubbing your toes on deck gear.

DINGHY BOOTS

Non-slip footwear

There are many types of specialist sailing shoes and boots available, but normal sneakers or trainers with flat, soft, rubber soles are fine to start with. Look for wide-grooved soles that provide the best grip on a wet deck. Do check that they don't leave marks on deck or you could be unpopular with the boat's owner!

Flexible short boots made from neoprene but with moulded soles are ideal for dinghy sailing, while leather or synthetic boat shoes are good on larger boats. Sailing boots are used on larger boats in rough or cold conditions.

Nonslip tread

SAILING BOOTS

Comfortable hands

Sailing gloves are a good idea when dinghy sailing. Hauling on ropes can quickly result in sore hands, especially when your hands and the ropes are wet. The best gloves have reinforced palms for gripping ropes. You can choose between styles with full or cut-off fingers. The latter allow you to manage intricate tasks that require the ability to feel with your fingertips.

GLOVES

Personal safety gear

AS WELL AS CHOOSING the right clothing, you must also think about your personal safety equipment. In a dinghy this means having suitable personal buoyancy to keep you afloat if your boat capsizes or if you fall overboard. If you sail a cruiser you will also need to have a safety harness for use in rough conditions and at night.

Personal flotation device (PFD)

A PFD is essential for anyone using a small boat, whether rowing a dinghy or dinghy sailing, to sailing a larger yacht, or windsurfing. Even if you are an excellent swimmer and conditions are ideal, you will find it impossible to stay afloat for long after capsizing or falling overboard unless you wear some form of buoyancy.

You can choose between a PFD and a full lifejacket. PFDs are less bulky than lifejackets and are the usual choice for dinghy sailors.

Do not go afloat in a dinghy without either a PFD or a lifejacket.

PFDs use closed-cell foam in a waistcoat-type jacket that is comfortable to wear. They are available in a variety of styles and sizes, but you must ensure that you buy one that is the correct size for your body weight.

> **DEFINITION**
>
> *A PFD is designed to provide some support when you are in the water, while a lifejacket will provide full support and should be designed to turn an unconscious person onto their back, to keep their face clear of the water.*

Some lifejackets use closed-cell foam to provide all their buoyancy, but they are very bulky and get in the way when dinghy sailing. Other types have some permanent foam buoyancy and can be further inflated with air if necessary. Cruiser sailors commonly prefer to use inflatable jackets. These have no permanent buoyancy at all but are inflated by mouth or a gas cylinder when needed. The gas cylinder can be activated either by pulling a cord or, in some models, will inflate automatically when immersed in water.

If you can swim, a PFD will satisfy most dinghy-sailing needs. If you can't swim, you should learn before taking up sailing!

PERSONAL FLOTATION DEVICE (PFD)

Staying on board

When you sail a cruiser, the most important item of personal safety gear is a safety harness. A lifejacket will keep you afloat if you do go overboard, but it is better to stay on the boat in the first place. Harnesses are available in several types. Some waterproof jackets have a harness built in that is always available when you are wearing the jacket, but a separate harness may be more useful since it can be worn at any time, even in conditions where you don't want to wear a jacket.

Some harnesses incorporate an inflatable lifejacket. These are popular as they are easy to put on, reasonably comfortable, and do not require you to wear two separate items of equipment. If you do buy separate items, however, try them on together outside all the gear you expect to wear in bad conditions. Make sure they fit well, don't interfere with each other, and are comfortable.

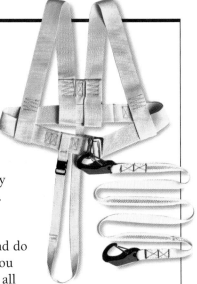

HARNESS

Important accessories

AS WELL AS HAVING the right clothing and safety gear, there are a few other items that can make a big difference to your comfort afloat:

1 One-third of body heat is lost through the head, so a warm hat or balaclava will make a big impact on colder days.

2 If you have long hair, carry a hairband or a hat to prevent it from being blown about and obscuring your vision, or getting caught in the rigging, which can be painful!

HAT

■ **Protect yourself from the sun** – *wear a hat and sunglasses to protect your head and eyes, and use a high-factor sunscreen to prevent sunburn.*

(3) A stainless steel knife that incorporates a shackle key is a useful tool to carry. Fit it with a length of line that can be looped around your wrist or tied around your waist.

KNIFE

(4) Protection from the sun is important when sailing because reflection from the water, even in light overcast conditions, can quickly burn unprotected skin. Good sunglasses that block UV are essential to protect the eyes, and it is often advisable to wear a hat to keep direct sun off your head. Attach sunglasses and hats by a light cord or retainer to prevent you from losing them. Remember to apply a high-factor sunscreen to all exposed skin before you go afloat and re-apply it at frequent intervals.

(5) It is easy to get dehydrated on hot days, so carry a bottle of water and take frequent sips. Take some fruit (non-squashable varieties, such as apples), a high-energy bar, or chocolate in case you get peckish, or in the event that the short sail you planned turns into a longer trip when the wind drops.

(6) Carry your gear in a small kit bag that is easily stowed. A waterproof bag is ideal.

A simple summary

✔ Staying warm and dry will greatly influence your enjoyment of sailing so make sure that you select the correct protective clothing for you.

✔ For your first few sails you can get by with normal casual clothing or sportswear that you probably own already.

✔ Modern gear is light and supple but it can be expensive, so choose the gear you need for the type of sailing you intend to do.

✔ Choose accessories that provide adequate protection for your hands and feet.

✔ Do not go afloat in a dinghy without some form of personal buoyancy.

✔ Do not sail a cruiser without equipping yourself with a safety harness.

✔ Remember to carry protection from the sun, including sunglasses, a hat, and sunscreen.

Chapter 4

A Simple Boat Guide

ONE THING THAT CAN CAUSE a problem for beginners is the language of sailing, but don't worry – it's not necessary to learn an entire nautical dictionary before you sail. Understanding the parts of a boat is a good introduction and is an important first step in learning to sail.

All sailing boats have basic parts in common: the hull is the body of the boat, providing buoyancy to float itself and to support you; the rig is the combination of mast and sails that produce the motive power; and the foils are comprised of a keel to stop the boat sliding sideways (and to provide stability in keelboats) and a rudder to steer the boat.

In this chapter...

✓ The hull

✓ The foils

✓ The rig

✓ Dinghy fittings

ALL SAILING BOATS HAVE SOME BASIC PARTS AND TYPES OF EQUIPMENT IN COMMON

The hull

BOAT HULLS COME IN ALL *shapes and sizes and you can even have more than one hull if you wish. You can choose from a wide range of designs including monohulls, catamarans, and trimarans. Fiberglass is the most commonly used material for constructing dinghy hulls, but moulded plastic and wood are also very popular. Despite the variety of boats available, most sailing dinghies have very similar features.*

> **DEFINITION**
>
> *Boats with one hull are known as* monohulls. *Catamarans have two hulls and* trimarans *have three. Most sailing dinghies are monohulls, but there are many types of small catamarans on the market, as well as a few small trimarans.*

Don't worry if the first dinghy you sail is a bit different from the one shown here – the way the boat works will quickly become obvious once you understand the basic layout.

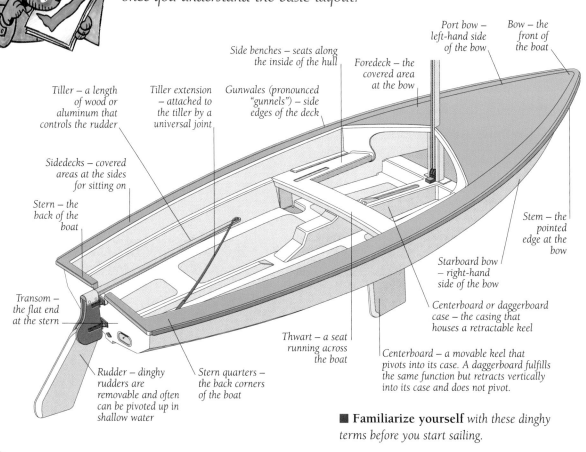

Side benches – seats along the inside of the hull

Foredeck – the covered area at the bow

Port bow – left-hand side of the bow

Bow – the front of the boat

Tiller – a length of wood or aluminum that controls the rudder

Tiller extension – attached to the tiller by a universal joint

Gunwales (pronounced "gunnels") – side edges of the deck

Sidedecks – covered areas at the sides for sitting on

Stern – the back of the boat

Stem – the pointed edge at the bow

Starboard bow – right-hand side of the bow

Centerboard or daggerboard case – the casing that houses a retractable keel

Transom – the flat end at the stern

Rudder – dinghy rudders are removable and often can be pivoted up in shallow water

Stern quarters – the back corners of the boat

Thwart – a seat running across the boat

Centerboard – a movable keel that pivots into its case. A daggerboard fulfills the same function but retracts vertically into its case and does not pivot.

■ **Familiarize yourself** with these dinghy terms before you start sailing.

The foils

UNSEEN AND OFTEN FORGOTTEN is the fate of a sailing boat's foils, yet they are as essential to the boat's performance as the sails. All sailing boats have two foils – a rudder and a keel. The rudder is used to steer the boat and the keel prevents the boat from slipping sideways when sailing.

The rudder is positioned at or near the stern of the boat. When the rudder is turned on its mountings, it deflects the water moving it. The force of the water on the rudder pushes the stern of the boat in the opposite direction to that in which the rudder has been turned.

RELATIVE TERMS

When we're ashore, we usually describe things, especially directions, as relative to ourselves, such as left or right, in front or behind. The key thing to remember when trying to understand the language of sailing is that when you're afloat these things are described relative to the boat or the wind. So the port side of a boat is defined as the left-hand side when facing the bow. It doesn't matter if you turn around, the port side always stays where it is!

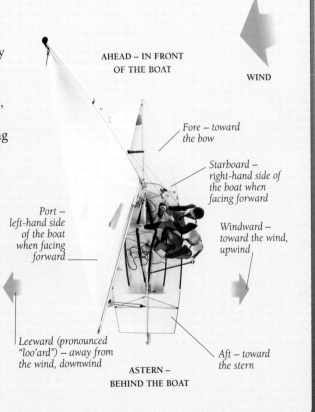

AHEAD – IN FRONT OF THE BOAT

WIND

Fore – toward the bow

Starboard – right-hand side of the boat when facing forward

Port – left-hand side of the boat when facing forward

Windward – toward the wind, upwind

Leeward (pronounced "loo'ard") – away from the wind, downwind

Aft – toward the stern

ASTERN – BEHIND THE BOAT

Steering the boat

Notice that the stern moves when you steer a boat, unlike a car or bike, which are steered by their front wheels. When a boat turns, it pivots around a point somewhere near its center, and the stern and bow swing in opposite directions. You need to remember this when you first learn to steer the boat.

Tiller or wheel?

The rudder can be controlled by a simple stick, called a tiller, or by a wheel. All dinghies use a tiller and this system is also used on some large boats because it is simple and gives the helmsman direct feedback. Larger boats use a wheel because their loads would be impractical to handle with a tiller. Wheel steering is much less sensitive than steering with a tiller and does not transmit as much feedback from the rudder, which you need when you are learning and beginning to get a feel for the forces acting on the boat.

Avoid learning to sail on a boat with wheel steering.

The role of the keel

Some form of keel is needed to prevent the boat from being pushed sideways by the wind. Most dinghies use a retractable wooden or fiberglass blade contained in a case, which is built into the centerline of the hull. If the blade is retracted vertically by sliding it up and down it is called a daggerboard. An equally common arrangement has the blade pivoting back and up into its case and this is called a centerboard.

INTERNET

www.sonar.org

This Sonar Class site features the popular 23 ft (7 m) International Sonar keelboat, which is popular for training and offers high-quality racing.

Keelboats usually have a keel that is fixed to or is an integral part of the hull, and is made of lead or iron to provide stability. In keelboats the weight of the keel keeps the boat upright, but dinghies do not need a weighted keel because the crew can move their weight around to stop the boat from capsizing.

The rig

MOST DINGHY RIGS *look quite similar although there are a few common variations that you will encounter. All dinghies have a mast, which is the vertical pole that supports the sail or sails. Most masts are supported by a number of wires that are collectively called the standing rigging, but some dinghies use simple freestanding – or unstayed – masts. These masts are usually placed into a tube that runs from the deck to the bottom of the hull, and are free to rotate.*

> ## Trivia...
> *Pulley systems used on boats are correctly called tackles (pronounced "ta'kles" if you're being fastidious) and use blocks – the nautical term for pulleys.*

Stayed masts

Masts that need standing rigging to hold them in place are called stayed masts and may be stepped (stood) on deck or on the keel (in this instance, the keel means the inside of the bottom of the hull). On most dinghies the standing rigging includes a *forestay* to the bow, as well as port and starboard *shrouds* leading to the side decks. Larger boats, including some small keelboats, also have a backstay, which runs from the top of the mast to the stern, and some have extra shrouds.

> ### DEFINITION
> *A forestay is a supporting wire joining the mast to the bow. The shrouds are the supporting wires that link the mast to the sidedecks.*

The most important sail on all boats is the large one behind the mast, which is called, unsurprisingly, the mainsail. Most mainsails are triangular but other shapes are used on a few dinghies, and on some cruisers.

Mainsail and jib

At the bottom of the mainsail, a pole, called a boom, is used to control the sail. The boom is attached to the mast by a fitting – called a gooseneck – that allows it to pivot from side to side and up and down.

Some dinghies intended for singlehanded sailing have only a mainsail, but most dinghies also have another sail that is set in front of the mast. This is called a jib and is always triangular.

> ### INTERNET
> **www.lasersailing.com**
>
> *The Laser Center produces some very popular monohull and catamaran dinghies.*

Mainsail – the large sail that is set behind the mast

Spreaders – aluminum or wooden tubes attached to the mast and the shrouds that add support to the mast

Boom – made of aluminum or wood, supports the foot of the mainsail

Hounds – where the forestay and shrouds terminate on the mast

Forestay – wire at the bow that supports the mast and jib

Jib – attached to the forestay by small clips called hanks

Mast – usually made of aluminum but can be wood. The mast can be stepped on deck or on the keel.

Shrouds – wires on port and starboard sides that support the mast

Gooseneck – the mechanism that attaches the boom to the mast

Mast step – the socket in which the heel of the mast sits

Shroud plates or bottlescrews – the adjusters used to attach the standing rigging to the boat and adjust their tension

Chainplates – the strong points on the boat to which the shrouds are attached

■ **Most modern** sailing boats, including many dinghies, keelboats, and cruisers, use a similar rig arrangement. Two triangular sails – a mainsail and a jib – are supported by a single mast to which a boom is attached, supporting the bottom edge of the mainsail.

Parts of a sail

Most mainsails and jibs are made from Dacron sailcloth cut into panels and sewn together. The sides and corners each have their own names. Each corner is reinforced to take the extra loads on these parts of the sail. The curved area of the sail that runs from the head to the clew on the leech is called a roach. Battens of wood or fiberglass slip into pockets along the sail to support the roach. Battens can be short (as shown on the diagram) or full length.

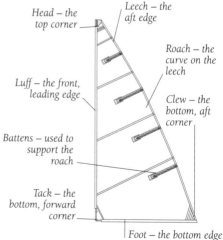

Head – the top corner

Leech – the aft edge

Roach – the curve on the leech

Luff – the front, leading edge

Clew – the bottom, aft corner

Battens – used to support the roach

Tack – the bottom, forward corner

Foot – the bottom edge

Controlling the sails

Each sail is hoisted – pulled up – by a rope or wire called a halyard. Other ropes, called sheets, are used to pull each sail in or let it out. For example, the mainsheet is the rope used to control the mainsail. A few other control lines are usually fitted for sail adjustment but, at this stage, you only need to know the basic controls.

The word sheet often confuses beginners since it seems logical for it to refer to sails. Forget logic, and remember that sheets are the most important ropes because they are your throttle and brake combined!

Because the mainsail is the largest sail, it can exert quite a strong pull on the mainsheet so, to make it manageable, the mainsheet is usually rigged with a pulley system to make it more powerful. Pulley systems are very common on boats and appear in a variety of uses.

Mainsheet arrangements vary, and may be attached to different parts of the boom and boat, but the principle is the same for all dinghies and you will quickly become accustomed to handling the type you sail.

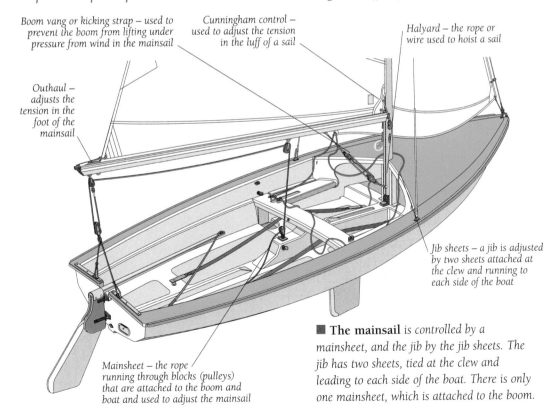

Boom vang or kicking strap – used to prevent the boom from lifting under pressure from wind in the mainsail

Cunningham control – used to adjust the tension in the luff of a sail

Halyard – the rope or wire used to hoist a sail

Outhaul – adjusts the tension in the foot of the mainsail

Jib sheets – a jib is adjusted by two sheets attached at the clew and running to each side of the boat

Mainsheet – the rope running through blocks (pulleys) that are attached to the boom and boat and used to adjust the mainsail

■ **The mainsail** is controlled by a mainsheet, and the jib by the jib sheets. The jib has two sheets, tied at the clew and leading to each side of the boat. There is only one mainsheet, which is attached to the boom.

Dinghy fittings

DINGHIES AND SMALL KEELBOATS *usually have a fairly simple layout, although racing boats often have much more complex control systems than family or general-purpose boats. When learning, you are likely to sail a simple boat with straightforward equipment and fittings.*

Fittings for controlling ropes

Dinghies generally benefit from a number of fittings designed to make life easier. Fairleads are used for altering the direction of a rope and may have a smooth eye or rotating pulley. Jib sheets, for example, are led through fairleads, one on each side of the boat, before being led through a cleat, which holds the rope firmly in place.

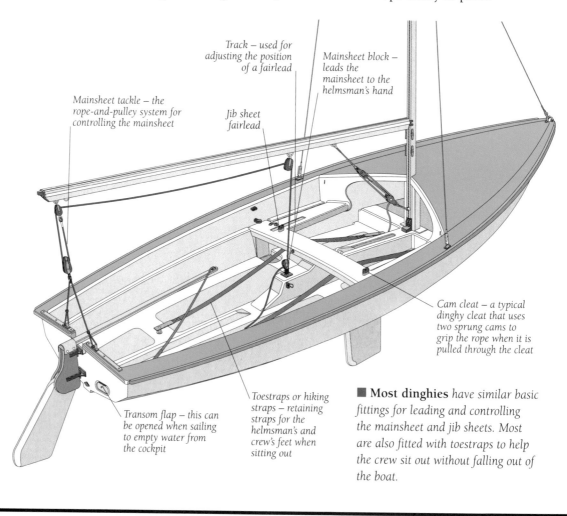

Track – used for adjusting the position of a fairlead

Mainsheet block – leads the mainsheet to the helmsman's hand

Mainsheet tackle – the rope-and-pulley system for controlling the mainsheet

Jib sheet fairlead

Cam cleat – a typical dinghy cleat that uses two sprung cams to grip the rope when it is pulled through the cleat

Transom flap – this can be opened when sailing to empty water from the cockpit

Toestraps or hiking straps – retaining straps for the helmsman's and crew's feet when sitting out

■ **Most dinghies** *have similar basic fittings for leading and controlling the mainsheet and jib sheets. Most are also fitted with toestraps to help the crew sit out without falling out of the boat.*

Stowed equipment

There is very little room for extra gear in most dinghies, but some basic equipment should be carried for convenience and safety. It must be stowed securely so that it cannot move even if the boat capsizes. If you sail on the sea, you should include an anchor and flares among your extra equipment.

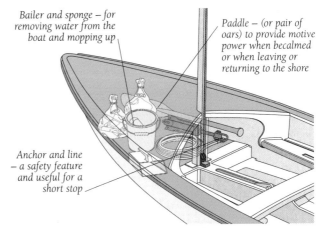

Bailer and sponge – for removing water from the boat and mopping up

Paddle – (or pair of oars) to provide motive power when becalmed or when leaving or returning to the shore

Anchor and line – a safety feature and useful for a short stop

■ **Under the foredeck** *is a good place to stow additional items of loose gear.*

A simple summary

✓ The language of sailing may sound complicated to start with, but it has developed over centuries and is designed to identify clearly any part of a boat, piece of gear, maneuver, or action on board.

✓ Boat hulls come in a range of shapes and sizes.

✓ All sailing boats have the same basic parts, and all work on the same principles.

✓ The keel and rudder are as important to the boat's performance as the sails.

✓ When you turn a boat, the stern swings one way as the bow swings the other.

✓ Most masts are supported by wires that are collectively known as the standing rigging.

✓ Sails are controlled by ropes that are called sheets.

✓ The large sail is called the mainsail. The smaller, triangular sail is called the jib.

✓ Most sailing boats are fitted with a range of standard, basic equipment.

PART TWO

A CLEATED LINE

LEARNING THE BASICS

WHEN YOU START LEARNING TO SAIL, your first steps are the most important. By learning the basics correctly, you will be well prepared for handling virtually any type of sailing boat as your experience increases. It is not necessary to learn any theory at this stage, but if  you can grasp the *basic principles* of how a sail harnesses the wind, you will probably find it easier to learn *how to handle* a sailing boat.

In this part, I'll tell you how to start and stop, how to stay upright, and what to do if you don't. You'll find out about steering the boat and changing course, as well as how to coordinate your actions with your crew. How to *stay safe* is an important part of your first lessons. You'll learn how to look after yourself and your crew, and how to stay clear of other boats you encounter.

Chapter 5

Before You Go Afloat

I KNOW THAT YOU ARE KEEN to get on the water and I promise that we're nearly there. But before you go afloat, there are a couple more things you should know. Sailing dinghies need to be prepared for sailing and, because they are usually stored ashore, they have to be moved to the water. There are ways of doing these tasks that can make your life much easier and minimize the chance of damage to the boat and your temper. This is also the time to talk a little about how sails work so that you understand why and how you must adjust them once you start sailing.

In this chapter...

✓ How a boat sails

✓ Preparing the boat for sailing

✓ Launching the boat

✓ Hoisting the sails

NOT ALL LAUNCHING SITES ARE AS CROWDED AS THIS ONE!

How a boat sails

UNDERSTANDING HOW A BOAT *manages to convert the wind into motive power is not essential when you are learning to sail, but it will help you to reduce the time spent in trial and error and will give you a good insight into what you are trying to achieve. Let's start by thinking of a boat's sail as a flag: If the sail is allowed to it will flap freely in the wind, just like a flag. Obviously, while it is doing this, it is not pushing the boat forward.*

How a sail works

To harness the sail's motive power, we pull the sail so that it takes up an *angle of attack* to the wind. When the sail is flapping like a flag, the wind is able to pass down each side without being diverted from its straight course. Once you have shaped the sail, the wind has to split at the sail's front edge and flow down both sides of the curved wing shape.

> **DEFINITION**
>
> *All sails need to be set at an angle to the air flowing over them. The angle between the front part of a sail and the wind is called the* angle of attack.

Unlike a flag, the sail can be controlled by its sheet. When we pull on the sheet, the sail is transformed into a curved, wing-like shape.

How wind moves around the sail

To see what happens next, try a simple experiment. You need a spoon and running water from a tap. Notice how the spoon is similar in shape to a curved sail. Hold the spoon by the tip of the handle and let the spoon hang with its back near the water stream. Move it slowly toward the running water. As soon as the spoon touches the water it is pulled further into the flow and you can feel the force causing the attraction. Now, look at the water below the spoon. See how the water curves around the back of the spoon and is diverted from its straight course.

The same thing happens to a sail. When you pull it into a wing shape with a small angle of attack to the wind, the air flows around both sides of the curved shape. The air travelling around the leeward side (back, convex side) speeds up. This is because it has further to travel around the outside of the curved sail than the air on the windward side (front, concave side) where the air moves more slowly. This speed difference creates a pressure drop on the leeward side and the sail is effectively sucked to leeward in just the same way as your spoon was sucked sideways.

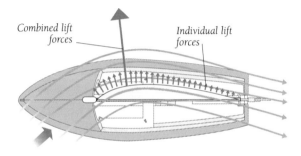

Combined lift forces

Individual lift forces

■ **Driving force:** *The individual lift forces on each part of the sail combine into a single lift force that acts roughly at a right angle to the boom. When the sail is pulled in tight, a large sideways component of the force is resisted by the keel to allow the relatively small forward component of the force to propel the boat.*

The force that pulls the sail to leeward is called lift and it acts at every point on the sail's surface. Because the sail is curved, lift at each point on the sail acts in a slightly different direction, but they all add up to one force acting through a single point. This point is called the sail's center of effort.

The keel plays its part

I have mentioned already that a boat's foils are as important as its sails. The reason for this is because not all of the lift produced by a sail acts in a forward direction. The force produced by a sail always has an element of sideways force in it, except when you are sailing with the wind directly behind you. At all other times the total lift from the sail is made up of two components – a sideways force and a driving force.

Because a dinghy does not have a deep hull and sits on the water as much as in it, the sail's lift will push the boat sideways as well as forward. In order to sail properly rather than moving crab-wise, we have to counter the sideways force somehow, and we do it by using a keel. The keel is an underwater wing and it behaves in exactly the same way as the sail above it, except that the keel moves through water.

Because the boat moves partly sideways, the keel is forced through the water at an angle of attack that causes lift. In this case, the lift is to windward, so it cancels out the opposite sideways force of the sail.

Keelboats have a fixed keel that is designed to be large enough to generate all the lift needed to counter the sideways push of the sail. Dinghies, however, need to be easily transportable and use a centerboard or daggerboard, which can be retracted. This allows you to adjust the amount of keel protruding under the boat to match the sail's sideways thrust. You will see how this works in practice when you go afloat for the first time.

Preparing the boat for sailing

THAT'S ENOUGH THEORY *for the time being. Let's get the boat ready for sailing. Preparing the boat is called rigging it, and it consists of getting the sails ready to hoist and making sure that everything you need is aboard before you set off. Now is the time that you will need to be able to tie a knot or two so turn to the Ropes and Knots appendix and read how to tie a bowline.*

Pronounced "bowlin", the bowline is the most useful of knots and you should try to master it early on.

All dinghies have a mainsail and most have a jib as well. The way these are attached varies from boat to boat but the principles are the same. Once you understand the basics of rigging, you will quickly sort out any differences in detail.

Rigging the mainsail

Sails are usually stored away from the boat in their sail bags. Take the mainsail out of its bag and unroll it inside the boat. Slide the battens into their pockets on the mainsail leech and make sure that they are located in the flap or elastic that holds the outer ends in place. If you're sailing a boat with an unstayed mast, you must fit the mainsail on the mast before stepping the mast. The sail has a sleeve at the luff (forward edge) into which the mast is slid before it is stepped in the boat. In most cases, though, the mast is already stepped and the mainsail is hoisted up it.

Fitting the sail to the boom

Some dinghy mainsails have a loose foot, and you only have to attach the tack and clew to their respective ends of the boom. It is more likely, however, that your mainsail has a rope – a boltrope – sewn along its foot. Slide the clew of the sail into the groove at the forward (mast) end of the boom and pull the clew along the boom. Make sure that only the boltrope goes into the groove and does not trap any folds of sailcloth alongside it. Fix the tack of the sail to the forward end of the boom with a shackle or a pin through the sail and the fitting.

■ **When the mainsail** *foot has been fed into the groove in the boom the tack is fastened in place, often with a pin through the boom.*

Pull the clew along the boom and fasten the clew outhaul. Sometimes this is adjustable while sailing but, on simple dinghies, it is usually a length of line attached to the end of the boom that is tied to the clew before you go afloat. Before you tie it off, pull the sail taut along the boom until the foot of the sail is reasonably tight and a small horizontal crease forms in the sail parallel to the boom. Then fasten the clew outhaul to the clew and take a couple of turns around the boom to prevent the boltrope at the clew pulling out of the groove.

■ **The halyard** is attached to the head of the sail, which is usually reinforced with an aluminum headboard to take the loads on the sail at this point.

Attaching the halyard

With the sail on the boom, run your hands along the luff from tack to head to check that the luff is not twisted. Then look up the halyard to make sure that it is not caught around anything aloft, and shackle or tie it with a bowline to the head.

Insert the boltrope at the head into the mast groove and pull it up a few inches (10 cm or so). Loosely fold the rest of the sail inside the boat and, if it is windy, tie the end of the mainsheet around it to prevent it blowing away.

Leave the mainsail like this until you are ready to hoist it (usually after you launch the boat). If you hoist it earlier, it will flap around out of control and could cause damage.

Rigging the jib

Start rigging the jib by attaching its tack to the bow fitting just behind the point where the forestay is fastened. This is usually done with a shackle or a lashing. The luff of the jib is attached to the forestay by clips known as hanks. Start at the tack and work your way along the luff, attaching each hank in turn to the forestay and making sure that the luff is not twisted between the hanks.

Attach each jib sheet to the clew of the jib using a bowline. You could use a shackle if the sheets have eyes in the ends but this is unnecessary and can cause damage or injury when the sail flaps around.

INTERNET

www.realknots.com/
knots/index.htm

If ropes and tying knots capture your imagination, this site will tell you all you need to know.

Lead the other end of each sheet back to its fairlead. If your dinghy has a large jib – called a genoa – that overlaps the mast and shrouds, lead each sheet outside the shrouds before passing it through the fairlead. If your jib does not overlap the mast, the sheets usually pass between the shrouds and the mast. Tie a figure-eight knot – another important knot – in the end of each sheet after it has been led through the fairlead to prevent the end running out.

Attach the jib halyard to the head, either by a shackle for a wire halyard or by tying a bowline if it is made of rope. Look up the mast before you fasten the halyard and make sure that it is not twisted or caught around anything. If you are not hoisting the sail straight away, gather it into a bundle and loosely tie a jib sheet around it to stop it from blowing around.

■ **Jib hanks** *are used to hold the jib luff to the forestay. They may be metal, plastic, or webbing.*

Checking the equipment

Now you have the sails rigged, take a look around the boat to make sure that all the essential gear is aboard:

1. The rudder, tiller, and tiller extension should be kept in the bottom of the boat, under the mainsail and boom, until you launch

2. If your dinghy is fitted with a daggerboard make sure it is in the boat

3. You should have a bucket or bailer and sponge in case you need to bail out water

4. There should be at least one paddle or a pair of oars

5. If you are sailing on tidal waters there should be a small dinghy anchor and a length of anchor rope

6. Put any extra clothing, water, and snack food you may need in a kit bag and tie it somewhere out of the way, such as under the foredeck

Make sure that each member of the crew is wearing a personal flotation device (PFD) or a lifejacket, and check that the bungs are in the drain holes in the transom and the buoyancy tanks.

Launching the boat

MOST DINGHIES ARE STORED ashore and have to be moved to the water and launched before you can go sailing. It is easy to damage the dinghy or hurt yourself when moving boats on the shore so you need to learn how to lift and move dinghies safely. Some dinghies have lifting handles, but most have only the inside or outside edges of the sidedecks for you to hold on to. Small dinghies can be carried by two people – one at the bow and one at the stern – or on opposite sides by the shrouds. If you're carrying a dinghy any distance, remember that most of the weight is in the front half of the boat so arrange the lifting power accordingly.

Check for hazards

It is not unknown for overhead power lines to be in the vicinity of dinghy parks or launching points, or for people to be killed when moving their boats. Always look up before you move the boat to check that your tall aluminum mast will not touch a high-voltage cable or other obstruction.

Never drag the boat on or off a launching dolly, as this is very likely to scratch the hull. Push the trolley down the beach or slipway until the boat floats off – but make sure that someone keeps hold of the boat or the painter (the rope attached to the bow).

> ### Trivia...
> The ease with which your dolly will move over different surfaces depends on its wheels. Small, solid wheels work well only on hard surfaces. If you need to launch across a beach choose larger, preferably inflatable wheels.

The best way of moving a dinghy between the boat park and the water is to use a launching dolly. Before moving a boat or leaving it on its dolly, make sure that it is sitting evenly on the support chocks, is slightly bow heavy on the dolly, and is tied on securely. When you use a launching dolly, make sure that you always float the boat on and off the dolly.

Never get into a dinghy while it is ashore or on its launching dolly. Your weight in the bottom of the boat when it is not supported by water may damage it.

■ **Once the boat** has been floated off its dolly, one crew member holds it while the other parks the dolly clear of the water.

Hoisting the sails

WHETHER YOU LAUNCH THE BOAT before or after hoisting the sails depends on the circumstances, as we will see in Chapter 10. For your first few sails, you should have an instructor or experienced sailor showing you how to get afloat. But for now, let's assume that your boat is still ashore on its dolly and has been parked at the water's edge with the boat pointing into the wind.

The boat must be pointed into the wind before you attempt to hoist the mainsail, although the jib can be hoisted whatever the wind direction.

Crew checks that the jib sheets are led correctly

Hoisting the jib

Pull on the jib halyard to hoist the jib. Pull hard until the forestay goes slack, then cleat the halyard and coil up the loose rope.

■ **If you are hoisting** the sails while the dinghy is still ashore, you should always hoist the jib before you hoist the mainsail.

Hoisting the mainsail

Now it's the turn of the mainsail. Make sure that the sail is loosely folded in the boat with the boom lying underneath. Do not put the boom onto the gooseneck yet and make sure that the boom vang is loose. One person should pull on the mainsail halyard while the other guides the sail's boltrope into the groove in the mast. In the last stages, one person should hold the boom up to keep its weight off the sail. When the mainsail reaches the masthead, cleat the halyard or pull it into the halyard lock if there is one fitted. Coil the loose halyard tail and stow it out of the way.

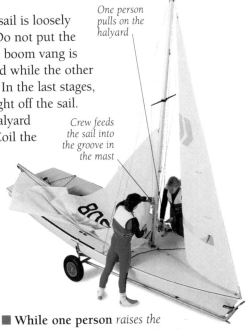

One person pulls on the halyard

Crew feeds the sail into the groove in the mast

Slide the boom onto the gooseneck and make sure that the mainsheet is free to run. The mainsail can then shake in the wind without filling and pulling the boat off its dolly. Attach the boom vang if it was not fitted earlier.

If your boat uses a lifting rudder, this can be fitted before launching. If it has a fixed rudder blade, lay it in the boat ready to be fitted as soon as possible when you are afloat. Lay it on the floor or it may be knocked out of the boat as the boom and mainsail flap in the wind.

■ **While one person** *raises the mainsail, the other makes sure that the boltrope feeds into the groove evenly and does not get jammed.*

A simple summary

✔ Sails create lift from the air blowing across them. This force drives the boat forward.

✔ A keel creates lift as it is pushed through the water, and this counteracts the sideways force produced by the sails.

✔ You should master knots such as the bowline and figure-eight.

✔ The sails must be rigged ready to hoist, and all the necessary equipment should be in the boat before launching.

✔ Dinghies are best moved around on shore with a launching dolly to avoid damage.

✔ Turn the dinghy into the wind before hoisting the mainsail.

Chapter 6

Afloat At Last

YOUR FIRST TIME AFLOAT will be full of new sensations and confusing activity. It will pass in a flash as you strive to get to grips with steering, trimming the sails, and keeping the boat upright. Your first impressions will probably induce a degree of nervousness, especially when the sails flap noisily and the boom swings above your head, but you will soon get used to these new experiences as you begin to relax and start to appreciate the art of sailing.

In this chapter...

✓ Your first time afloat

✓ Starting and stopping

✓ Staying upright

✓ Steering the boat

77

RELAX WHEN YOU GO AFLOAT – AFTER ALL, YOU'RE DOING IT FOR PLEASURE

Your first time afloat

THIS IS NOT THE TIME *to be worrying about the intricacies of leaving the shore under sail. In practice, your instructor or an experienced friend should take you out to the sailing area before letting you loose at the controls.*

Setting the scene

For our purposes, let's assume that you and a crew are sitting in your dinghy in the middle of a nice empty stretch of water. The sun is shining, the water is warm, and there is a gentle breeze providing ideal conditions for learning to sail.

When the boat is stopped with the sails hoisted, they will flap in the wind and the boom will swing from side to side. Do not hold the boom to stop it swinging about or the mainsail will fill with wind and you will start sailing before you are ready.

Where to sit

You are going to be the helmsman on your first sail and you must sit where you can see the sails and steer the boat. The best position is on the windward sidedeck, far enough forward to stop the end of the tiller from hitting your legs when you pull it towards you. From there, you will be able to see the luffs of jib and mainsail and you will have a good view ahead.

Hold the end of the tiller extension in your aft hand and the mainsheet in your other hand. You can hold the tiller extension in an overhand or underhand grip, whichever is the most comfortable and natural for you, but holding it like a dart works well in dinghies. Many keelboats have a tiller extension with a handle on the end and, in this case,

■ **In light winds**, *the crew sits to leeward to balance the weight of the helmsman to windward.*

you can fold your fingers through the handle. Whichever way you choose to hold the extension, be careful not to grip it too tightly. A sure sign of a nervous beginner is when their fingers turn white as they grip the extension too hard!

Holding the tiller extension too tightly restricts your wrist movement and makes the boat difficult to steer.

The role of the crew

Your crew should sit just in front of you as long as there is enough wind in the sails to allow you both to sit on the windward side. The crew adjusts the jib using the jib sheets, and moves his or her weight to keep the boat upright while allowing you to stay sitting on the windward sidedeck.

GETTING INTO THE BOAT

Small dinghies are not very stable so be careful when getting in and out. The trick to avoiding an early bath is to step into the middle of the boat and keep your weight as low as possible. By the middle, I mean on the centerline, about halfway between bow and stern. If you have to step down into the boat from a dock, consider sitting or kneeling on the edge of the dock before getting into the boat. Use the shroud or mast for support but don't pull the boat over toward you. Once you are in the boat, keep your weight low, and be careful not to move too far to one side until you have gotten used to the amount of stability your dinghy has. If the water is deep enough, putting the centerboard or daggerboard fully down will make the dinghy a bit more stable. In a two-person dinghy, both people have to coordinate their movements. Many dinghies will capsize if both people move to the same side when their weight is not counterbalanced by the wind in the sails.

Crew pushes boat off and climbs aboard

■ **When you launch** *from a slipway or beach, the helmsman gets in first and the crew pushes the boat toward open water then climbs aboard over the windward side.*

When you take your turn at being crew, you'll learn that you have to stay alert, adjusting your weight frequently as the wind varies in strength and direction. By comparison, the helmsman has an easy job since he can rightly claim that he needs to sit in one place in order to steer properly. Be gentle on your crew because it will soon be his turn to be helmsman!

■ **After changing her course** *and turning onto a run, this solo sailor adjusts her sails and daggerboard to retain speed and balance.*

Getting moving

Let's start sailing. Make sure that the centerboard is at least halfway down, keep the tiller in the middle of the boat, and pull in the mainsheet. Tell your crew to pull in his jib sheet – the leeward one. Pull the sheets in until both sails stop flapping. Watch the luff of each sail and pull the sheets until the flapping stops at the luff. The boat will immediately move forward. Congratulations, you are sailing, but in which direction?

The points of sail

The direction in which a boat is sailed is often described by its angle to the wind. Collectively, the different angles are called the points of sail. For each point of sail, or angle to the wind, you must adjust the sails, the centerboard position, and the crew position to keep the boat sailing fast, upright, and under full control.

When you are sailing close-hauled – as close to the wind as you can – the sails are pulled in tight and the centerboard is put right down to stop the sideways force, which is at its maximum on this point of sail. This also means that the heeling force is at its highest so the crew weight must be moved to windward to keep the boat upright. As you turn on to points of sail further away from the wind, the sails are let out, until they are fully out when you are on a run. As you let the sails out, the sideways force is reduced so the centerboard can be pulled up progressively. The heeling force also reduces so the crew weight is moved inboard.

Your first few minutes steering a boat under sail should be done on a beam reach, since this is the easiest point of sail to get used to. Look at the points of sail diagram (opposite) and you will find that you can sail on a beam reach in two different directions. The same is true for all the other points of sail except a run. We have to distinguish between the two possibilities and we do this by also describing which *tack* the boat is on.

DEFINITION

The word tack *has several meanings in sailing but, in this case, it describes the position of the wind and mainsail relative to the boat. If a boat is on port tack, the wind is blowing over the port side and the boom points out to starboard. On starboard tack the wind blows over the starboard side and the boom points out to port.*

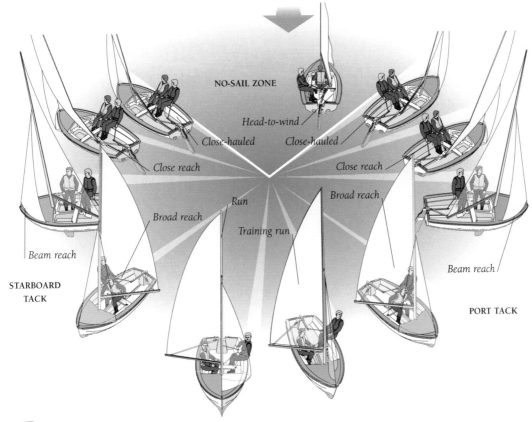

NO-SAIL ZONE

Head-to-wind

Close-hauled   *Close-hauled*

Close reach   *Close reach*

Run   *Broad reach*

Broad reach   *Training run*

Beam reach   *Beam reach*

STARBOARD
TACK   PORT TACK

a **No-sail zone** It is impossible to sail directly into the wind. Most boats only manage an angle of 45° either side of the true wind direction.

b **Head-to-wind** When you turn too far into the no-sail zone, you end up head-to-wind and the boat will stop before starting to move backward.

c **Close-hauled** This is as close to the wind as it is possible to sail. Sails are pulled in tight and the centerboard is put fully down.

d **Close reach** Turn from a close-hauled course, away from the wind by about another 20°. The sails are eased out and the centerboard is raised about a quarter.

e **Beam reach** Sailing across the wind with it blowing directly over the side of the boat. Both sails are eased halfway out and the centerboard is halfway up.

f **Broad reach** On a broad reach, the wind comes over the port or starboard quarter of the boat. Sails are eased well out and the centerboard is only a quarter down.

g **Training run** This is 5–10° off a true run but is safer for novices. Sails are eased right out, with the boom kept just off the leeward shroud, and the centerboard is kept at a quarter down.

h **Run (or dead run)** Sailing directly away from the wind. The sails are eased right out and the jib can be pulled to the opposite side from the mainsail, called wing and wing.

Starting and stopping

YOU ALREADY KNOW how to start sailing – simply pull in the sails until they stop shaking and the boat will move forward. Few things are so simple, but do remember to keep the tiller in the middle when you pull the sails in, otherwise the boat will start to turn as soon as the sails fill.

Helmsman pushes the tiller to turn head-to-wind

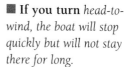

Adjusting the centerboard

You must also remember to put the centerboard down so that the boat moves forward rather than sideways. Beginners often forget this point and find they are moving, but not in the direction they expected. The amount of centerboard that must be lowered depends on the point of sail you are on, but for your first few attempts at steering the boat you should choose a beam reach and put the centerboard at least halfway down.

■ **If you turn** *head-to-wind, the boat will stop quickly but will not stay there for long.*

Learning to stop

If starting is simple, stopping requires a bit more thought, since the only brakes available are the natural forces of wind and tide. The simplest way to stop is to turn onto a close reach and let both sails out fully. This is known as lying-to.

The crew must be ready to move to balance the boat

Alternatively, you can turn the boat head-to-wind. The sails will shake along the centerline and the boat will come to a stop. Unlike the lying-to position, however, this is not a stable situation. The boat will be blown backward by the windage of the flapping sails and the bow will fall off in one direction or another – depending on the position of the rudder. When the bow is far enough away from the wind, the sails will fill and it will start to sail.

■ **If you point the boat** *on a close reach and let out both sails, the boat will stop and will lie fairly steadily in this position until you are ready to start again.*

When lying-to, it is vital that you turn the boat to a close reach. If the boat is allowed to point further off the wind, you will not be able to spill all the wind out of the mainsail.

Staying upright

A DINGHY SAILS FASTEST (and is easiest to control) when it is sailed upright. This sounds straightforward, but it is the key to handling a sailing boat well and requires considerable awareness of the forces acting on the boat.

When you look at a boat from behind, you can understand how the sideways force from the sails is significantly higher than the opposite sideways force from the keel. This vertical separation of the two opposing forces causes the boat to heel and eventually to capsize if you and your crew do not counter it with your weight.

Using your weight

Cast your mind back a few pages to when we talked about the sideways force created by the sails and the opposing force produced by the keel. You and your crew must move your weight, by sitting in or out, to balance the heeling force accurately. Since the wind is always shifting in strength and direction, you need to be vigilant to changes and be aware that, whenever you change your point of sail, you will have to move your weight in or out.

Always remember that an instant cure for heeling too far to leeward is to let the sheets go so that the sails flap and spill wind. If everything seems to be going totally wrong, let the tiller go as well. Even at the point of capsize, there is always a good chance that the boat will stay upright if you don't interfere!

Do not make the classic mistake of hanging on to the sheets for grim death while the boat heels further and further, until it eventually capsizes.

■ **When you are sitting out,** *tuck your feet under the hiking straps so that you can lean out without overbalancing. Adjust the hiking straps, if necessary, so that you can sit out comfortably.*

Adjusting your position

Sailing upwind or on a reach in light winds, the helmsman sits to windward and the crew balances the boat by sitting to leeward. As the wind increases, the crew moves into the middle of the boat, then up to the windward side to sit out alongside the helmsman. On a broad reach or run, the heeling force is almost zero, so the crew sits in the middle of the boat or on the opposite side to balance the helmsman's weight.

Check your position fore and aft. If you sit too far aft, the transom will drag in the water, while if you sit too far forwards the bow will dig in. In either case you will slow down and steering will become harder.

If your crew sits just aft of the windward shroud and you sit next to him with your legs clear of the tiller, you will be in the right position for most conditions.

Trivia...

Racing crews sit alongside each other when sitting out and try to centralize their weight halfway along the boat. This reduces wind resistance and allows the bow and stern to lift easily.

Steering the boat

THE RUDDER IS YOUR MAIN *steering control and you move it by pushing or pulling on the tiller or tiller extension. Remember that the boat will turn in the opposite direction to the way you push the tiller. This means that if you push the tiller to starboard the boat's bow will turn to port, and vice versa.*

For the rudder to work it needs water flowing past it.

Steering made simple

You can't steer unless you are moving. The faster you sail, the more effective and sensitive the rudder becomes due to the increased speed of water across it. Get used to steering by sailing the boat on a beam reach first. Pick a spot ahead of the bow on the horizon and use it as a reference mark to steer for. Now, gently push the tiller away from you. Do not watch the tiller when you push it but look at the horizon in front of the bow. As the boat turns, you will see the bow swing across the horizon away from your reference mark. When the boat has turned about 20°, pull the tiller back to the centerline and then toward you so that the bow swings back the other way. Once you are pointing at your reference mark again, put the tiller back in the middle of the boat.

A natural tendency for many beginners is to put the tiller over and then forget to straighten it when the boat has turned far enough. Remember that the boat will continue to turn for as long as the tiller is pushed or pulled from its central position.

Getting used to your boat

The first thing to get used to in a new boat is the sensitivity of that particular boat's steering. It varies according to the design of boat, with high-performance dinghies being more sensitive than general-purpose dinghies. Rudder sensitivity varies according to the speed at which you are sailing. In light winds, the boat moves slowly and the rudder is less effective so the boat turns slowly. In stronger winds, with the boat sailing quickly, the rudder is in fast-flowing water and the smallest movement of the tiller will produce a quick turning response. So, in light winds, expect to push or pull the tiller further, and hold it there longer, than when you sail in stronger winds.

INTERNET

www.boats.com

Check out this US portal for lots of useful information about boats.

A simple summary

✔ Get an instructor or an experienced sailor to take you to the sailing area before you take over the controls.

✔ Get comfortable with sitting in the boat and holding the tiller and mainsheet before you pull in the sails.

✔ Sail on a beam reach, using the rudder to steer and adjusting the sails to start and stop.

✔ Adjust the sails, centerboard, and crew weight according to the point of sail you are on.

✔ Move your weight in and out of the boat in order to balance the wind in the sails and to keep the boat upright.

✔ Get used to the sensitivity of the steering of the boat you sail, and practice using the rudder to steer the boat accurately.

Chapter 7

Changing Course

SAILING IN ONE DIRECTION is fine to start with but it soon becomes a bit limiting if you do not know how to change course! Now that you are getting accustomed to the controls, and to steering the boat in a straight line on a beam reach, you are ready to explore all the points of sail. As you do so, you will also learn the two most important sail maneuvers – tacking and jibing – and you will be well on your way to mastering the basics of sailing.

In this chapter...

✓ Turning the boat

✓ Learning to tack

✓ Learning to jibe

✓ The five essentials

THE WAY YOUR BOAT RESPONDS WILL TELL YOU HOW WELL YOU'RE SAILING

Turning the boat

AS WE HAVE SEEN, the rudder is the main steering control but it is not the only one. The way the sails are trimmed, the position of the crew, and the amount the centerboard or daggerboard is lowered all influence how the boat turns. Some of these influences can be so powerful that they may overcome the force of the rudder, preventing the helmsman from turning the boat in the direction he wishes.

Using the rudder

Because you nearly always sit on the windward side of a dinghy when you are steering, this means that if you are *luffing up* you must push the tiller away from you. If you are *bearing away*, remember to pull the tiller toward you.

Try to keep the movement smooth when you push or pull on the tiller. Whenever the rudder is turned, it acts as a brake as well as a turning control. If you put the tiller over too far, or move it very rapidly or jerkily, you will slow the boat down.

Using the sails

Sails have an important steering effect that you can easily demonstrate for yourself. With the boat pointing on a beam reach but with both sails let out as much as possible, let go of the tiller and pull in the mainsheet quite quickly. You will see the boat start to move forwards while also turning toward the wind. Let the mainsheet out and reposition the boat on the beam reach with both sails let out fully.

Now, get your crew to pull in the jib sheet while you let go of the tiller. This time the boat will move forward and turn away from the wind. The effect will probably not be as powerful as when you pulled in the mainsheet because the jib is usually a lot smaller than the mainsail, but it will still be very apparent as long as you keep the boat upright when you try it.

A boat tries to turn in the opposite direction to that in which it is heeled. So if you both move your weight to heel the boat to windward, it will turn to leeward and vice versa.

Using your weight

Your weight also affects the steering. Try steering on a beam reach, with both sails trimmed properly, then sit out hard to heel the boat toward you, while holding the tiller extension loosely. As the boat heels toward you, it will turn away from the wind. Now, try heeling it to leeward by moving your weight inboard slightly. Let the tiller extension slide through your fingers and the boat will immediately turn toward the wind.

SHEETING THE MAINSAIL IN AND OUT

When your crew sheets in the jib, he has two hands available. When you sheet in the mainsail, however, you have to control the tiller extension at the same time. How you do this depends on whether your dinghy has a center or an aft mainsheet.

Center mainsheet

1 Control the tiller

Hold the tiller extension with your fingers on top and your palm underneath.

2 Pull in the sheet

Rotate the tiller extension across the front of your body. Pull in as much sheet as possible using your forward hand and then swing the tiller hand down to grasp the sheet.

3 Reach down to pull in further

Hold the sheet and tiller extension in the tiller hand and swing the tiller extension as far aft as you can without repositioning the tiller. With your sheet hand, grasp the mainsheet near the block. Pull as far as you can, then repeat to pull in more sheet.

■ **When you have** *swung both sheet and tiller extension aft, reach down with your sheet hand to pull in another armful of mainsheet.*

Aft mainsheet

1 Start to pull in the sheet

To sheet in, pull the mainsheet across your body as far as you can.

2 Hold with your tiller hand

Trap the mainsheet under the thumb of your tiller hand. This allows you to let go with your sheet hand and reach across your body to grasp the sheet again.

3 Continue to sheet in

Repeat as necessary until the sail is sheeted in sufficiently.

■ **By trapping** *an aft mainsheet under the thumb of your tiller hand, reach across with your sheet hand to pull in more mainsheet.*

Using the centerboard

Finally, you can experiment to see the effect the centerboard or daggerboard has on the way the boat turns. With the boat sailing on a beam reach, pull the centerboard fully up. The boat will immediately slide sideways and heel less than before – you will have to move your weight inboard to keep it upright. Now, try turning the boat toward the wind by pushing the tiller away from you. You will find that the boat turns less quickly or positively than when the centerboard is fully down.

A centerboard's effective area moves backward or forward along the fore and aft line, and this also has a steering effect on the boat. The boat will tend to turn away from the wind as the centerboard is raised, and toward it as it is lowered.

LUFFING UP

To luff up, push the tiller away from you and then centralize it when you have turned onto the new course. Pull both sails in until they stop shaking at their luffs and they are set correctly for the new course. Get your crew to lower the centerboard to the correct position for the new course and move your weight outboard to balance the increased heeling force.

Sails are about halfway out

Crew has to sit out further

Sails are pulled in tight

1 **Beam reach**

Start by sailing on a beam reach with the sails set correctly, the boat upright, and the centerboard halfway down.

2 **Close reach**

Luff up to a close reach. Pull in the sails until they stop shaking at the luff. Put the centerboard three-quarters down.

3 **Close-hauled**

Luff up to close-hauled. Pull both sails in and fully lower the centerboard. Center the tiller when you are on course.

Remember, a daggerboard is moved straight up and down, but a centerboard pivots backward and forward as it is raised and lowered.

Practice turning

So far we have experimented with the turning controls while sailing on a beam reach. Now it is time for you to explore the other points of sail and to practice changing course. Try to change course smoothly, moving the tiller gently and adjusting the sails, crew weight, and centerboard position as you make the turn.

Trivia...

We refer to courses that are closer to the wind than a beam reach as "upwind" courses, and those further away from the wind as "downwind" courses.

BEARING AWAY

To bear away, pull the tiller toward you and then centralize it when you have turned to the new course. Ease the mainsheet and jib sheet to let both sails out until they are set correctly on the new course. Get your crew to raise the centerboard to the correct position for the new course and be ready to move your weight inboard as the heeling force decreases.

Sails are about halfway out

Crew moves in to balance the boat

Mainsail is let right out

1 Beam reach

Start sailing on a beam reach with the sails set correctly, the boat upright, and the centerboard halfway down.

2 Broad reach

Bear away to a broad reach. Position the sails correctly and raise the centerboard to about one-quarter down.

3 Training run

Bear away further to a training run. If the jib attempts to cross to the windward side, luff up slightly to keep it to leeward.

Learning to tack

THE TACKING MANEUVER is used whenever a course change involves turning the bow through the wind. When you are learning, you will start by sailing on a beam reach, with the wind on one side of the boat and then tacking onto the opposite beam reach, with the wind on the other side of the boat. Tacking from one beam reach to the opposite beam reach involves a turn of 180°, and it will take some time for the boat to turn through this angle. It is important that the boat is sailing as fast as possible before you start the maneuver and that you continue to steer throughout, or you may fail to complete the turn, stopping in the head-to-wind position. This is known as being caught in irons.

Knowing your role

As the helmsman it is up to you to decide when to tack, to be responsible for ensuring that the new course is clear, and for making sure that your crew is ready. After the tack, you must check the sail trim, boat balance, and the new course.

The crew, if you have one, is responsible for releasing the jib sheet, picking up the new sheet, moving across the boat, and sheeting in the jib on the new side as the boat completes the turn. The crew can cross the boat facing forward or aft. If you are sailing a singlehanded dinghy with only a mainsail to control, you can ignore all the references to a crew and a jib.

■ **These Sonar keelboats** *are tacking as they race to windward. Being able to tack well, with minimum loss of speed, is an important sailing skill, but it is vital when racing.*

Center or aft mainsheet

During a tack, you need to change hands on the mainsheet and the tiller and move across the boat, while simultaneously keeping control of both tiller and mainsheet. In an aft mainsheet dinghy, the helmsman should cross the boat facing aft. When using a center mainsheet, the helmsman can face forward during the tack. This allows him to look ahead as the boat turns.

TACKING

Handling the tiller extension and the mainsheet during a tack is often one of the most difficult skills to learn. When I taught myself to sail, I spent hours practicing ashore with a stick and some rope to stand in for the tiller and the mainsheet! Don't worry if at first you end up with tangled arms, sheet, and tiller. The task is difficult because you need to change hands on the tiller and mainsheet while moving from one side of the boat to the other.

When you are sailing a center mainsheet boat, you should change hands after you have sat down on the new side. This seems strange at first because it means holding the tiller extension behind your back as you sit down, but it will soon become natural.

Go through the following steps when you are tacking with a center mainsheet arrangement:

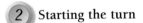

Sails are properly trimmed before the tack

Helmsman pushes the tiller over further

Helmsman calls out "helms-a-lee" when he pushes the tiller away

1 **On a beam reach**

The helmsman checks the area to windward and alerts the crew by saying, "Ready about".

2 **Starting the turn**

Crew checks the area, uncleats the jib sheet, and says, "Ready". The helmsman starts the turn.

3 **Into the tack**

When the jib flaps, the crew releases the old jib sheet and picks up the new one.

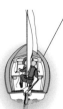

Helmsman and crew cross the boat at the same time as the boom

Crew sheets in the jib as it blows across to the new side

Sails are properly trimmed for the new course

4 **Head-to-wind**

As the boat turns head-to-wind, helmsman and crew cross the boat, ducking under the boom.

5 **Through the tack**

Helmsman and crew sit down on the new side and the crew sheets in the jib.

6 **New course**

The helmsman keeps the boat turning onto the new course and then straightens the tiller.

Tacking from close-hauled

When learning to tack, you usually do so from one beam reach to the other, since it gives you more time to complete the maneuver. In normal sailing, however, you usually tack from one close-hauled course to the other because tacking is an integral part of beating to windward. When you are trying to reach an upwind destination, you must sail close-hauled with the wind on one side, then tack and sail close-hauled with the wind on the other side. In this way, you will zigzag your way to windward. Tacking from close-hauled to close-hauled involves a turn of only 90° and will happen much more quickly than tacking from a reach to a reach. You have less time to complete the tack and you will find that, on your first few attempts, you probably turn too far through the tack and end up further off the wind than the intended close-hauled course. Try to be in the middle of the boat as, or just after, the boom crosses the centerline. Don't forget to duck as you move across the boat so that the boom passes safely over your head.

To move across a boat, simply watch the end of the boom and begin to change sides when it approaches the centerline.

Common problems

Knowing when to move across the boat often causes problems for beginners. Since your weight is needed to keep the boat upright once the sails fill on the new tack, it is important that you move at the right time. Another common problem is not completing the tack. Many beginners forget to steer throughout the turn and lose control of the tiller while they are moving across the boat.

TACKING AND JIBING COMMANDS

There are many strange-sounding sailing terms, but the key ones have an important purpose and are generally understood by all sailors. When tacking, the helmsman calls, "Ready about" or "Prepare to tack" to warn the crew to prepare for the tack. The crew should reply, "Ready" to let the helmsman know that he is free to tack. The helmsman then calls, "Helms-a-lee" when he pushes the tiller over to let the crew know that he is starting to turn the boat. Some people call out "Helms-a-lee" or "Lee-oh," or some other similar expression, which is fine as long as everyone understands exactly what is meant. The equivalent jibing commands are "Ready to jibe" (or "Stand by to jibe") and "Jibe-oh."

Keep the tiller pushed away from you as you move across the boat and do not centralize the tiller until you have sat down on the new side. Wait until the boat is on the new course and then center the tiller.

Tips for tacking

- Do remember to check that the area you will turn into is clear of obstructions.
- Remember to check that your crew is ready before starting the tack.
- Push the tiller over and keep it there.
- Don't rush across the boat. The maneuver takes longer than you may think. Wait until the boom swings toward the center of the boat, and then start to move.
- The crew must not pull in the new jib sheet until the jib has blown across to the new leeward side.
- Keep steering through the maneuver until you are on the desired course.

IN IRONS

This refers to those occasions when the boat fails to complete a tack and ends up stopped head-to-wind. This can happen if:

- The boat was not sailing fast enough before the tack
- The helmsman didn't steer the boat completely through the tack
- The crew pulled in the new jib sheet too early, causing it to fill on the wrong side and stop the boat

The solution is to wait until the boat moves backward, then push the tiller away from you. This will reverse the flow of water over the rudder and the bow will move in the direction you push the tiller. If your crew also pulls the jib to the opposite side to the tiller, the wind will catch it on its "back" side. This will help push the bow in the desired direction and is known as "backing the jib." As soon as the boat is pointing in the right direction, center the tiller and get your crew to sheet in the jib on the correct side. If you are sailing a singlehanded dinghy with no jib, push the boom out to "back" the mainsail.

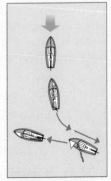

■ **When the boat** *starts to move backward, push the tiller away from you. The boat will turn, leaving you sitting on the new windward side and ready to sail away.*

Learning to jibe

NOW THAT YOU HAVE MASTERED tacking, it is time to try jibing. *Both maneuvers have the same result: the boat is turned to bring the wind to the other side. However, when jibing, the boat is turned downwind until the stern passes through the wind. This means that jibing is quicker and feels more violent than tacking. When tacking, the sails flap harmlessly while the boat is head-to-wind but during jibing, the sails are always full of wind. As the boat turns beyond a run, the wind gets behind the mainsail leech and quickly blows the sail over to the other side.*

The speed with which the mainsail and boom swing across the boat during a jibe means that it is very important that you move your weight quickly to the new side. If you are slow to move, especially in a strong wind, a jibe can end in a capsize.

Staying in control

As the helmsman, it is up to you to decide when to jibe. You must make sure that the new course is clear and check that the crew is ready, just as you do before a tacking maneuver. Your crew is responsible for using his weight to balance the boat through the jibe and for sheeting the jib from one side to the other.

Before a jibe, make sure that the centerboard is raised so that it is no more than one-quarter down or preferably less.

Preparing to jibe

If the centerboard is any further than one-quarter down, the boat will try and luff violently as the boom swings across and the boat may trip over the centerboard and capsize. If your boat has a daggerboard rather than a centerboard, make sure that it is not raised so far that it catches on the boom or boom vang as the mainsail swings across. If it does, a capsize is inevitable unless the wind is light.

When you have decided to jibe, bear away until the jib hangs limply behind the mainsail – indicating that you are on a dead run. Then, luff up slightly until the jib fills on the same side as the mainsail. You are now on a training run which, when you are learning, is the best starting point for the maneuver.

JIBING

The method for handling the tiller extension and the mainsheet during a jibe is similar to the procedure for tacking. Follow these steps when you are moving through a jibe, with a center mainsheet arrangement:

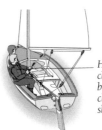

Crew concentrates on balancing the boat

Helmsman checks the boom is just clear of the shroud

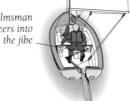

Helmsman steers into the jibe

1 **Training run**

Check that the area the boat will turn into is clear and call out, "Stand by to jibe."

2 **Starting the jibe**

The crew checks for other boats, replies, "Ready," and prepares to move his weight.

3 **Ready to jibe**

The helmsman bears away onto a dead run and moves into the middle of the boat.

Helmsman centers the tiller as the boom swings over

Helmsman changes hands on tiller and sheet

Set sails correctly for new course

Crew adjusts the jib sheet on the new side

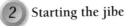

4 **Jibing**

Helmsman and crew should be in the middle of the boat when the boom swings across.

5 **After the jibe**

The helmsman sits down on the new side and the crew adjusts his position to balance the boat.

6 **New course**

After the jibe, you are likely to be on a broad reach and can now steer to your chosen course.

- Swing the tiller extension around so that it points to the opposite side of the boat. Push the tiller to the windward side. Put your aft foot into the middle of the boat.
- When you see that the mainsail is about to swing across, move to the middle of the boat, pivoting on the balls of your feet so that you face forward, and crouching to avoid the boom as it swings overhead.
- Center the tiller as the boom passes overhead and move to the new windward side. Sit down and change hands on the tiller extension and the mainsheet.

The five essentials

WHATEVER TYPE OF DINGHY you sail, there are five essential elements for efficient sailing. They are sail trim, centerboard position, boat balance, boat trim, and the course steered. Whenever one of these is changed, you should quickly review the other four elements and adjust them if necessary.

Sail trim

Check sail trim by easing the sails out until they shake along their luffs, then pull them in until the shaking just stops. To make it easier to check sail trim, fit telltales to the sails. Telltales are strips of wool or nylon sewn or glued about 6–9 inches (15–23 cm) back from the luff on each side of the sail. These light streamers fly in the wind stream passing the sail and indicate whether the stream is smooth or turbulent. When the telltales on both sides of the sail stream aft along the sail, it is set correctly. If the windward telltale breaks away and flies high, the sail is too far out and you should pull in the sheet. If the leeward telltale breaks away and flies high, the sail is too far in so let out the sheet.

Centerboard position

Remember that the closer you sail toward the wind, the more the centerboard should be lowered until it is fully down when you are close-hauled. Sideways force is zero on a run so, as you turn away from the wind, you should raise the centerboard until it is almost fully up when you are running. Always keep a small amount down otherwise it can be difficult to steer.

Boat balance

All boats sail fastest when they are upright, so you and your crew must move your weight to counteract the heeling force from the sails. The heeling force is greatest when you are sailing

■ **Expert dinghy sailors** *automatically and constantly check and adjust the five essential elements, in order to keep the boat sailing at maximum speed and under full control.*

close-hauled, so expect to be sitting out on the sidedeck in all but the lightest of winds. As you turn away from the wind, the heeling force reduces and your crew can move into the boat, ending up on the opposite side to you when you are sailing on a run.

Boat trim

Remember to check your fore and aft position occasionally. It is common for beginners to sit too far back in the boat, so take a look over the transom to check that the wake is not very disturbed, which would indicate that you are sitting too far aft. In light winds, you can move forward to trim the boat slightly down by the bow for extra speed, and in strong winds it helps to move back slightly to allow the bow to lift easily on waves.

On course

Beginners often concentrate so hard on the boat, they tend to forget how important it is to keep an eye on their course and to check for any obstructions in their path. Use a land or seamark to help you steer a straight course and sail with your eyes looking ahead of the boat rather than watching the tiller or mainsheet as you adjust them.

A simple summary

✓ When changing course in a sailing dinghy, you have to adjust the sails, centerboard, and crew position as you steer onto the new course.

✓ As you turn toward the wind, the heeling force increases, and as you turn away from the wind, it decreases.

✓ Tacking involves turning the bow through the wind when changing course from one tack to the other.

✓ Jibing involves turning the stern through the wind when changing course from one tack to the other.

✓ You will need to master different movements depending on whether the boat you sail has a center or an aft mainsheet.

✓ To sail a dinghy well you must pay attention to the five essentials: sail trim, centerboard position, boat balance, boat trim, and the course you are sailing.

Chapter 8

Safety Matters

Dinghy sailing is not a dangerous sport – provided you are not allergic to getting wet – and you can help keep it that way by taking sensible precautions and learning the basic safety skills. All sailors have to remember that, ultimately, they are responsible for their own safety. Even if you are sailing with safety boats close by there can be no guarantee that you will not be forced to rely on your own abilities at some point. The further away from the shore or assistance that you sail, the more important it is that you can deal with any problems and take care of yourself.

In this chapter...

✓ Man overboard

✓ Recovering from a capsize

✓ Avoiding other boats

WORK AS A TEAM WHEN YOU ARE RECOVERING FROM A CAPSIZE

Man overboard

IT IS ACTUALLY QUITE RARE for someone to fall overboard from a dinghy, but, if it does happen and you are left alone in the boat, it is vital that you know how to rescue the person in the water without capsizing in the process.

The most likely cause of someone falling overboard is a hiking strap breaking or coming undone, so make it a habit to check yours before you go afloat.

When a person falls out of the boat, it is usually as much of a shock to the person left aboard as it is to the one in the water. The first step is to stop the boat from capsizing now that part of the weight that was balancing it is in the water. If you are steering when your crew falls overboard, your task is easier because you are already in control of the boat. You are in a position to let the mainsheet out quickly to spill wind and keep the boat upright. If you are crewing and your helmsman falls overboard, you have to react very quickly to move aft, grab the tiller, and get the boat under control.

Knowing what to do

Once the boat is under control, the next step is to get back to the person in the water as quickly as possible, while staying in control of the dinghy. To achieve this, you need to have practiced the recovery routine regularly. Practice will also teach you the skill of being able to sail a boat slowly and to stop it at an exact point. The more proficient you are, the easier it will be to handle the boat instinctively while keeping your eye on the person in the water.

■ **An approved personal flotation device** *will keep you afloat. Even so, it can be very difficult to spot someone in the water.*

Getting into position

All the textbooks tell you that the most important factor during a man overboard recovery is to keep the person in sight constantly so that you always know where they are. This is true, and may be achievable in a larger boat with several people on deck, but it is almost impossible when you are alone in a dinghy. During the maneuver, you will have to tack to return to the person's position and, at that point, you are likely to lose sight of them.

RETRIEVING A MAN OVERBOARD

The safest method of returning to the person in the water is to turn the boat immediately onto a beam reach and sail away from him or her, just far enough to give yourself room to maneuver. Keep checking the person's position as you sail away so that you do not lose them among the waves.

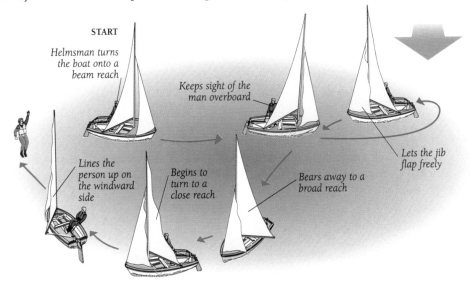

START

Helmsman turns the boat onto a beam reach

Keeps sight of the man overboard

Lets the jib flap freely

Lines the person up on the windward side

Begins to turn to a close reach

Bears away to a broad reach

1 Taking control

When someone falls overboard, the person left in the boat must regain control. Let the jib sheet out so that the jib flaps during the maneuver, and turn the boat onto a beam reach.

2 Planning action

Sail away from the person for about ten to fifteen boat lengths. Give yourself long enough to assess the situation and room to maneuver during the next part of the operation.

3 Tacking back

Leaving the jib flapping, tack the boat onto the reciprocal beam reach, and make sure that you still have the person in sight.

4 Making room

Bear away onto a broad reach. Your intention is to get far enough to leeward of the man overboard so that you have room to luff to a close reach on the final approach.

5 Controlling speed

About five boat lengths from the person and to leeward of him, turn to a close reach. This will give you full control of your course and speed. Use the mainsheet to control your speed.

6 The recovery

Make your final approach so that you can stop the boat with the person by the windward shroud. In this position, the boat will lie quietly with sails flapping as you retrieve him.

If you are the person in the water remember how difficult it is for the person aboard to see you. Keep calm, hold one arm above your head, and blow your lifejacket's whistle to attract attention.

When you approach the person in the water, make sure that you stop the boat with them positioned on its windward side. If you try to pick them up on the leeward side, there is a risk that the boat will drift on top of them, or that you will capsize as you try and get them aboard. If you try to bring them aboard too far aft, the bow will probably blow off downwind and the boat will start sailing again.

Your man overboard should take hold of the windward gunwale. You can then give the tiller a flick to windward before letting go of it and moving forward to help him aboard. This flick will help prevent the boat turning head to wind or even tacking around the person in the water.

Pulling someone aboard

Move to just behind the windward shroud and grasp the person under the armpits. Leaning toward him will depress the side of the boat toward the water, and, if you lean back and pull, you should be able to drag the person's upper half into the boat. From there he can be rolled into the boat. If you have trouble getting the person back aboard, drop a loop of the jib sheet over the side for him to use as a step into the boat.

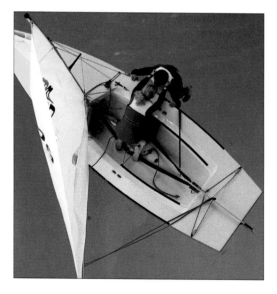

■ **Recover the person** *just behind the windward shroud and grasp him under the armpits to pull his top half into the dinghy.*

Do not be tempted to jibe the dinghy in an attempt to get back to a person in the water quickly; this could easily result in you capsizing some distance from him, putting you both in greater danger than before.

Practicing the maneuver

It is important to practice this maneuver regularly so that you know what to do if this situation ever arises. Obviously, you shouldn't use a real person in your practice sessions, but you can create a suitable substitute using a fender tied to a large container (at least 7 gallons, or 25 liters), or several smaller containers tied together. Fill the containers almost fully with water and they will drift in a similar way to a real man overboard. Try throwing the containers over on all points of sail until you are confident that you can return accurately from whatever point of sail you start on.

Don't stop practicing until you can bring the boat to a complete stop, alongside the bottles, on virtually every attempt. Even when you are confident in your abilities, practice this skill occasionally to make sure that it is second nature. Also, try the maneuver whenever you sail a new boat as it is a great way to learn how it reacts.

Recovering from a capsize

DINGHIES ARE PRONE TO CAPSIZING *because they rely on the weight of the crew for their stability under sail. Capsized and inverted boats are a common occurrence among high-performance dinghies, and even the more stable, general-purpose dinghies can capsize if mishandled. Because capsizing is always a possibility, it is important that you learn how to right a capsized boat and practice the skill regularly.*

The most important thing to remember when you capsize is always to keep hold of the boat and never attempt to swim to shore. A capsized boat is far easier to spot than a swimmer's head and the shore is usually further away than it looks.

Reasons for capsizing

Sailing dinghies can capsize either to windward or to leeward. The leeward capsize is the most common and usually happens when the boat is allowed to heel so far over that water pours over the leeward gunwale. It usually happens quite slowly but, once a capsize becomes inevitable, you and your crew should allow yourselves to drop into the water between the boom and the hull. If you try to hang on to the boat in order to stay out of the water, the dinghy is likely to turn upside down, making recovery harder.

The windward capsize happens when the boat rolls heavily to windward, typically when sailing on a run or during a jibe. When the boat heels to windward it naturally tries to turn away from the wind, the roll increases, and it capsizes to windward – on top of you and your crew. This type of capsize is usually quicker and more violent than a leeward capsize and you may not have any time to react.

Recovering from a capsize

When you right a capsized boat, you should pull it up toward the wind. This way the boat will be more stable when it comes upright, with the crew already in the boat and the helmsman climbing in over the windward shroud.

During a capsize recovery, you and your crew will be out of sight of each other for much of the procedure, so keep talking to each other to make sure that you know what is happening and make sure that the other person is safe.

If, after the capsize, the mast is pointing toward the wind with the hull downwind of it the wind will get under the sails as soon as you start to right the boat. The boat will probably immediately flip over the other way when you try to right it. To avoid this, stand on the centerboard and lean back enough to pull the mast just clear of the water and hold it there. This will result in the hull turning round so that the rig lies downwind. You can then safely right the boat.

RIGHTING A TWO-PERSON DINGHY

The standard method for righting a two-person dinghy is known as the scoop method. The name comes from the fact that one person is scooped aboard as the other person pulls the boat upright. The weight of one person in the boat as it is righted makes it more stable and helps prevent it capsizing again.

Crew makes sure centerboard is lowered

Checks rudder is secured to the boat

1 **Safety first**

Check that your crew is safe and is not trapped under the boat or sails. Begin to move toward the transom so that if the boat inverts, you will not be trapped underneath.

2 **Rudder-check**

At the transom, check that the rudder has not fallen off its fittings. Use the mainsheet as a safety line as you swim around the bottom of the boat to the centerboard.

The boat will be slow to right at first, but when the mast and sails have been pulled clear of the water it will come up quite quickly. As the boat comes upright, your crew will be scooped aboard. You can often scramble aboard by the windward shroud as the boat comes upright. If not, the crew can help you aboard, but he must be careful not to move too quickly because the boat will be relatively unstable with water in it. Once you have righted the boat, tidy up any loose gear and bail the water out before sailing off. If self-bailers or transom flaps are fitted, you should open them and start sailing slowly on a reach so that they can empty the boat.

Useful tips

When you capsize, always keep the following points in mind:

1. Don't panic if you find yourself under the mainsail or jib when the boat capsizes. Raise your hand above your head to lift the sail clear of the water and make an air pocket. Keeping your hand above your head, paddle out from under the sail.

2. If you find yourself under the hull of an inverted boat, you'll find plenty of air inside the hull. Move to the outer edge and reach down and grasp the gunwale edge. Pull yourself under the sidedeck and emerge outside the hull.

3. If you cannot pull the boat upright, lower the mainsail and try again. If all attempts fail and you find yourself becoming tired, climb onto the hull, tie yourself on with the end of a sheet, and wait for rescue.

Crew finds the end of the top jib sheet and throws it to the other person

Crew holds on to a thwart or hiking strap, without putting weight on the boat

Pulls steadily on the jib sheet to right the boat

3 Throwing the sheet

Tell your crew when you are at the centerboard and have him pull himself along the inside of the boat. Once he has thrown you the jib sheet, let go of the mainsheet.

4 Getting into position

Your crew should float inside the hull, head toward the bow. He should ensure that the mainsheet is free so that the mainsail can flap when the boat is righted.

5 Righting the dinghy

Climb onto the centerboard using the jib sheet to help you. Position your feet on the part close to the hull. Lean back with straight arms and legs and pull on the jib sheet.

RIGHTING AN INVERTED BOAT

Modern dinghies, especially high-performance ones, are often very prone to invert when they have capsized. This is because they usually have a high amount of built-in buoyancy in the sides of the boat rather than in the bow and stern. This helps them to come upright with very little water in them, but also causes them to float very high on their sides when capsized. If they invert, their decks can form a seal with the water and the resistance of the sails underwater also makes them slow to right. Sometimes the centerboard will retract when a boat turns upside down, which makes righting the boat more difficult, but still possible. The two-person technique for righting an inverted boat is to bring it up so that it is lying on its side, before proceeding with the scoop method already described:

1 Initial action

One of you should find the jib sheet on the leeward side and throw it across the hull, forward of the centerboard. The heaviest person should swim around to the windward side of the boat to grasp the end of the jib sheet. The other one should swim to the stern.

2 Using your weight

The heavier person then climbs onto the windward gunwale and tries to pull the centerboard down. He leans back and pulls on the centerboard or jib sheet. The other person crouches on the windward corner of the stern to help break the seal between decks and water.

INVERTED DINGHY

3 Joint effort

As the boat starts to come up, the person near the stern gets ready to move inside the boat, when it is on its side, for a scoop recovery. If the heavier person has trouble pulling the boat onto its side, the other person should swim to join him and climb onto the gunwale, grasp the centerboard or jib sheet, and add his weight to the effort. Remember that a steady pull is most effective.

CAPSIZED DINGHY

4 Righting the boat

With the boat on its side, the recovery continues with the scoop method. Because you started off by standing on the windward gunwale of the inverted boat, the boat will come up onto its side with the mast pointing downwind. This will allow you to right the boat toward the wind, which makes the recovery much easier and will help prevent the boat capsizing again.

Righting a singlehanded dinghy

Righting a singlehanded dinghy is much easier if you don't end up in the water when the boat capsizes. Many singlehanders float quite high in the water when capsized, and it can be difficult to reach and climb onto the centerboard without a jib sheet to pull on. In a leeward capsize, try and climb up over the top gunwale as the boat capsizes and step onto the centerboard. If you do this quickly enough, the boat can be up and sailing again in seconds and you can even stay dry!

If you do end up in the water, perhaps after a windward capsize, swim around to the centerboard and wrap your arms over it. If you can't climb up onto the board, simply hang your weight on it and the boat should slowly come upright. As soon as you can reach the gunwale, grasp it and pull yourself aboard.

■ **If the dinghy capsizes** *to leeward, make every effort to move quickly over the high side to step onto the daggerboard. This is the quickest way of getting sailing again.*

Some singlehanders can be righted by depressing the bow as deeply as possible. The boat may then rotate itself into its normal upright position. Try this in practice to see if it works for your boat.

Mast in the mud

If you capsize and invert in shallow water, your mast may hit the bottom. If the bottom is soft mud, the mast may dig in and you will find it very difficult to right. Be careful not to put extra weight on the hull as this could break or buckle the mast. If you cannot pull the boat onto its side quickly, your only option may be to ask for a tow to pull the boat upright. Make sure that the helmsman of the towing boat knows what he is doing or mast damage could result. Take the towline over the hull and tie it to a chainplate. If possible, pull the boat up against the wind. The towing boat should motor very slowly away from the boat at right angles to it. This should pull the mast clear of the mud as the boat rotates onto its side.

Avoiding other boats

ONE OF YOUR MOST IMPORTANT responsibilities when you are in charge of a boat is to avoid a collision with other craft. All craft on the water are governed by the International Regulations for the Prevention of Collisions at Sea, often referred to as the "Col Regs" or "the rules of the road."

When you are racing you have to obey rules set by the International Sailing Federation (ISAF), but the Col Regs always take precedence.

INTERNET

www.uscg.mil

The United States Coast Guard web site provides a lot of information relating to general boating safety and outlines the official rules of boating.

When you start to sail, it is sufficient to know only the basic rules shown here, but you should be aware that the full rules are more complex and cover every eventuality of boats meeting. As you gain experience, and especially if you sail larger boats, you should learn the rules in more detail.

In any situation, one boat has the duty to keep clear and the other has the duty to stand on – or hold its course.

Trivia...

When you start sailing, it can sometimes be difficult to remember which tack you are on. You can solve this problem by marking your boom as shown. If the boom is over the starboard side, you are on port tack and must give way to a boat on the opposite tack. If the boom is over the port side, you are on starboard tack and have the right of way.

When it is your job to keep clear, it is most important that you do so in plenty of time and make your intentions obvious. Make a big alteration of course and always try to pass behind the other vessel rather than ahead. Keep a good lookout all round and try to anticipate the actions of others. When in doubt of how to proceed, keep clear but make your intentions obvious so that you do not confuse the crew of the other boat. Remember that when you are underway, you must keep clear of any boat at anchor or on a mooring, and any boat that is stopped.

Giving way

In general terms, a power boat usually must give way to a sailing boat but, in practice, this means power boats of a similar size to your boat. It does not apply to big ships, which in coastal waters are often restricted in their ability to maneuver. Large ships cannot maneuver quickly, have to keep to deep water channels, and may also have a blind spot close under their bows in which your small boat cannot be seen. Keep a lookout for fishing boats, as you have to keep clear of them too!

■ **Crowded waters:** *Popular sailing areas are often very crowded on summer weekends and you may have to negotiate numerous other craft. You may encounter commercial shipping, large racing fleets, fishing boats, and boats at anchor, so it is important that you learn the basic rules and stay alert.*

Even a yacht in a narrow channel approaching a marina under power may have no room to maneuver, so you should keep clear if you are in a small and easily maneuvered dinghy. Also note that when you are under oars, you are classed as a power-driven vessel and it is your duty to keep clear of sailing boats.

Sailing boats meeting

When boats are on opposite tacks, the boat on port tack must keep clear of a boat on starboard tack. The port-tack boat should tack or bear away to pass behind the starboard-tack boat. The starboard-tack boat should hold its course.

When boats are on the same tack, a windward boat must keep clear of a leeward boat. The leeward boat should hold its course. Always change course to pass behind the other boat rather than trying to cut across its bow.

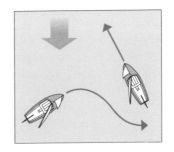

■ **These two boats** *are approaching each other on opposite tacks. As there is a risk of collision, the port-tack boat must keep clear of the starboard-tack boat.*

■ **When two boats** *are both sailing on the same tack – here a starboard tack – there is a risk of collision. The windward boat needs to alter its course to keep clear of the leeward boat.*

In a channel

When moving along a channel or fairway, all boats – under power or sail – should keep close to the starboard side of the channel in whichever direction they are going.

If you have to cross a busy channel or shipping lane, always cross at right angles to the channel in order to get clear as quickly as possible.

Overtaking

When one boat is overtaking another, the overtaking boat must keep clear. This applies even if you are under sail and are overtaking a power boat.

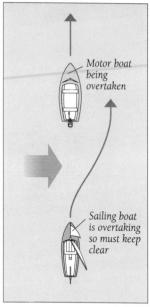

Motor boat being overtaken

Sailing boat is overtaking so must keep clear

■ **If you are overtaking** *any type of boat, you must keep clear.*

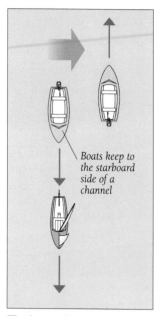

Boats keep to the starboard side of a channel

■ **Always keep to** *the starboard side of any river or channel.*

Power boats meeting

When two boats under power (or oars) are approaching head-on, both boats must turn to starboard so that they pass each other port to port.

When two boats under power (or oars) are crossing, the boat on the other's starboard side has right of way. In other words, if you're on the right you are in the right. The give-way boat should pass behind the right-of-way boat.

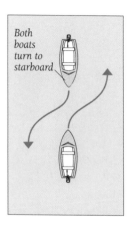

Both boats turn to starboard

■ **If you are** *approaching another power boat head-on, or nearly so, both boats should alter course to starboard so that they pass each other along their port sides.*

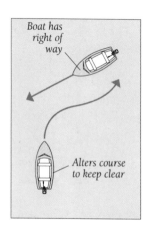

Boat has right of way

Alters course to keep clear

■ **In a crossing** *situation with another power boat, you must decide which boat is on the other's starboard side. That boat should hold its course while the other keeps clear.*

Stay alert

It is very easy to become so engrossed with your own sailing that you forget to keep a good lookout. Remember to check carefully all around the boat every few minutes and be particularly cautious if you see a large ship within sight. A ship traveling at 20 knots (see Chapter 20 for an explanation of the nautical speed unit) will travel 1 mile in only 3 minutes. If you do not keep an eye on it regularly, you could get a nasty surprise as the ship interrupts your pleasant sail.

Make sure that you keep a safe distance from any craft on moorings or at anchor. If you are sailing in shallow water, or just off a popular beach, keep a lookout for swimmers in the water and stay well clear. Similarly, watch out for fishermen on the shore or in small boats. Their lines may extend some distance and you will not be popular if you tangle with them.

Try to anticipate the actions of other boats around you and remember to look astern regularly as it is remarkably easy to overlook even a large ship when it is approaching you from behind.

A simple summary

✔ Man overboard does not happen very often but you should practice the recovery method until it becomes automatic.

✔ If you fall overboard you should raise an arm and blow your whistle to attract attention.

✔ Don't stand on your rights when in danger of collision with a large boat or ship – they may not have seen you!

✔ When you are in charge of a boat, you are responsible for keeping clear of other boats and you must always keep a good lookout all around your boat.

✔ Any sailing dinghy can capsize, so it is important to learn how to right the boat and to remember that you must always stay with the boat, even if you cannot right it.

PART THREE

USING A SPINNAKER INCREASES THE THRILL

IMPROVING SMALL BOAT SKILLS

ONCE YOU HAVE LEARNED THE BASICS of boat handling, you can start to expand your skills. Every sailor must have an understanding of *wind and tide* and now is the time to start learning how to use weather forecasts and tidal information. At this stage, you will start to explore the art of small boat seamanship – getting to and from the shore, using moorings, and anchoring will be added to your *repertoire of skills*.

By now, you will want to find out how to make a boat sail faster. You can start to develop expert skills, including roll tacking and jibing, and learn how to use a spinnaker or an asymmetric. I'll tell you about different types of boat, such as the singlehanded dinghy, the catamaran, and high-performance dinghies and keelboats. If you are at all competitive, you can start to *test your skills* against others on the race course.

Chapter 9

Respecting Wind and Tide

WHEN WE ARE ASHORE, especially if we live in an urban environment, we tend to take the weather for granted. When you sail, however, you are much more aware of the weather and its implications for your pleasure and your safety. You may be surprised at how quickly it can change, and how frequently the wind can vary in both strength and direction. If you sail on tidal waters you will also discover that the entire body of water is in virtually continuous movement, both vertically and horizontally. The tides add a new dimension to sailing that is both challenging and rewarding.

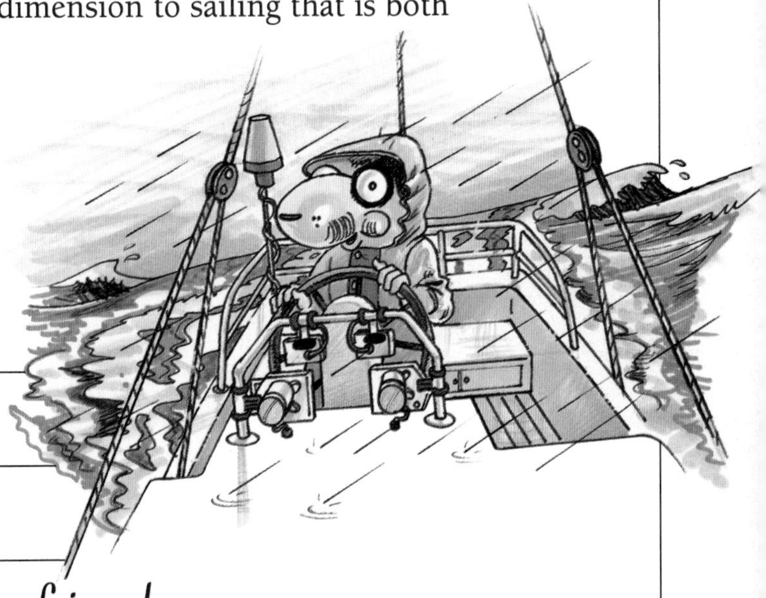

In this chapter...

✓ Weather basics

✓ The local picture

✓ Understanding tides

✓ Making the tide your friend

A GOOD BREEZE GIVES A FAST RIDE FOR EXPERIENCED DINGHY SAILORS

Weather basics

WHEN WE GO SAILING, *the weather is the most important factor to take into account. It may not matter if it is cold or raining, except that it may cause discomfort, but the strength and direction of the wind and any forecast changes will be of considerable importance, as will a forecast of reduced visibility or fog.*

You should choose conditions of light to moderate wind for your first few sailing trips. Avoid going afloat if the forecast is for winds to increase significantly or for visibility to deteriorate. If fog descends while you are sailing, get ashore quickly if possible, or sail into shallow water, where there is less danger of colliding with a larger craft.

Do not go sailing in a dinghy on the sea in poor visibility – you may easily become disoriented.

WORLD WEATHER

The earth's equatorial regions receive far more heat from the sun than the poles. If the heat was unable to circulate, the tropics would get hotter while the poles would get colder. The earth's weather stabilizes global temperatures. Excess heat is moved from the equator toward the poles by air movement caused by changes in pressure as the air is heated and cooled. Air that is warmer than its surroundings rises, while colder air falls. This, together with the earth's rotation, results in winds that blow around areas of low and high pressure.

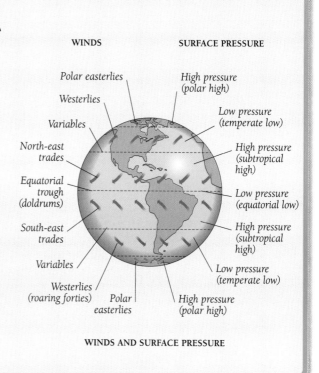

WINDS

Polar easterlies
Westerlies
Variables
North-east trades
Equatorial trough (doldrums)
South-east trades
Variables
Westerlies (roaring forties)
Polar easterlies

SURFACE PRESSURE

High pressure (polar high)
Low pressure (temperate low)
High pressure (subtropical high)
Low pressure (equatorial low)
High pressure (subtropical high)
Low pressure (temperate low)
High pressure (polar high)

WINDS AND SURFACE PRESSURE

Wind strength

Wind strength is of vital importance to sailors. It is generally described using the Beaufort Scale, which defines wind strength in "forces." It describes the effects of each force on both sea and land, making it easy to judge the strength of the wind by simple observation. Force 3 is the ideal strength for learning to sail. The boat will sail well without being difficult to handle. Less wind, on the other hand, will cause the boat to sail slowly and to be less responsive and, of course, stronger winds make the boat harder to handle and increase the risk of capsizing. The Beaufort Scale continues up to Force 15, but, at this stage in your sailing career, anything above Force 6 should be of academic interest only.

From a dinghy sailor's point of view, Force 6 is a very strong wind and only experienced dinghy sailors should venture out in winds of this strength.

RECOGNIZING WIND STRENGTHS

Force	Description	Effects on water	Signs on land	Wind speed
0	Calm	Mirror-smooth water; drifting conditions.	Smoke rises vertically; flags hang limply.	Less than 1 knot
1	Light air	Ripples on water; sufficient wind to maintain motion.	Smoke drifts with the wind.	1–3 knots
2	Light breeze	Small wavelets with smooth crests – sufficient to sail steadily and upright. Wind is felt on your face.	Light flags and windvanes respond; leaves rustle.	4–6 knots
3	Gentle breeze	Large wavelets with crests starting to break. Most dinghies will sail at hull speed. Planing is possible with fast dinghies.	Light flags extended; leaves and small twigs move.	7–10 knots
4	Moderate breeze	Small waves with frequent white horses. Crew fully extended. Beginners should head for shore.	Small branches move; dust and paper raised.	11–16 knots
5	Fresh breeze	Moderate waves with frequent white horses. Fun conditions if you are experienced. Capsizes common if you are inexperienced.	Small trees sway; the tops of all trees move.	17–21 knots
6	Strong breeze	Large waves start to form and spray is likely. This is a dinghy sailor's gale – only experienced crews should race, with good safety cover.	Large trees sway; wind whistles in wires. Difficult to use umbrellas.	22–27 knots

Wind direction

As you gain experience, you will find that you automatically monitor the direction of wind by the feel of it on your face, and by other clues around you. Until this becomes automatic, remember to keep checking the wind direction using all available signs.

Once afloat, keep checking the wind direction by looking at the wind indicator at the top of your mast or on other boats. Look at flags on the shore and ripples or waves on the water. Check the direction of smoke from chimneys ashore.

Remember that the wind shifts frequently, even in stable weather. It can be bent from its true direction by trees, tall buildings, hills, or even large ships. A river valley often bends the wind causing it to blow up or down river.

Ripples or small waves are caused by the wind blowing across the water surface and show the direction of the wind quite accurately.

Offshore or onshore

Whether the wind is *offshore* or *onshore* can make a great difference to your trip. If the wind is onshore you will feel its full force and it may cause waves to build up on the shore if it is moderate or strong. It will make it harder to launch a dinghy and sail away from the shore but, once away from the beach, the waves should calm down, and an onshore wind will make it much easier to return to the shore. Also, there will not be a danger of being blown away from your base.

> **DEFINITION**
>
> *An offshore wind is, as the name implies, a wind that blows, either directly or at an angle, off the shoreline. An onshore wind is the opposite: it blows, directly or at an angle, onto the shoreline.*

If the wind is offshore it may be difficult to judge its true strength from the shore, especially if it is sheltered by high ground inland. As you get further from the shore, the strength is likely to increase and could be more than you feel comfortable with.

When the wind is blowing off the shore, there is often a calm patch close to the shore. Beyond this you will feel the full force of the wind and waves, which is difficult to estimate from the shore.

It will be easy to launch a dinghy in an offshore wind as there will not be any waves on the shore and you will blow off the shore as soon as you launch the boat. Getting back could be more difficult and there is a danger that you will be blown away from your base and be unable to return. Do not sail in offshore winds for your first few trips, unless there is a safety boat, in case you need a tow.

The local picture

WEATHER CONDITIONS CAN VARY considerably over a very small distance due to the effects of local geography, so it is important to check the actual conditions in the area in which you are going to sail.

■ **These dinghies** in *Mission Bay, California, are sailing in ideal learning conditions. The light onshore wind is not strong enough to create waves.*

Most areas have what is called a prevailing wind – a direction from which the wind blows for a large percentage of the time. Although the prevailing wind is the common wind direction, the movements of weather systems mean that you cannot rely on the wind remaining in the prevailing direction.

Always check the weather forecast before you go afloat. Weather forecasts are available from several different sources but many do not include sufficient information on wind conditions for sailors.

Always use a sailing forecast that covers your sailing area in as much detail as possible. Many sailing clubs and harbor-master offices display the local forecast, and you can always ask them for advice.

INTERNET

weather.noaa.gov/
www.weather.ec.gc.ca
www.meto.gov.uk
www.meteo.fr

The national weather centers of many countries are good starting points for online weather information.

Local conditions

Get to know the area in which you usually sail, and study both the general forecast and shipping or small-craft forecasts. Check the actual weather against the forecast conditions on a regular basis, and you will soon build up a picture of how local factors influence both wind speed and direction in your local area.

It is important to know the limitations of your experience and always to sail within them. Ask the advice of experienced sailors, especially those with good local knowledge. If in doubt, stay ashore – it is better to be safe than sorry.

Understanding tides

IF YOU SAIL ON INLAND WATERS, you will not be concerned with tides. However, if you sail on a river – even away from its tidal stretches closer to the sea – there will be some current to contend with. Current is the flow of water down river toward the sea and, on some rivers, it can get very strong, especially if heavy rain has flowed into the river upstream.

When you sail on the sea in an area with significant tidal effect, the tide becomes the main factor to consider along with the wind strength and direction.

Tides are caused by the gravitational pull of the moon (and, to a lesser extent, the sun) on the surface of the water. In most parts of the world, this pull causes two high tides and two low tides every 24 hours. In a few areas there is only one high and low tide each day.

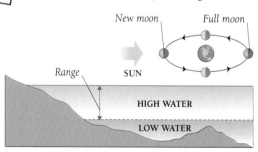

■ **During a spring tide,** *when the sun, moon, and earth are in line with each other, the difference between the high and low tide is at its greatest level.*

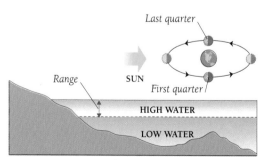

■ **During a neap tide,** *when the sun, moon, and earth are at right angles to each other, the difference between the high and low tide is at its lowest level.*

Spring tides and neap tides

The gravitational pull of the sun and moon is greatest at the periods of the full and the new moon, when the sun, earth, and moon are in line. These are the times of the highest high tides and the lowest low tides, known as spring tides. Spring tides occur approximately every 2 weeks.

At the in-between times, when the moon is in its first and last quarters, the sun, earth, and moon are at right angles to each other and the gravitational pull is less. At these times the lowest high tides and the highest low tides occur; these are called neap tides. Neap tides also occur approximately every 2 weeks, in between successive spring tides.

At spring tides, the amount of water that has to move between high and low water is a lot greater than the amount of water moving at neap tides.

The difference in height between a low tide and the next high tide is called the tidal range. The tidal range is greatest at spring tides and smallest at neap tides.

Tidal current

The rise and fall of the tide causes a *tidal current*. Whenever you are plotting a position or planning a course to sail, you will need to know the strength and direction of the tidal stream.

Because of the difference in range between spring and neap tides, you will find that the tidal current always runs much faster during spring tides than during neap tides. The positions of tidal currents that have been measured are marked on nautical charts.

DEFINITION

The difference in height of the sea's surface between low tide and high tide causes a horizontal movement of the water called a tidal current. This stream flows along coasts and up and down estuaries and rivers.

The tidal range and the consequent tidal currents are much larger in some parts of the world than others. Places like Maine or Alaska, or the Bay of Fundy in Canada, have very large ranges and very strong tidal currents. When you are sailing in places like these you have to take much greater account of the tide than when you are sailing in places like the Caribbean, where the range is small.

Flood tides and ebb tides

When the tide is rising toward high tide, the current is said to be flooding, and when it is falling toward low tide, the current is said to be ebbing. The flood tide runs up rivers and estuaries and then reverses at high tide so that the ebb tide runs back toward the sea. In areas that have two high tides and two low tides every 24 hours, each flood tide and each ebb tide will last for approximately 6 hours, although there can be significant local variation in this average duration.

Trivia...
Unlike the wind direction, the direction of the tide is always described according to the direction in which it is flowing.

When you sail during spring tides, take greater care than usual, or you may find yourself surprised by the extra strength of the tidal current.

Making the tide your friend

MANY PEOPLE WORRY *about sailing in tides but there is no need to do so. The important thing is to understand the tide and to use its effects to assist you.*

Before you go afloat, find out the direction in which the tidal current is running and at what time it will turn. Make sure you have a copy of the local tide table that will show the time of high and low waters, and, if in doubt, ask an experienced sailor for advice before you go afloat. Plan your trip so that you can sail back to your base with the tide when you are ready to return.

Once afloat, check the direction of the tidal stream by looking at keelboats at anchor or on moorings — they normally lie head to tide. Beware of looking at dinghies, power boats, or multihulls because they do not have keels and will tend to lie head-to-wind.

THE TIDE'S EFFECT

It is always sensible to try to sail with the tide in your favor. When the tide is with you, your speed over the ground (relative to the bottom) is a combination of the tide's speed and your speed through the water. If you sail at 5 knots in the same direction as a 2-knot tide, your speed over the ground is 7 knots. If you turn around and, still sailing at 5 knots, sail against the tide, your speed over the ground will drop to 3 knots. To help picture this scenario, imagine walking along a conveyor belt. When you walk in the direction the belt is moving, you will cover the distance to your destination quickly. If you walk against the flow of the moving belt, it will take you a long time to get anywhere because the belt will attempt to take you back the way you came.

When you are sailing directly with or against the tide, the tide affects your speed over the ground but it does not alter the course you sail. Now, imagine that you are sailing across a channel along which a tide is flowing. If you head straight across the channel, the tide will sweep you some way downtide before you get to the other side. If you want to go straight across, point the boat uptide so that it crabs across the channel, being swept sideways by the tide as it moves forward.

Simple observation

Learn to spot signs for yourself, rather than relying on tide tables. If the shoreline is wet it means the tide is going out, while if it is dry the tide is coming in. Look at boats on moorings to check the direction of the tidal current. Unless the wind is very strong and the tide weak, moored keelboats will lie head to tide. Look at buoys and posts in the water. You will see the direction of the tide by a bow wave or wake trailing off the buoys. In strong tidal streams, buoys lean in the direction the tide is flowing.

Making use of the tide

Tidal currents always flow fastest in deep water, so if you are trying to sail against the tide seek out the shallower water at the edge of the channel. If the tide is with you then pick the deeper water and make maximum use of the help the tide will provide.

The tide also flows fastest on the outside of bends in rivers or channels and around headlands or obstructions that stick out into the tidal stream. Be careful to avoid areas where a fast-moving tidal current is constricted in any way, such as by a headland or uneven seabed, as these can cause rough water on the surface.

Take an anchor!

When you are sailing in tidal waters, make sure that you carry an anchor aboard in case the wind drops or you have gear failure. In these circumstances, an anchor may be the only way to avoid being carried away from your base by the tide. Tell someone ashore of your plans and your expected time of return so that, should you get into trouble, there is someone who can summon assistance if you fail to return.

A simple summary

✔ Wind direction and strength are key factors when you plan a sailing trip.

✔ Avoid sailing a dinghy in poor visibility or fog.

✔ As a beginner, try to sail in winds of about Force 3.

✔ Be careful when sailing a dinghy in offshore winds.

✔ Always get a local sailing forecast before you go afloat.

✔ Make sure you know the state of the tide when sailing in tidal waters.

Chapter 10

Small Boat Seamanship

NOW THAT YOU HAVE LEARNED the basic techniques of sailing, you will be able to sail the boat reasonably proficiently around a simple course in open water. You will be able to tack and jibe and you know how to stop the boat and get sailing again. So far you will have had an instructor or an experienced friend sail you from the shore to clear water, but now it is time to begin to master the seamanship skills that are needed when getting underway and returning.

In this chapter...

✓ To and from the shore

✓ Using moorings

✓ Anchoring

✓ Under tow

SMALL BOATS LIKE THESE MIRROR DINGHIES ARE IDEAL FOR SAILING FROM A BEACH

To and from the shore

LEAVING FROM AND RETURNING TO the shore can be the trickiest part of your sailing trip. The shoreline presents a very solid obstacle that can be a hazard if you do not handle your dinghy carefully and leave or approach properly. As well as avoiding obstacles on the shoreline, you must also watch out for other boats moving in the same area as you and for boats on moorings or at anchor nearby.

If you have doubts about your ability to leave or return to the shore safely under sail, consider whether it would be easier to row or paddle between the shore and deep water, hoisting or lowering the sails in clear water away from hazards.

ROWING AND PADDLING

Most modern sailing dinghies have no provision for rowing, but many older dinghies and some newer, general-purpose dinghies can be rowed. You will need a pair of oars and a pair of oarlocks. These are fitted into plates in each gunwale and act as pivot points for the oars. Rowing takes practice, so do not be dismayed if your first attempts result in you going around in circles. Most sailing dinghies use paddles as their alternative means of propulsion. Paddling is less efficient than rowing but is useful for short distances, and the paddles are much easier to store in the boat than the longer oars. Dinghies can be paddled by one or both crew members – the design of the boat will determine the most efficient way of paddling.

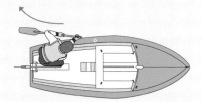

■ **When you row,** *you should sit on the thwart and face aft. Rowing is a useful skill for every sailor, so take the time to practice.*

■ **When you paddle,** *sit in the stern and face forward. It may be easier to paddle backward – experiment to see what suits you.*

Before you make any attempt to leave or return, it is a good idea to look around the area and identify any potential hazards – obstructions that could cause the wind to change in direction or strength, and strong tidal currents. It is always a good idea to plan an escape route, especially when you are arriving at the shore. This way, if your approach goes wrong, you can abort the approach and go round to try again.

If other boats are performing the same maneuver that you are about to undertake, watch them carefully for clues as to how your boat will behave.

Leaving in an offshore wind

A *weather* or *windward* shore is the easiest to leave from since the wind will help blow you clear of the shore and the water will be flat as it is sheltered by the land. The details of how you leave the shore will depend to some extent on whether you are leaving from a beach, a launching ramp (a ramp running down from the shore into the water), or a dock (a floating walkway alongside which boats can be tied), but the principles for a safe departure remain the same. Always keep the boat head-to-wind while you are launching, so that the sails continue to flap without any wind in them.

> **DEFINITION**
>
> *If the wind is blowing off the shore it is called a weather or windward shore. If the wind is blowing onto the shore it is called a lee shore.*

Using the beach or launching ramp

If you are leaving from a beach or launching ramp, you can usually hoist both sails before you launch the boat. Make sure that the jib sheets and the mainsheet are loose so that both sails are able to flap freely while you lift the boat into the water or use your dolly. If you prefer, you can launch the boat first and then have your crew hold the boat by the bow, head-to-wind, while you climb in and hoist both sails.

■ **If you use a dolly or trailer** *on a launching ramp, park it out of the way once you have launched.*

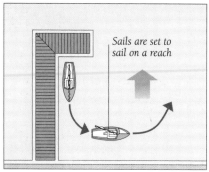

■ **Leave from a dock** *with the sails hoisted and the rudder and centerboard lowered, push the bow off, and sail away.*

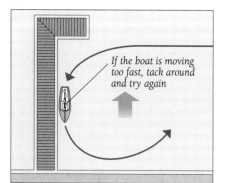

■ **Approach a dock** *on a close reach and turn head-to-wind to stop. It is sensible to have an escape route planned.*

Using a dock

If you are leaving from a dock, it is normal to launch the boat with the sails down, then put it alongside the dock before hoisting the sails. An advantage of leaving from a dock is that there is often sufficient water next to the dock to allow you to lower the centerboard and rudder before you sail away. When you leave from a beach or launching ramp, you will start in shallow water and may need to sail out a little way before lowering the foils. Once you have the boat in the water with the sails hoisted, it is quite an easy matter to sail away as the wind will help by pushing you off the shore.

Arriving in an offshore wind

When the wind is blowing offshore, you need to sail to windward and tack to reach your landing point. The way you approach will depend on the depth of the water close to the shore. If it is shallow, you must raise the centerboard and rudder enough to clear the bottom as you approach. If you have to raise the centerboard as you arrive, remember that the boat will slip sideways, so do not expect to sail too close to the wind in the final stages. Arriving at a dock is often easier than coming into a beach or launching ramp, since the water is often deep enough for you to keep the rudder and centerboard fully down.

Leaving in an onshore wind

Leaving from a lee shore is more difficult than from a weather shore because the wind tends to blow you back onto the shore. There may also be waves breaking on the shore, making it difficult to sail away. If you are launching from a beach or launching ramp, and the water close to the shore is deep, hoist your sails first. If it is shallow, your crew should stand in the water and hold the boat head-to-wind while you hoist the sails.

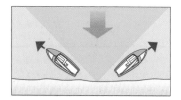

WIND DIRECTLY ONSHORE

WIND AT AN OBLIQUE ANGLE

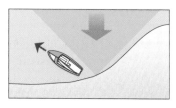

WIND ON A CURVED SHORELINE

MANEUVERING IN TIDES AND CURRENTS

If there is a current or (river or tidal) present, it may complicate your leaving and arriving maneuvers. If the water is shallow, the effect of a current will be weak or nonexistent; if the water is deep, the effect could be quite significant. The safest way to handle this situation is to always leave and arrive by pointing into the tide or current. If this means that the wind is aft of the beam when you are pointing into the tide, you should choose to drop the mainsail and leave or arrive under jib only.

When the wind is blowing onto the shore, you will have to sail away on a close-hauled or close-reaching course. This means that you need your centerboard right down. However, if the water is shallow, you will not be able to lower the centerboard fully until you get some way offshore. If the wind is blowing onto the shore at an angle, leave on the tack that takes you offshore the most quickly.

As you sail away from the lee shore, lower the rudder and have your crew lower the centerboard as far as possible, but be careful to avoid hitting the bottom.

If you are leaving from a dock, launch the boat with the sails down and hoist them once the boat is alongside the dock and pointing into the wind.

Arriving in an onshore wind

When you approach a lee shore, the wind will be behind you and all you have to do is sail straight for the shore. The difficult part is stopping, and dealing with waves that are likely to be present in even moderate winds.

Never attempt to land on a lee shore in strong winds unless you are very experienced. The waves are likely to be steep and breaking, and they can easily overwhelm a small boat.

When you approach a lee shore, you have the choice of doing so under full sail or under jib alone. Usually it is safer to plan your final approach under jib alone, which allows you to come in under full control and at slow speed. In a singlehanded dinghy with a single sail, you have no choice but to approach under full sail unless you have the ability to lower the sail afloat, which is unusual in singlehanded dinghies.

When you arrive at a beach or launching ramp, make sure that you get out of the boat on the windward side. If you jump out on the leeward side, a breaking wave or a strong gust of wind could easily push the boat on top of you and cause injury. Make sure that you get the boat out of the water as quickly as possible so that the waves breaking on the shore don't swamp the boat or cause it to grind to the bottom.

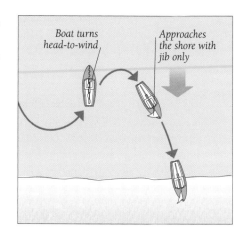

Boat turns head-to-wind

Approaches the shore with jib only

■ **When approaching a lee shore,** *it is safest to turn head-to-wind and lower the mainsail before coming in under jib alone. Get the boat ashore quickly.*

Using moorings

IF YOU SAIL a larger, general-purpose dinghy it may be kept afloat on a mooring rather than being brought ashore in between sailing trips. Even if your dinghy is usually brought ashore, you may need to pick up a mooring for a brief stop so it is a useful skill to learn and good practice for sailing the boat at slow speeds.

Leaving a mooring

If you sail in nontidal waters and there is no current, a boat tied to a mooring will always lie pointing head-to-wind. This makes leaving and returning to a mooring quite easy. Simply hoist both sails, cast off (undo) the mooring, and sail off.

If there is a tide or current, the situation may be more complex. The way a dinghy lies on a mooring will depend on the strength of the tide, current, or wind and the amount of boat below the water for the tide to grip.

■ **When leaving a mooring,** *the crew passes the buoy aft to the helmsman to help turn the boat onto the desired course.*

Before you decide how to leave a mooring, lower the centerboard. The increased area underwater will give the tide more grip on the boat and will make it more obvious whether the wind or tide has the most effect.

If the wind and tide are not in the same direction and the boat lies on its mooring head to tide, you have to decide how to leave the mooring. There is a simple rule that will show you how to do this.

If the wind is blowing from ahead of the beam, hoist both sails before leaving. If the wind is on or aft of the beam, leave under the jib alone before turning head-to-wind to hoist the mainsail.

Arriving at a mooring

When the time comes to return to a mooring, the same principles apply as when leaving. First, decide how your boat will lie once you have picked up the mooring. The best way to do this is to look at boats on other moorings. Pick boats that are similar to yours and check to see if they are lying head-to-wind or if they are being influenced by the tide. Assume that your dinghy will lie in a similar position once tied up and decide where the wind will be.

If the wind will be well ahead of the beam when you are tied up, it is safe to approach the mooring under mainsail and jib. If the wind will be on or aft of the beam always approach under jib alone.

At a mooring, if you pick up the mooring buoy while the mainsail is full of wind, the boat will try and sail in circles around the buoy. This is fun for spectators but far less amusing for those on the boat.

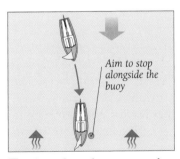

Aim to stop alongside the buoy

■ **When the tide** *is against the wind, approach a mooring under jib alone, letting it flap to stop.*

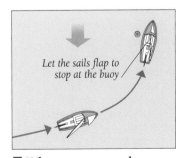

Let the sails flap to stop at the buoy

■ **When you approach** *a mooring upwind, sail on a close reach and aim to stop by the buoy.*

Never attempt to pick up a mooring by sailing downwind under mainsail and jib. You may pick up the mooring but you won't be able to stop the boat, because the mainsail will stay full of wind.

Anchoring

ANCHORING IS RARELY USED in dinghies but it is a skill that can be very useful in an emergency, when the wind drops and the tide is against you, or just for a short stop or lunch break. Since an anchor should always be carried when sailing in tidal waters, it makes sense to practice how to use it.

The most common type of anchor for use in a dinghy is a folding one, such as a grapnel anchor. Although they are not very efficient, they are easy to stow and do not take up much space. You will also need a length of rope equal to about five times the depth of water in which you intend to anchor. If you don't have a long enough rope, known as an anchor rode, extend it by tying on your jib sheets or any other ropes in the boat.

ANCHORING A DINGHY

The same procedure for leaving and approaching applies to anchoring as to moorings. In nontidal waters, the boat will lie head-to-wind when at anchor, just as it would on a mooring. You can approach and leave the anchorage under mainsail and jib. In tidal waters, decide how the boat will lie under the influence of wind and tide and approach accordingly. When you are anchoring, decide where to anchor and approach that spot either under mainsail and jib, or under jib alone. When you wish to leave the anchorage, follow the same procedure as when leaving a mooring, recovering your anchor by hauling it up as you leave.

1 **Approach with no tide**

Approach under mainsail and jib on a close reach and let the sails out to stop. Lower the anchor over the side until it reaches the bottom.

2 **Anchoring**

Pay out the anchor rode until you have let out about five times the depth of water. Lead the rode through a fairlead at the bow.

3 **Stowing**

When the boat has dropped back on its rode, check that the anchor is holding, then lower and stow the sails and raise the centerboard.

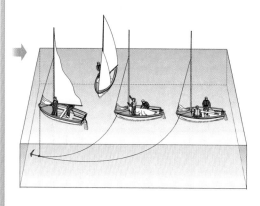

Under tow

THERE ARE TIMES when you need a tow, perhaps from the club's safety boat. Be careful when accepting a tow from a stranger, especially if their boat is a large power boat. They may not understand how to tow a sailing dinghy, and serious damage could be done if the tow is not handled properly.

The painter (the dinghy's bow rope) should be rigged so that it can be passed to the towing boat. It needs to be at least as long as the dinghy and should be tied around the mast and led through a bow fairlead.

The safest way to be towed is astern of the tow boat. It is possible to tie a dinghy alongside the tow boat but this usually results in damage except for a short tow in very calm conditions. When you are being towed astern, lower your sails and pull your centerboard almost fully up. Leave the rudder in place and steer to follow the wake of the towing boat.

If several boats are being towed, the painter of each should be tied to the boat ahead around a strong point at the stern, such as the hiking strap attachment point. Each boat removes its rudder except the last boat, which should steer to follow the wake of the towing boat.

INTERNET

www.apparent-wind.com/sailing-page.html

This is Mark Rosenstein's sailing page – one of the oldest sailing-related sites on the Web. It contains a large number of links to other Web-based sailing resources.

A simple summary

✔ Learn to row or paddle so that you can maneuver your boat without sails.

✔ Plan your departure from and return to the shore with care.

✔ A weather shore is easiest to leave from and the safest to return to.

✔ A lee shore can be dangerous to approach in a strong wind and with breaking waves.

✔ Always check the relative directions of wind and tide when anchoring or using a mooring.

✔ When you are under tow always steer to follow the tow boat.

Chapter 11

Sailing Faster

Now that you have mastered the basics of dinghy sailing and seamanship, the next step is to improve your skills by spending as much time on the water as possible. Nothing will improve your sailing as much as sailing itself. Only time spent in a boat can refine your skills and teach you the finer points about boat handling and sail trim. As you progress, you can start to sail in stronger winds and to learn some techniques that will be rewarded by better performance – especially if you sail one of the more responsive modern dinghies.

In this chapter...

✓ Working with the wind

✓ Upright is fast

✓ When to rock and roll

✓ Sailing in strong winds

TO SAIL FASTER, MOVE YOUR WEIGHT FURTHER OUT TO KEEP THE BOAT UPRIGHT

Working with the wind

THE WIND IS YOUR MOTIVE POWER, *so the more you understand about its behavior the easier it will be to control the boat and to sail efficiently. When you start sailing, you will probably take the wind for granted but you will quickly learn that it is never truly steady in strength or consistent in direction.*

To complicate matters, you feel the true direction of the wind only when you are stationary. As you begin to move, the wind you experience changes direction from the true wind. The wind you feel when you are moving is called the apparent wind.

Understanding the difference between the true wind and the apparent wind will help improve your sailing skills.

True and apparent wind

The true wind, as the name suggests, is the real wind direction as shown by flags on flagpoles or smoke from chimneys. As soon as your boat starts moving it creates its own wind, which combines with the true wind to form the apparent wind. Imagine walking with a lit candle on a still day – the flame will blow back toward you. This demonstrates that anything moving through the air will create its own wind, blowing opposite to the direction of travel.

The important things to remember about true and apparent wind are:

● The apparent wind is the wind that affects your sails and boat when you are moving
● Wind indicators on your boat will show the apparent wind, while wind indicators on shore or on moored boats will show the true wind direction
● The speed of the apparent wind is different from the true wind speed
● When you sail on upwind courses, the apparent wind is stronger than the true wind, but when you sail downwind, the apparent wind speed is less than the true wind

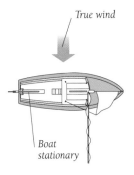

True wind

Boat stationary

■ **When a boat** is *stationary you feel the true wind. When the boat starts moving it creates its own wind, which combines with the true wind to create the apparent wind.*

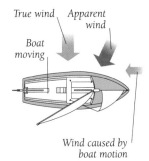

True wind   Apparent wind

Boat moving

Wind caused by boat motion

■ **The apparent** *wind always comes from further forward than the true wind, except when you sail on a run, when the direction is the same.*

Wind shifts

Wind direction is rarely constant for long, even in a stable weather situation. It is quite usual for the wind direction to shift backward and forward every few minutes on either side of a general direction. This may be by only a few degrees, but it can often be by 10–20°, or even more. At other times, the wind will shift permanently to a new direction that may be quite different from its original direction.

Wind shifts are particularly important when you are sailing to windward as they can either shorten your course or add considerable distance to it.

Headers and lifts

Wind shifts are known as headers and lifts. In a header, the wind shifts further ahead and if you're sailing to windward, it forces you to bear away to keep the sails full and the boat moving. If you were pointing at your destination before the heading shift, you will find that you now have to tack to reach it.

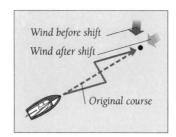

Wind before shift

Wind after shift

Original course

■ Here the boat *was sailing close-hauled and was pointing at the mark, but after the heading shift the boat must tack to reach the mark.*

In a lift, the wind shifts further aft and, unless you spot it and luff up immediately, you'll find yourself sailing too far off the wind. I'm sure you have already noticed that a header on one tack is a lift on the other tack.

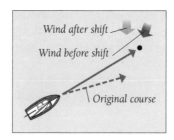

Wind after shift

Wind before shift

Original course

■ Here the boat *was sailing close-hauled but could not point at the mark. After the lifting wind shift, the boat can point directly at the mark.*

Checking your course

Spotting a large wind shift is not difficult, but smaller wind shifts can be hard to see unless you use a compass or a landmark as a reference point. Use a compass, if your boat is fitted with one, to keep checking your course when you are sailing close-hauled. The course will vary a bit as you steer upwind, but if it changes by 5° or more you may be experiencing a wind shift and should decide if it is a header or a lift.

If you are sailing to an upwind destination and will have to tack to reach it, you will sail the quickest course if you tack when you are headed. If the wind then shifts back, it will head you again on the other tack. You will then be able to tack again and make more ground to windward.

If you do not have a compass but can see land when you look ahead, you can use a landmark to check your course. Pick some recognizable feature ahead of the boat and check your course relative to it fairly frequently. If you are lifted or headed, the landmark will appear to move to one side or other of the bow, indicating whether you are on a lift or a header.

Sail trim

When you start sailing, it can be difficult to get used to the need to constantly adjust sail trim to suit changes in wind direction and strength, but it will soon become automatic.

If you sail high-performance dinghies, you will find that they accelerate or slow down very quickly when the wind strength changes – this in turn causes the apparent wind to shift backward or forward. Sail trim or the boat's heading must be adjusted each time this happens so that the sails remain set at their optimum angle.

Controlling twist

As well as keeping the sails set at the correct angle to the wind by watching the luff, or using luff telltales, you also need to adjust the leech tension in each sail to control the amount of twist, which affects the power you get from the sail.

The easiest way to check mainsail leech tension is to have leech telltales sewn near the end of each batten pocket. When these all stream aft, with the top telltale occasionally folding to leeward of the leech, the sail is set correctly.

> **DEFINITION**
>
> Twist *is the difference in the angle of the sail to the wind between the bottom of the sail and its top. Mainsail twist is controlled by mainsheet or vang tension. The more tension in either, the less twist there will be. Jib twist is controlled by the fore and aft position of the fairleads, and sheet tension.*

If the top telltale stays permanently folded behind the leech, it means the sail is stalled and the mainsheet or vang should be eased a little to allow the sail to twist more and keep the telltale just flying.

Twist in the jib can be set using leech telltales, although these are harder to see than on the mainsail. Otherwise, you can adjust the sheet tension and fairlead position to keep the curve on the jib leech parallel to the curve on the lee side of the mainsail.

■ **Leech telltales** *are strips of nylon sewn to the leech of the mainsail to show how the wind flows off the sail. They should stream aft with the top one flicking behind the sail occasionally.*

Leech telltales are sewn near the batten pockets

Upright is fast

JUST ABOUT THE MOST IMPORTANT FACTOR when sailing
a dinghy is to keep it upright. Dinghies not only sail fastest when they are
upright, or just slightly heeled to leeward, but they are also easier to steer. As
we have seen, a boat tries to turn when it is heeled, and, if you allow the boat to
heel too much, the turning force may become so large that you cannot counter
it with the rudder.

When you start sailing, you will probably find it quite difficult to keep the
boat upright consistently. You will be juggling with tiller and mainsheet and
trying to coordinate your movements with those of your crew. Only
practice will help make your actions smooth and confident, so aim
to spend as much time in the boat as possible.

I find that it takes me a while to become fully accustomed to a
boat I haven't sailed before, but, especially if I'm racing, I usually
develop the necessary feel for a new boat after a few hours. Each
boat has different characteristics, but once you have sailed one for
a while in various conditions you should find that you adjust to it,
and your boat-handling skills will become automatic.

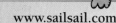

INTERNET

www.sailsail.com

Visit this UK site for links to
dinghy and keelboat classes
and for a good summary of
the latest racing news.

Using your weight

The first step in keeping the boat upright is to use the combined weight of yourself and
your crew effectively. As you gain experience, you will feel more confident to sit far out,
using the hiking straps to keep you securely in the boat. As soon as
the wind is strong enough, you and your crew should sit out as
hard as you can to balance the boat.

Allow yourself to relax when you use hiking
straps. Find a comfortable sitting out position
from where you can see the sails and the waves
ahead of the boat.

Many high-performance dinghies use one or more
trapezes to allow you to move your weight further out of
the boat. Using a trapeze is not difficult but it requires practice and a
degree of athleticism. Ask an instructor or an experienced friend to
steer the boat and show you how to get in and out on the trapeze.

DEFINITION

A trapeze is a wire running
from the mast, just above the
shrouds, with a ring at its
bottom end. The ring attaches
onto a hook on a trapeze
harness worn by the crew,
and sometimes the helmsman.
If a trapeze is fitted, there
will be two wires, one on
each side of the boat, for each
person who will be trapezing.

When you are trapezing, keep your front leg straight and bend the rear one at the knee slightly. This helps you to resist the forward pull of the trapeze wire and stops you from being catapulted around the bow, especially when the boat slows down quickly.

Playing the sheets

The most effective way to keep the boat upright, especially when the wind is strong and gusty, is to ease the sheets as the boat heels. In your efforts to keep the boat level, the mainsheet is your most important tool. Because the mainsail is

■ **Sailing upright,** *the helmsman sits out hard using the hiking straps while his crew uses a trapeze to get his weight even further outboard.*

by far the largest sail, easing or pulling in the mainsheet will have the most effect. Use the mainsheet as your heeling control by easing it out when a gust causes the boat to heel, then pull it in again as the gust passes.

■ **To keep the boat upright,** *this singlehanded sailor sits out and trims the mainsheet.*

In gusty winds, you will need to constantly trim the mainsail to keep the boat level. Usually, you would not do the same with the jib sheet since the jib is smaller and has less of a heeling effect than the mainsail. Except in very strong winds, keep the jib trimmed using its luff telltales or watching the luff, and keep the boat level using the mainsheet.

As you know, the heeling force is greatest on a close-hauled course, diminishing as you bear away on to courses further off the wind. You therefore have to be more responsive to dealing with gusts when you are sailing on upwind courses, by easing the mainsheet as necessary.

Luffing through gusts

When you are sailing on upwind courses, there is another option to reduce heel during gusts. If you turn the boat toward the wind (or luff) as the gust hits, without adjusting the sheets, the sails will spill wind sufficiently to reduce the heeling force. As the gust passes, bear away to your original course. It requires a delicate touch on the tiller to keep the boat sailing fast and upright, so practice this skill until it becomes automatic. I find it one of the most satisfying sailing skills, as it allows you to sail upwind fast and upright in strong and gusty winds.

When a gust hits, the true wind speed increases and the apparent wind shifts aft. You should therefore always luff through a gust when sailing to windward. When you are sailing on other points of sail, you should always ease the sheets.

Bearing away through gusts

When you are sailing on an offwind course the heeling force is lower than when you are sailing close-hauled, but in stronger winds you still need to be able to deal with gusts. The trick is to ease both sheets and bear away when a gust hits and the boat heels more than you can compensate for with your weight. By bearing away, the heeling force is reduced because the extra force of the gust is turned into a positive, forward drive. Done properly, you will find that the boat will accelerate with the gust while staying upright. As the gust passes, you can luff back to your original course and sheet in again.

When to rock and roll

WE KNOW IT IS IMPORTANT to keep the boat upright, but there are times when heeling can increase speed. In light winds, for example, it can be an advantage to heel the boat slightly to leeward by moving your weight inboard. This helps keep the sails still because their weight holds them in shape. You should also heel the boat when you are tacking and jibing in light winds.

ROLL TACKING

A boat usually slows down during a tack, but in light winds you can maintain speed or increase it by roll tacking. Rolling the boat as you tack causes the sails to be dragged through the air, and this drives the boat forward.

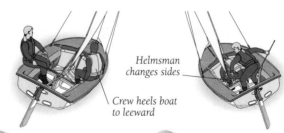

Helmsman changes sides

Crew heels boat to leeward

1 **Into the tack**

Heel the boat to leeward before the tack so it turns into the tack without much use of the rudder.

2 **Through the tack**

As the boat comes head-to-wind, roll it hard to windward then change sides and pull it upright.

ROLL JIBING

In the next chapter we will see how you can use a spinnaker to increase speed when sailing downwind, but if you sail without a spinnaker you can use a roll jibe to maintain speed through a jibe in light winds.

Heels the boat to windward

Stays on windward side

Moves to new side

1 **Before the jibe**

Heel the boat to windward so that it turns into the jibe without much use of the rudder.

2 **Through the jibe**

Stay sitting on the side as the boat turns through the jibe but be ready to move quickly.

3 **After the jibe**

As the boom swings over, move to the new side and sit out to pull the boat back upright.

Sailing in strong winds

WHEN YOU START SAILING, you should not sail in strong winds, but as you gain experience you will inevitably end up sailing in windier conditions. To start with you will probably feel that Force 4 is windy enough, but as your skills improve you will feel more confident and start to enjoy the thrill of dinghy sailing in strong winds.

Sailing a dinghy, particularly a fast, responsive one, is brilliant fun in strong winds and I can thoroughly recommend that you give it a try at least once, with an experienced friend if necessary, even if your ambition is to sail keelboats or cruisers.

Always remember that the design of the boat, the wind direction relative to the shore, and any tidal current all influence the way conditions are experienced. A high-performance boat will be harder to control in strong winds than a more stable dinghy, and the presence of large waves kicked up by a strong wind blowing against the tide will make boat handling more difficult.

Rough weather imposes considerable strain on the boat, sails, and equipment so do not go afloat without checking all the gear and making sure that your clothing is suitable for the conditions.

Reefing the sails

One way of maintaining control in rough weather is to reduce the size of the sails. Some dinghies have smaller sails that can be used when the wind is strong, and some general-purpose dinghies have sails that can be reefed – this is when a sail is reduced in size so that it is more manageable in a strong wind. Most high-performance dinghies have no facility for reefing or for using smaller sails, so do not sail this type of boat in strong winds until you have more experience and can be sure that a safety boat is in attendance.

Reefing the mainsail

Most general-purpose dinghies can be reefed by partly rolling the mainsail around the boom to reduce the amount of sail exposed to the wind. This is far easier to do when you are rigging the boat, although it can be done afloat in an emergency.

When you reef the mainsail, you should reduce the size of the jib in order to maintain the balance between the two sails. Sometimes it is possible to reef the jib by partially rolling it around the forestay but it is better to use a smaller jib if you have one.

Area of sail to be reefed

UNREEFED SAIL   REEFED SAIL

The way you reef the mainsail will be determined by the particular arrangement on your boat. Ask your instructor or an experienced sailor if it is possible to reef the mainsail on your boat and how it should be done for best results.

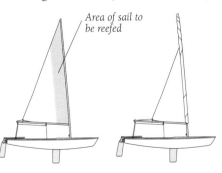

Area of sail to be reefed

UNREEFED SAIL   REEFED SAIL

Reefing an unstayed mast

If you sail a dinghy with an unstayed mast, as is common on many singlehanded dinghies, you can reef the mainsail by rolling it around the mast. Once you have done this, you should then attach the clew to the boom.

Experiencing planing

Once you start to sail in winds of Force 4 or more, you will soon experience the unforgettable thrill of planing. A dinghy planes when it reaches a speed that creates enough lift under the hull to raise the boat onto its own bow wave.

A light dinghy with a large sail area will plane readily as soon as the wind reaches Force 3 or above, and many heavier dinghies will plane if there is sufficient wind.

The best way to experience planing is to begin by sailing on a beam reach in a wind of at least Force 3 or stronger, depending on the type of boat you sail. With the boat sailing fast on a reach, the sails correctly trimmed, and the centerboard no more than halfway down, wait for a gust to arrive. As you feel the wind strength increase, bear away slightly, ease both sheets a little, and sit out hard to keep the boat upright.

Planing technique

If you make sure that the boat is upright as the gust hits, you should feel the bow lift and the boat accelerate as it begins to plane. As you do so, move your weight aft slightly to help the bow lift. Your speed will increase dramatically and the apparent wind will shift forward as the boat lifts onto the plane, so be ready to sheet both sails in to keep them correctly trimmed. The extra speed will make the rudder more efficient and you will find that quite small movements of the tiller will be sufficient to keep the boat on course. As the gust passes, the boat may come off the plane. Keep it planing as long as possible by luffing slightly as the gust passes. When the boat stops planing, move your weight forward again to the normal position.

Boat handling

Sailing in strong winds will test your skills but will teach you more about boat handling than a dozen outings in light or moderate conditions. When you first go out in strong winds, start by sailing on a reach to help you get a feel for the conditions.

Keep the boat upright and moving as fast as possible. This will give you the most control. Watch for gusts approaching. Be prepared to ease the sheets and bear away to keep the boat upright as the gust passes.

Once you are comfortable handling the boat on a reach, turn to a close-hauled course and sheet the sails in gently as the boat turns so that the boat stays upright without heeling. It is important that you keep the boat as upright as possible, so you should constantly trim the mainsheet to prevent heeling.

In the strongest gusts, the mainsail may have to be let out until it flaps across most of its width, in order to spill enough wind to prevent the boat heeling. Keep the jib sheeted in tightly except in the strongest gusts, when it should be eased slightly until the gust passes.

■ **Sailing in strong winds** *and big seas requires concentration and careful boat handling to be able to sail fast and upright.*

If you are sailing in large waves, steer through them by luffing up as you climb up the wave face, and then bearing away as the bow passes through the crest, before sailing down the other side.

Now bear away to a broad reach and enjoy the fun of sailing downwind in a strong wind. Be wary of sailing on a dead run in a strong wind. It is a difficult course to steer because there is no heeling force to balance against and there is always the danger of an unplanned jibe.

The boat will sail faster and be more stable if you sail on a broad reach, where there is sufficient heeling force to allow the helmsman and crew to both sit to windward and well aft. This will prevent the bow from digging in.

A simple summary

✓ The best way to learn to sail faster is to spend as much time in the boat as possible.

✓ Keep a dinghy upright to achieve maximum speed and ease of handling in most conditions.

✓ Roll tacking and roll jibing allow you to maintain speed in light winds.

✓ When you are sailing, remember that the wind you feel is the apparent wind, not the true wind.

✓ In strong winds, some dinghies can be reefed to make them easier to handle.

✓ Planing is great fun and most dinghies are capable of it in medium or strong winds.

Chapter 12

Have Fun Downwind

DOWNWIND SAILING IS FUN because after the effort of sailing upwind – and not for nothing is it called "beating" – it is a great pleasure to bear away and sail with the wind. The apparent wind drops, it feels warmer, and, when it is windy, there is less spray flying around. The boat is easier to keep upright as the heeling force is reduced, and you can sail directly for your destination. If you're feeling lazy, you can take it easier downwind than upwind, but, if you choose to, you can add to the excitement by setting a lightweight downwind sail to increase your speed.

In this chapter...

✓ Downwind sails

✓ Setting a spinnaker

✓ Jibing a spinnaker

✓ Dropping a spinnaker

✓ Sailing with an asymmetric

SAILING FAST DOWNWIND UNDER A SPINNAKER IS TRULY EXHILIRATING!

Downwind sails

THERE ARE TWO TYPES *of downwind sail used aboard dinghies, keelboats, and cruisers. The most common is the* spinnaker, *which is recognizable because of its billowing shape and colorful appearance. The other type is the asymmetric spinnaker, sometimes called a gennaker or, on cruising boats, a cruising chute.*

Spinnakers were originally used only on downwind courses, but modern sailcloth and new shapes allow high-performance boats to carry a spinnaker or an asymmetric on a beam reach.

The shape of a spinnaker or asymmetric is determined by how the sail panels are cut and sewn together. Spinnakers designed for sailing downwind are generally cut with a fuller shape, a wide mid-section, and a broader head. Those designed for reaching are flatter and narrower.

Dinghy spinnakers have to be good general-purpose sails as only one spinnaker is taken afloat, but larger keelboats, cruisers, and racers may well have two or more specialized spinnakers to suit a range of conditions.

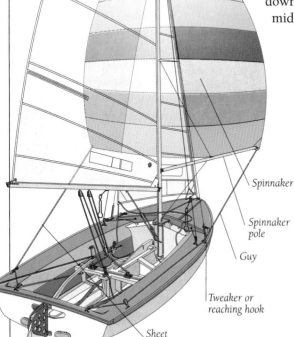

Spinnaker

Spinnaker pole

Guy

Tweaker or reaching hook

Sheet

Asymmetric sails

An asymmetric is a cross between a large genoa and a spinnaker – and is often called a gennaker. Unlike a spinnaker, an asymmetric is not symmetrical about its centerline, hence the name, but it has a distinct luff and leach. Depending on the design of the boat and sail, an asymmetric is usually set from the bow or from the end of a bowsprit (a spar sticking out ahead of the bow). Occasionally, it can be set from a spinnaker pole.

SAILING WING AND WING

As an alternative to using a spinnaker, you can improve your speed downwind by sailing wing and wing – sailing with the jib on the opposite side of the boat to the mainsail. On a run, it is easy to pull the jib across to the windward side, where it will catch the wind instead of hanging in the wind shadow of the mainsail.

It can be difficult to keep the jib set in this position, but this is solved by using a short pole, called a whisker pole, to boom out the jib. The whisker pole clips to a ring on the front of the mast and usually has a point on the other end that pushes into the cringle (the reinforced ring) at the jib clew. Tension on the jib sheet stops the pole from slipping out of the clew. Without the whisker pole, it is hard for the crew to keep the jib set in this way and it's more critical that the helmsman steers an accurate course. Make sure that you remove and stow the whisker pole before you jibe or luff up higher than a broad reach.

Setting a spinnaker

MANY SAILORS ARE VERY WARY of using a spinnaker because of the sail's reputation for being troublesome to set and use. It is true that the sail demands respect, but personally I really enjoy using a spinnaker or asymmetric and can thoroughly recommend that you learn how to use one properly.

There is no need to fear spinnakers as long as you follow a few simple rules. Learn a routine for hoisting, flying, and dropping the sail and it will add to your fun and give you much additional power.

Spinnaker gear

The systems for stowing, hoisting, and lowering a spinnaker range from an improvised system on an older boat to a sophisticated launching system on a high-performance racing dinghy. Arrangements for stowing the spinnaker pole also vary. In some boats, the pole is stowed in the boat, while others stow the pole in brackets fitted to the boom.

A good system allows you to hoist and lower the spinnaker quickly, with the minimum chance of a foul-up. It also allows you to stow the sail neatly, without twists, ready for hoisting again. Normally, the type of system is dictated by the design of the boat.

Apart from the spinnaker itself, you also need a spinnaker pole, a halyard and stowage system, and a pair of sheets that lead from each clew outside all the rigging to blocks and cleats on the sidedecks.

The sheet on the windward side of the boat is called the guy. As you jibe, the old sheet becomes the new guy and vice versa.

The turning blocks for the sheets are usually placed as far aft as possible on the sidedecks, with a hook – known as a reaching hook – just aft of the shrouds. The guy is led under this hook to hold it down and out of the way of the crew sitting out or trapezing. Sometimes a tweaker (also known as a twinning line) is used instead of a reaching hook. This is comprised of a small block that runs along the spinnaker sheet (to which a light line is attached). The line runs through a block on the gunwale just aft of the shroud and then to a cleat where it can be adjusted. There is a tweaker on each side of the boat. When in use, the tweaker on the guy is pulled tight to hold the guy down by the shroud, while the tweaker on the sheet is left slack.

Packing a spinnaker

Most modern dinghies are fitted either with a pouch stowage system on either side of the mast or with a chute system at the bow. With a pouch system, the dinghy is fitted with two light fabric pouches, one either side of the mast. The spinnaker is hoisted straight out of the pouch it is stowed in and must be packed carefully to avoid twists.

■ **Hoist the spinnaker** *when you are ashore and then have the crew stow it carefully into a pouch as you lower the sail.*

THE SPINNAKER POLE

When the spinnaker is in use, the spinnaker pole is fitted onto a ring on the front of the mast. The outer end is clipped onto the spinnaker guy. The pole is held horizontal by an uphaul (or topping lift) and downhaul, with which you can alter the height of the outer end. At each end of the pole is a fitting with a retractable plunger that allows it to be attached to the mast and the guy. When it is not in use, the spinnaker pole can be stowed in the boat or in brackets on the boom. In the latter case, the downhaul and uphaul are often attached to a ring that can slide along the pole to allow it to be stowed with the uphaul and downhaul permanently attached.

MARKING THE SPINNAKER SHEETS

It is a good idea to mark the sheets so that you can pre-set the spinnaker before hoisting, lowering, and jibing. To do this, hoist the spinnaker on land and set it symmetrically across the bow of the boat. Cleat the sheet and guy and mark the point where they pass through the fairlead or cleat with a marker pen. To make hoisting easier, put another set of marks on the sheets. With the sail hoisted ashore and the boat stern to wind, take one of the spinnaker clews to a point just forward of the forestay – about 3 ft (1 m) – and pull the sheet tight. Mark it where it passes through the fairlead or cleat. Repeat the process with the other sheet.

Many high-performance dinghies use a chute system because it allows for quick, easy, and twist-free hoisting and lowering. Built into the boat, the chute is a bell-shaped opening set into the foredeck in front of, or just behind and to one side of, the forestay. A long fabric sock or rigid plastic tube runs from the chute under the foredeck and contains the spinnaker when it is stowed.

When the spinnaker is hoisted, it emerges from the chute at the bow. A retrieval line, which runs through the tube and mouth and is tied to the middle of the spinnaker, is pulled to lower it. The halyard and retrieval lines are usually a continuous length of rope.

Avoid attaching the halyard to the wrong corner. It is embarrassing to hoist the spinnaker or asymmetric upside down but it is easily done – as I know all too well!

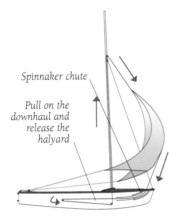

Spinnaker chute

Pull on the downhaul and release the halyard

■ **When you pack into a** *chute, hoist the spinnaker ashore then pull on the retrieval line and let out the halyard to pull the sail down into the chute.*

Avoiding twists

Whichever stowage system you use, it is important to pack the sail properly to avoid twists. Start at one of the lower corners, attach the sheet, and then run your hands along the foot until you reach the other lower corner. Attach the other sheet and then run your hands along the next side until you reach the head, to which you should attach the halyard. Now bundle up the middle of the sail and pack it into its pouch. If you are using a chute, attach the retrieval line to the eye in the middle of the sail and pull the sail into the chute.

Hoisting a spinnaker

Always steer onto a broad reach or run before hoisting a spinnaker. Remember that you and your crew have to continue to sail the boat and keep it balanced while dealing with the spinnaker. In most dinghies the halyard is led back to the helmsman, so you will usually handle the hoisting and lowering while your crew attaches the pole.

You will find it easiest if you stand in the middle of the boat, steering with the tiller between your knees while you hoist. Your aim should be to hoist the spinnaker and get it under control as quickly as possible. If you stow your spinnaker in pouches, it is easier and faster to hoist if it is stowed in the leeward pouch. Where possible, pack it in the pouch that will be to leeward when you are ready to hoist.

When you have to hoist from the windward pouch, you must steer onto a run or the sail may blow between the forestay and mast.

If you are hoisting from a chute, your crew can fit the pole while you hoist the sail straight out of the chute. Since the sail emerges at the bow there is no danger of it ending up on the wrong side of the forestay. As soon as the sail is hoisted, cleat the halyard and pick up the sheet and guy to set the sail while your crew deals with the pole.

LEEWARD HOIST

To hoist from a leeward pouch, the sail is pulled out of the pouch by the halyard. While you hoist the sail, your crew should pull on the guy to pull the clew toward the forestay. As soon as the sail is hoisted, you can fill it by trimming the sheet and guy, and cleating the guy, while your crew is fitting the pole.

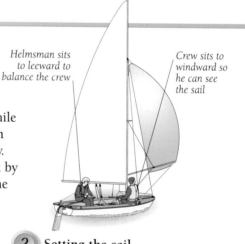

Helmsman sits to leeward to balance the crew

Crew sits to windward so he can see the sail

1 Hoisting

As the sail goes up, the crew attaches the pole to the guy, fits the uphaul and downhaul, and puts the inboard end of the pole on the mast ring.

2 Setting the sail

As soon as the sail is hoisted, the helmsman cleats the halyard and picks up the sheet and guy to set the sail. The crew finishes fitting the pole and puts the guy under the reaching hook and cleats it. He takes the sheet from the helmsman and sits on the windward side.

WINDWARD HOIST

Crew fits pole

If you are hoisting from the windward side, you have to get the spinnaker up and around the forestay to the leeward side as quickly as possible. This is made more difficult if you sail any course other than a run.

In a windward hoist, your crew should delay attaching the pole until the sail is hoisted so that he can help with the hoist. He should pull the sail, in a tight bundle, out of the pouch and hold it in his outboard hand before following the steps below:

1 Hoisting

While holding the sheet, the crew throws the sail forward. The helmsman hoists the sail rapidly. The crew pulls the sail around the forestay.

2 Setting the sail

When the sail is up and to leeward of the forestay, the helmsman takes the sheet and guy, and the crew attaches the pole. The crew then puts the guy under the reaching hook, cleats it, and takes the sheet from the helmsman to trim the sail.

Trimming a spinnaker

When sailing with a spinnaker, the crew is responsible for adjusting the sheet to keep the sail trimmed. A spinnaker can greatly affect the steering of a dinghy, especially in strong winds. If it is not trimmed correctly, it can add great heeling and turning forces that can capsize the boat or make it very difficult to steer. You and your crew must work together and communicate effectively to keep the boat upright and moving fast.

The key to trimming a spinnaker is to keep the sail symmetrical about its centerline. This means that the clews should be kept level at the same height above the water and the sail should be encouraged to fly as far from the mainsail as possible to allow air to pass freely between them.

Start by setting the angle of the pole just forward of a right angle to the apparent wind. This means that the pole is brought aft, using the guy, as the boat sails further downwind, and is eased forward as the boat luffs toward a reach.

On a reach, the pole will be eased right forward but should always be kept off the forestay otherwise it may bend or break.

The crew should adjust the pole angle using the guy, which should be led under the reaching hook in order to keep it out of the way of the crew sitting on the windward side. Alternatively, the tweaker – if fitted – can be pulled tight. The guy can be cleated once the correct pole angle has been set. The height of the pole end can be adjusted with the uphaul and downhaul. Raise or lower the outer end of the pole to keep it level with the other corner of the sail. In light winds, the outer end usually has to be lower than it will be in stronger winds in order to keep the clews level.

Fine-tuning the spinnaker

When the spinnaker is set correctly the crew should be able to ease the sheet until the luff starts to curl back on itself, about halfway up the luff. The point at which the luff starts to curl is the optimum trim for the sail. As the boat constantly accelerates or decelerates, the apparent wind shifts forward or backward and the spinnaker sheet must be continually trimmed to keep the spinnaker on the edge of curling. This requires considerable concentration from the crew, who must not take his eyes off the spinnaker.

The crew should sit to windward to get a good view of the spinnaker luff and the helmsman should sit to leeward if necessary to balance the crew's weight.

It is important that the crew trimming the spinnaker understands how to handle gusts, otherwise the power in the spinnaker can overcome the effect of the rudder when the helmsman tries to steer.

When a gust hits, the crew should ease the spinnaker sheet as the apparent wind moves aft. This will curl the luff and allow the boat to accelerate. If he doesn't ease the sheet the boat will heel and develop weather helm, making it difficult for the helmsman to stay on course or bear away with the gust. The apparent wind will shift forward again as the boat accelerates, and the crew must be ready to sheet in to help prevent the spinnaker collapsing. When the boat slows down again, remember that the apparent wind will shift aft and the sheet must be eased to keep the spinnaker correctly trimmed.

If the spinnaker does collapse, it will be necessary to pull in a lot of sheet to get it to fill again. As soon as it fills, ease the sheet, as it will now be significantly over sheeted. Don't be surprised if you have to ease lots of sheet out in order to set the sail with a curl in the luff.

INTERNET

www.sailingsource.com
www.madforsailing.com

These are useful sites for news and articles on sailing.

Jibing a spinnaker

JIBING WITH A SPINNAKER SET *is a maneuver that requires plenty of practice so that your actions become automatic and the procedure can be completed smoothly. It is important to keep the boat upright and to complete the jibe as quickly as possible to prevent the spinnaker getting out of control or the boat getting out of balance.*

JIBING

To prepare for the jibe, you must bear away to a run while your crew adjusts the sheet and guy to set the spinnaker square across the bow. If the sheets are marked, as described previously, they can be set at the jibing position quickly and easily. The crew should remove the guy from the reaching hook and the boat is then ready to be jibed.

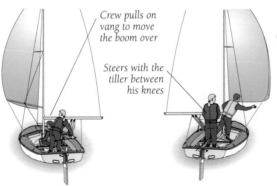

Crew pulls on vang to move the boom over

Steers with the tiller between his knees

Crew fits pole on new side

1 Into the jibe

The mainsail and jib are jibed first, with the boat pointing dead downwind. The crew helps the boom over by pulling on the vang. He sheets the jib loosely on the new side and then deals with the pole.

2 Through the jibe

The helmsman stands in the middle of the boat and takes control of the guy and sheet. He keeps the boat on a run while the crew takes the pole off the mast, clips it onto the new guy, and pushes it out towards the new side.

3 After the jibe

The crew removes the old guy from the pole and fits the pole onto the mast ring. After putting the guy under the reaching hook and cleating the guy, he takes the sheet and trims the sail while the helmsman steers onto the new course.

Although it may contradict your instinct, always jibe when the boat is traveling as fast as possible. This way the apparent wind will be reduced by the boat's own speed downwind and the loads on all the sails will be minimized.

Dropping a spinnaker

WHEN A POUCH SYSTEM IS USED you have the choice of lowering into either the windward or leeward pouch. The safest method is to drop into the windward pouch as this keeps the crew's weight on the windward side.

To lower the sail into the windward pouch, steer onto a broad reach or run and stand in the middle of the boat ready to lower the halyard. Your crew should unclip the pole from the mast, remove the uphaul and downhaul, and unclip the pole from the guy. He should then pull down on the luff of the sail as you lower it, stuffing it into the pouch. When all the luff is in the pouch, he should pull in the rest of the sail and hook the halyard under the reaching hook to stow it. Finally, any slack is taken out of the sheets and they can then be cleated.

Only drop the sail into the leeward pouch if you are going to need it in that pouch for a later leeward hoist. Steer onto a run while your crew moves to leeward and pulls on the sheet until he can reach the clew. He should release the guy and pull the sail down under the boom and into the leeward pouch. Once the sail is in the pouch, and the halyard stowed under the reaching hook, the crew can remove the spinnaker pole and stow it.

Lowering into a chute

Dropping a spinnaker into a chute is easier than using pouches. While you release the halyard and pull on the retrieval line to drop the sail, your crew should pull hard on both the sheet and guy. This will pull the foot tight against the forestay, allowing the middle of the sail to enter the chute first. As soon as the middle of the sail has entered the mouth of the chute, your crew can release the sheet and guy and remove and stow the pole.

■ **Dropping a sail into** *a windward pouch, the helmsman lowers the sail and the crew gathers it into the pouch.*

Sailing with an asymmetric

AN ASYMMETRIC SPINNAKER can be stowed and launched from a chute or from pouches depending on your boat's layout. In most dinghies the sail is flown from a retractable bowsprit (a spar projecting from the boom), although in larger boats it may be flown from the bow, a bowsprit, or a spinnaker pole.

An asymmetric is trimmed with two sheets. The lack of a spinnaker pole makes the sail easier to hoist and lower and means you do not need to worry about adjusting a pole. The sheets lead to the rear quarters and may be fitted with tweakers that move the sheet lead forward when sailing on a broad reach.

Hoist the sail while your crew pulls a line to launch the bowsprit to its extended position and also pulls the tack of the sail to the end of the bowsprit. To drop the sail, reverse the procedure. The sail is jibed just like a jib. As the boat turns through the jibe, the old sheet is eased well out and the new one is sheeted in as the sail blows across to the new side.

An asymmetric is best suited to a high-performance dinghy since this type of sail is not at its best on a dead run – a course that very fast dinghies rarely sail.

■ **Asymmetrics** *are often used on high-speed dinghies that achieve fast speeds when broad reaching.*

A simple summary

✓ Downwind sailing is more fun with a spinnaker or asymmetric.

✓ Sail wing and wing if you don't want to use a spinnaker.

✓ Always ensure that the spinnaker is not twisted when you pack it.

✓ Concentrate on watching the luff when you trim a spinnaker.

✓ Try to trim the spinnaker with a small curl on its luff.

✓ Hoist, jibe, and drop a spinnaker quickly so that you keep control.

Chapter 13

Adding Variety

Now that you have come to grips with the fundamental skills of sailing, and have developed your abilities with time spent practicing, I recommend that you try out some other types of daysailers. One of the great things about sailing is the huge variety of boats and the many different types of sailing you have to choose from. Before you make a decision about which is best for you, try out some of the boats you haven't sailed before. If you started sailing in a two-person boat, you could try a singlehander, a catamaran, or one of the new breed of high-performance dinghy.

In this chapter...

✓ Singlehanded sailing

✓ Sailing catamarans

✓ High-performance dinghies

✓ Sailing small keelboats

MANY SINGLEHANDED DINGHIES ARE LIGHT, RESPONSIVE, AND EXCITING TO SAIL

Singlehanded sailing

THERE ARE A LOT OF ADVANTAGES to sailing singlehanded. In many ways, it is the purest form of sailing since you alone are responsible for all aspects of boat handling. You have no one to help or blame – and no one to argue with – but you can take all the credit for success. You will certainly develop your skills quickly when you sail singlehanded, and you can sail when you want without having to find a crew to accompany you. Sailing alone may be a disadvantage, however, if you enjoy the social aspects of sailing with a crew or if you do not have sufficient confidence in your abilities.

Many people choose to sail singlehanded to avoid having to organize crew and because singlehanded boats are usually cheaper to buy and maintain. They are usually smaller and lighter than two-man dinghies and can often be transported on a car roof rack. They are generally quick to rig and you can be sailing within minutes of arriving at a venue.

■ **Singlehanded sailing** *puts you in complete control. These light dinghies respond rapidly to your movements and actions with the controls.*

Most singlehanded dinghies have a mainsail but no jib. The mainsail is set on a mast that is stepped much further forward than in dinghies with two sails.

Often, the mast of a singlehanded dinghy is unstayed and flexible, so that it can bend to give an efficient sail shape. The flexibility helps to release excess power in strong winds by increasing twist in the mainsail.

Rigging a singlehander

A few singlehanded dinghies have stayed masts, and their mainsails are rigged in the same way as two-man dinghies, but most have unstayed masts. They usually come in two pieces that are slotted together before the sail is fitted. The mast is then slid into the pocket in the mainsail luff and stood upright, before being stepped in the boat, with the sail blowing freely. Often, the mainsail on these boats is loose-footed, which means that the foot is only attached to the boom at the tack and clew. After the boom is fitted onto the gooseneck, the clew outhaul is attached and the sail is ready to go.

On the Laser, and other similar dinghies, the mast is held in place – in case of a capsize – by the Cunningham control line. Most singlehanded dinghies use a daggerboard rather than a centerboard. Make sure this and the rudder are in the boat before launching.

Launching

A singlehander is launched in the same way as a two-man dinghy except you have to do the job on your own. If your boat has an unstayed mast with a sleeved sail then this must be rigged before launching, while the boat is kept as close to head-to-wind as possible. If the boat has a conventional mast and sail arrangement, you can hoist it before or after launching, depending on the conditions.

If there is no one to help you remove the dolly once the boat is afloat, and to bring the dolly to you when you return, you will have to tie up the boat while you deal with the dolly.

Sailing a singlehander

Singlehanded dinghies are light and sensitive to changes in trim and balance. You must be ready to move your weight in and out, and fore and aft, to keep the boat upright. Because there is only one sail, it is important that it is always properly set. You will need to get used to adjusting its shape with the outhaul, Cunningham, mainsheet, and vang.

It is on downwind courses that singlehanded dinghies behave most differently from two-man boats. With only one sail, there is increased weather helm – a tendency for the boat to turn to windward. Compensate for this by heeling the boat to windward until the helm is neutral – it requires good balance and skill to maintain this heel downwind.

Because singlehanded dinghies are usually very light, they plane easily offwind. Since you don't have to coordinate your actions with those of crew, these boats are great fun to sail downwind in waves, as they react instantly to tiller movements and accelerate rapidly.

Tacking a singlehander

The key to tacking well in a singlehander is good timing and smooth movements across the boat. Your movements are the same as in a two-man dinghy but the boom is often very low on these boats – you will have to duck to get under it as you cross the boat.

Ease the mainsheet gently as you turn through the wind, and don't move off the windward side too early in the tack. Wait until the boom is approaching the centerline, with the boat heeled toward you, before crossing the boat, then move quickly and get your weight out over the new windward side as the boat completes the tack. Sit out hard and pull the mainsheet back in as the boat comes upright.

Jibing a singlehander

Before a jibe, it is essential that the boat is moving as fast as possible. If you're sailing downwind in waves, wait until the boat is accelerating down a wave face before you jibe. You should have the daggerboard up as far as possible but don't pull it up so far that it catches on the boom or vang when you jibe.

If the vang was set up tight before the jibe, ease it a bit to help prevent it from hitting the water after the jibe and causing you to capsize. Your actions through the jibe are the same as in a two-man dinghy, but there is only one of you to balance the boat through the maneuver so you will have to move quickly. With the boat sailing fast on a very broad reach or run, turn into the jibe and give a sharp tug on the mainsheet to start the boom swinging across. As it does so, straighten the tiller and get your weight out on the new side.

INTERNET
www.laserinternational.org
This is the site of the International Laser Class.

Sailing catamarans

CATAMARANS ARE AVAILABLE in a variety of sizes and styles to suit all ages and skill levels. They have two narrow hulls connected by two beams – a trampoline is fitted between these. Due to their wide beams, they are much more stable than monohull dinghies, and their narrow hulls and light weight mean that they offer little resistance and are easily driven.

Catamaran sails

Some catamarans use a loose-footed mainsail set without a boom. In this case, the multipart mainsheet tackle attaches directly to the clew rather than the boom, and it runs on a full-width traveler on the rear beam.

Catamaran masts are often designed to rotate so that they have an efficient angle to the wind on all points of sail. A mast spanner is used by the crew to control the mast's angle of rotation.

Many catamarans are fitted with one or two trapezes, just like high-performance single-hulled dinghies, and many use an asymmetric spinnaker to increase speed downwind. They have twin rudders, one at the stern of each hull, and their tillers are connected by a tiller bar. A long tiller extension is attached to the middle of the tiller bar.

Most catamarans have large mainsails, often with battens that run full length from luff to leech, together with a much smaller jib that is usually tall and narrow. The most important thing to get used to in a catamaran is the much greater speed potential. Watch for approaching gusts, because the catamaran will accelerate rapidly when they hit and, if you are not prepared, you could be taken by surprise. Because of their extra speed capability, you can get very wet when you sail a catamaran. If you are considering sailing one regularly, think about investing in a good wetsuit or drysuit.

■ **Hobie cats** *are very popular and are a good introduction to the high-speed fun of catamarans, whether you want to race or sail just for pleasure.*

Catamaran performance

Catamaran sailors usually fit a wind indicator on the forestay bridle so that the helmsman can constantly check the direction of the apparent wind while looking forward. Because catamarans sail so fast, there is a much bigger difference in direction between the true and apparent wind than you experience when sailing most other dinghies. As a result, catamarans always sail downwind in a series of zigzags, much the same as when tacking upwind. Sailing dead downwind is very slow for a catamaran, but sailing at an angle of about 135° to the true wind will cause the speed of the catamaran to pull the apparent wind forward until it is on the beam.

Catamarans are more stable than conventional dinghies and jibing is easier, but they can still capsize – often in a very spectacular way. This usually happens when sailing offwind, when it is possible to cartwheel the boat over its leeward bow or pitchpole it – it digs its bows in and capsizes stern over bow.

Tacking and jibing

Tacking a catamaran is a bit different from tacking a dinghy because their lightness, coupled with the turning resistance of the two hulls, causes them to stop very quickly when they reach head-to-wind. It is worth reviewing the method of recovering from being "in-irons," because you are likely to have to use it when learning to tack a catamaran.

Don't try to tack a catamaran from a reach to a reach. Always sheet in to a close-hauled course and get up to speed before trying to tack.

Jibing a catamaran is easier than jibing a dinghy because of the greater stability, but you must ensure that you have plenty of room for the maneuver and that the boat is under full control before you start the jibe.

Each type of catamaran has its own characteristics and idiosyncrasies, just like the various monohull classes. The best way to learn how to sail one well is to take a catamaran course at a sailing school, or crew for an experienced sailor.

High-performance dinghies

HIGH-PERFORMANCE IS A RELATIVE TERM *that changes as new boats appear on the scene and new gear or techniques are developed to allow dinghy crews to control increased power and sail at faster speeds. Only a few years ago, a few classic International and Olympic classes were regarded as the pinnacle of high-performance dinghies. Then, along came lighter and stronger materials and new designs, and we now have much faster dinghies, some of which test even the best crews to the limit of their skills.*

With their development has come a new type of short-course racing dinghy that offers plenty of thrills and spills. These boats are definitely not for novices, but there is no reason why you shouldn't aspire to sail one once you have mastered the skills involved in sailing a fast boat with a trapeze and a spinnaker or asymmetric.

This will introduce you to the increased speed and help you develop the skills needed to keep a fast boat under control. Offer to sail as crew on board a really fast boat before deciding if high-performance dinghies are for you.

■ **A Laser 4000** *is a good starting point if you want to progress to the fastest dinghies. It will teach you the boat-handling skills needed to sail the fastest examples of the type.*

Sailing high-performance dinghies

The techniques for sailing a high-performance dinghy depend on its sail-area-to-weight ratio. The very light, high-powered dinghies require more careful handling than their less extreme cousins. They require techniques, especially downwind, that are similar to those used when sailing a catamaran. This is because their high speed, like that of a catamaran, causes the apparent wind to move further forward than on slower dinghies.

Nearly all of the very fast designs use an asymmetric rather than a regular spinnaker. Like catamarans, they should be sailed downwind in a series of jibes, keeping the apparent wind well forward for maximum speed.

Before you rush out to buy a high-performance boat, be sure to decide what type of sailing you will want to do most of the time.

JUDGING A BOAT'S SPEED

Boat speed is determined by the strength of wind, the sail area, and the weight of the boat complete with its crew. In other words, the more sail area you have and the less your boat weighs, the faster you will go.

Comparing types

High-performance boats are much lighter than general-purpose dinghies, have more complex rigs, and shallower hull shapes. A heavier, general-purpose dinghy will be slower on all points of sail. Both types perform better on some points of sail than others – reaching courses are faster for both types than close-hauled or running courses.

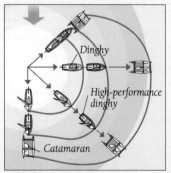

A polar diagram shows the potential speed of a boat for a specific wind strength. Each type of boat will have a unique polar curve for a particular wind speed. Racing yachts use polar curves to predict the speed they should attain on any point of sailing and trim and tune the boat accordingly.

■ **The curves** *in the polar diagram above show the potential speeds for each type of boat on the various points of sailing.*

If you really enjoy just sailing around in a dinghy or cruising around your local area, then a high-performance boat is not for you. Even if you want to race, it is not necessary to buy the latest type of fast dinghy. Most popular classes provide good club-level racing and many give world-class competition. In fact, slower boats often provide closer, more tactical racing.

If, however, you want to sail as fast as possible and are prepared to spend a lot of time capsizing, then there is plenty of choice among the latest lightweight dinghies. Decide where you want to sail and pick a class that is raced there. Then join a club and crew for others before buying your own boat.

> ## Trivia...
> The Olympic Games is the pinnacle of competitive sailing. All types of sailing are represented in the Games, including singlehanded sailing, high-performance dinghies, catamarans, and keelboats.

Sailing small keelboats

SMALL KEELBOATS are similar to dinghies in that they have open cockpits and are designed for day sailing or racing, but they differ significantly in that they have a fixed and weighted keel. This gives them greater stability and they are less dependent on crew weight to keep them upright.

> ## DEFINITION
> Sport boats *are small keelboats – typically 23–30 ft (7–9 m) – that share many characteristics with high-performance dinghies. They are lightly built and have large rigs, and they usually have an asymmetric spinnaker set on a retractable bowsprit. They are often sailed with between four and six crew and are intended to be fast, day-racing boats. All the techniques used to sail high-performance dinghies are needed to make a sport boat perform well, and they give good racing.*

The amount of stability provided by the keel varies between different designs. Crew weight is still very significant in some designs, especially modern boats that tend to be wider than older designs.

In the lighter keelboats, and especially the type known as *sport boats*, crews still use their weight to help keep the boat upright. There are others, however, that rely more on keel weight, and their crews may sit in the boat. There is a wide range of keelboats to choose from, and, if you are interested in sailing a keelboat, you are bound to find a class that suits your needs.

All the sailing techniques you learned in a dinghy will also serve you well when sailing a small keelboat, but you will notice some differences. Your weight will have less of an impact, but, if you are racing a keelboat, weight is still an important consideration.

The fixed keel means that you don't have to remember to adjust a centerboard or daggerboard, but it also means that you cannot retract the keel, so be careful when you are sailing in shallow water.

Learning in a keelboat

Maneuvers take longer in a heavier, larger boat and the loads on sheets are higher, so you may need to use winches to sheet in the jib. Although they are heavier than dinghies, many modern keelboats will plane in stronger winds and give exciting sailing.

A keelboat is a good alternative to learning to sail in a dinghy. Most keelboats have more space than a dinghy, with sufficient room for an instructor to sail with you. You will not have to worry about the risk of capsizing, but you will have to handle a larger, heavier boat with higher equipment loads and this may seem more daunting than a smaller boat. If you are keen to race, you will find plenty of choice among the keelboat classes. Many of them provide very close and competitive racing but remember that you will need more crew for a keelboat than for a dinghy.

■ **A sport boat** *offers fast and exciting sailing without the physical demands of a high-performance dinghy, but at greater cost.*

A simple summary

✔ Try out a variety of different types of boat before deciding which is right for you.

✔ If you sail a very high-performance dinghy you will capsize a lot but the thrill will more than compensate.

✔ Singlehanded dinghies offer the simplest form of sailing, and there is no crew to worry about.

✔ Small keelboats can be good to learn in, and the best ones offer very close and highly competitive racing.

Chapter 14

The Fun of Racing

IF YOU HAVE ANY COMPETITIVE INSTINCT at all then there is a good chance that you will enjoy dinghy or keelboat racing. Personally, I enjoy racing all sizes of boat as much as I enjoy cruising – which is a lot! Most people tend to fall into one or other of the racing and cruising camps but there is no reason why you can't enjoy both. You will learn more about how to get the best performance out of your boat through racing than you will from thousands of miles of cruising. If you aspire to developing expert skills, or are attracted by the challenge and thrill of competition, then join a club, pick a suitable class, and come and join the racers.

In this chapter...

✓ Tuning your boat

✓ Types of courses

✓ Starting well

✓ Sailing the course

NOTHING BEATS RACING FOR TEACHING YOU HOW TO SAIL WELL

Tuning your boat

SUCCESS IN RACING *is achieved by being good in three key areas: boat speed, boat handling, and tactics. It is possible to win in a slow boat by handling it better or sailing a faster course than others, but it is a hard route to success.*

It is not much use having the fastest boat in the fleet if your boat-handling skills or tactics are not up to snuff. However, a fast boat can make an average sailor look really good, while a slow one will humble an expert, so time spent preparing your boat and tuning it for best performance is time well spent.

■ **When you have spent time** *fine tuning your boat, you can enjoy the buzz of racing, knowing that you can push your boat to the limits of its performance.*

Tuning a boat is similar to tuning a car for best performance. Your aim is to refine and adjust all the elements on your boat that affect its speed so that you have the best performing boat in the fleet – or at least one that is as fast as the top boats.

Minimizing weight

Boats, like cars, are constrained by their power-to-weight ratio. This means that you must do all you can to increase drive, reduce drag, and eliminate unnecessary weight. Weight is one variable that is often taken for granted. After all, surely the boat must weigh the same as other, seemingly identical boats? In fact, it is quite common for boats to be heavier than their class's minimum weight rule.

Fiberglass boats can absorb moisture if they are left afloat, or even when stored ashore if water is allowed to collect in the boat. Many sailors forget the importance of weight and allow unnecessary gear to accumulate in boat lockers. It is worth noting that even on the largest offshore racing yachts, skippers go to amazing lengths to minimize weight, such as banning any personal gear other than sailing clothes, or even cutting toothbrush handles in half! These weight savings may seem very excessive but top sailors understand the detrimental effect of unnecessary weight on a boat's speed.

Reducing drag

Drag from the air is caused by poorly set sails and by the wind resistance of the boat, rig, and crew. Try to minimize drag by sitting close alongside your crew to help reduce your windage, and make sure that there is no unnecessary gear above deck. Buy the best sails you can afford and learn to set them properly.

A critical issue to be aware of is underwater drag. The underwater parts of the hull, centerboard, and rudder must have a perfect finish and be free from any blemishes that would disturb the flow of water. If the surfaces are not totally smooth on your boat then lightly sand them until any imperfections are removed.

Check your hull and foils regularly – feeling with your fingertips is the best way to pick up irregularities – and repair any damage.

In light winds and flat water, when the boat is not sailing at its maximum speed, the surface drag of the underwater surfaces have a big effect on the boat's resistance, so surface imperfections will be particularly detrimental in these circumstances.

Tuning your rig

The key to increasing your boat's drive is to tune your rig so that it can deliver the power you need across a range of wind strengths. In light and moderate winds, your aim is to get the maximum power possible out of the rig. As the wind increases, the available power will start to become greater than your ability to balance the heeling force when you are sailing upwind.

You will now have too much power when sailing upwind and, at that point, you will need to be able to reduce the heeling force without increasing drag from flapping sails or a heavily heeled boat. If your rig is well tuned, it will deliver power when it's needed yet will bend to flatten the mainsail and reduce the heeling force as the wind increases.

On a downwind course, there is far less heeling force so you can use the power of strong winds to increase your speed – as long as you can stay in control of the boat!

Seeking advice

Many classes and their leading sailmakers publish tuning aids to help newcomers set up their boats, and leading sailors are often happy to help novices learn to tune their rig. Ask the best sailors in your class or at your club for advice, and aim to set your boat up in exactly the same way as the top boats before you start experimenting for yourself. This will help you achieve good performance quickly and will prevent you getting too confused by all the variables that combine to make a fast set-up.

Your aim is to set the boat up to achieve the maximum speed possible in light, medium, and strong winds, so that you can concentrate on boat handling.

DEFINITION

Pre-bend is the amount of bend set in the mast before you start sailing, and it has a large effect on the shape of the mainsail.

Choosing and fitting sails

If you are able to invest in new sails, choose a sailmaker who makes sails for the winning boats, tell him what mast you are using, and ask for information on how to set up your mast to suit the mainsail. You need to know how much to rake your mast and how much *pre-bend* should be set in the mast.

Rake your mast aft using the measurement provided by your sailmaker or class experts, then adjust the spreaders and the shroud tensions to set the recommended pre-bend. If possible, get an expert to help you and ask them to explain the effect of their adjustments. Each different class has its own optimum settings. Things that work well in one type of boat may not work in another. This can be confusing, but keeping in mind a few basic rules will help you work through the idiosyncrasies of your boat.

If you need to increase the bend in the mast, there are a number of options. You can increase the shroud tension; angle the spreaders further aft; or increase the spreader length – doing the opposite of this will reduce mast bend.

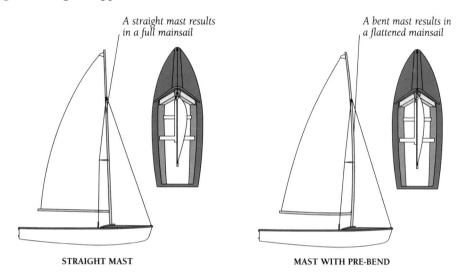

A straight mast results in a full mainsail

A bent mast results in a flattened mainsail

STRAIGHT MAST

MAST WITH PRE-BEND

WEATHER AND LEE HELM

When a boat is upright, trimmed correctly fore and aft, and the sails are accurately set, there should be little or no tendency for the boat to turn. This is referred to as having a balanced helm. If you let go of the tiller, the boat will continue on a straight course. If the boat turns to windward when you let go of the tiller, it has weather helm. If it turns to leeward, then it has lee helm. In practice, it is easier to sail a boat with a small amount of weather helm as this gives some feel to the steering. Lee helm is to be avoided because it makes the boat difficult to sail, and if the tiller is dropped by accident the boat will not automatically turn into the wind and stop, as it would if it had weather helm.

Making adjustments

If your boat has a centerboard, you can adjust the helm balance while sailing by adjusting the centerboard rake (the angle at which it is inclined). Lift the centerboard slightly to reduce weather helm and lower it to eliminate lee helm. When you tune your boat, you should adjust the mast rake to give the desired helm balance.

Types of courses

SAILBOAT RACING TAKES PLACE *on a variety of courses, ranging from short courses that take an hour or less to complete to round-the-world races lasting several months. Most dinghy and small keelboat races take place around triangular or sausage-shaped courses; inflatable turning points are usually laid for the race, although some clubs may use fixed navigation marks instead. The length of each leg of the course can vary depending on the size of boat being raced and the location, but it is typically between 1 and 2 miles (1.5–2 km).*

The start line is usually arranged between a committee boat and a buoy. The race officers are based on the committee boat and use sound and visual signals (flags or shapes) to indicate the time remaining before the start.

The best type of start line is one that is laid square to the wind, with the first mark of the course laid directly upwind from the start line. If the wind is fluctuating it can be a difficult job laying a square line and, in most cases, one end of the line is closer to the wind than the other.

Sometimes a club may use a starting line where a buoy marks the outer end but the inner end is on the shore. Depending on the angle of the shore, it is often impossible to change the angle of the line significantly. It is unlikely to be square to the wind and the first leg may not be directly upwind. Indeed, you may find yourself starting on a reach, or even downwind on some occasions, depending on where you are racing.

Racing details

Details of the course for each race, together with other important information about starting signals and other aspects of the race, will be contained in the Sailing Instructions that will be issued by the organizing club. You should also have a copy of the International Yacht Racing Rules.

Starting well

THE START IS THE KEY *to any race. While it is possible to recover from a bad start, it is much easier to do well in the race if you make a reasonable start. Make sure you know exactly where the starting line is and sail along it between the buoy and the committee boat to see if you can identify the end closest to the wind.*

There are several ways of visually checking the angle of the line, but for your first few races you will probably have your hands full keeping clear of all the other boats, watching for signals from the committee boat, and working out what is going on.

■ **The start** *of a race often involves jockeying for a good position close to the starting line. Boats will be in close proximity and you must be precise in your boat control.*

Take a look at what the best sailors are doing. Pick one boat that you know is a regular winner and stick close to it.

If you have a crew, make him responsible for monitoring the time to the start. He will need a good watch with a countdown feature that should be set at the first signal. This is known as the warning signal and it is commonly given 10 minutes before the starting signal. The most crucial factor is to be on the start line when the starting gun is fired. This may seem obvious, but few novice racers manage to be anywhere near the line at the start.

At the starting line

Keep an eye on the boat you have picked to be your guide and try to stay close by. Most boats will be sailing slowly as they attempt to gain the best position and this is where your own slow-speed handling skills will be tested. Do not be tempted to sail up and down the line at full speed, but concentrate on staying close to your guide. Avoid getting too close, though, because if there is a collision your experienced competitor is likely to be unfriendly to say the least! Never try to start a race on port tack when you are learning, since all the other boats approaching the line on starboard tack will have right of way over you.

Trying to keep clear of a whole fleet while making your own start is not recommended until you have much more experience. Plan to make your final approach to the line close-hauled or on a close reach on starboard tack. Adjust your speed by allowing the jib to flap and by spilling wind from the mainsail. If you are lucky, and have managed to get close to the line, the final few seconds before the starting gun will see the boats either side of you pulling in their sails, luffing to close-hauled, and accelerating toward the line. Watch them carefully and go with them. Pull in your sails, sit out to keep the boat upright, and concentrate on getting the boat up to maximum speed as quickly as possible.

At the crack of the gun

The starting gun fires and you're off. If it has all gone well, and you are lucky, you will be up among the fleet and there will be boats to either side of you. Try to ignore them and concentrate on sailing fast. They will all spread out in a few minutes and you will have more room to maneuver. However, it is more likely, if you are beginning your racing career, that you will have been late for the start and the majority of the fleet will already be some way ahead of you. Don't worry, this is quite normal and you will soon learn how to improve your starting skills. Concentrate on your boat speed because there will be other opportunities to catch up.

INTERNET

www.racingrules.org

This is a useful site for learning about the rules that govern all types of sailboat racing.

Sailing the course

AS WE HAVE SEEN, *racing courses can vary considerably in their layout and number of turning marks, so make sure you know the course you should be sailing. It is quite common for boats to make a mistake going around the course and it is very frustrating when you lose a race by heading for the wrong mark.*

Assuming that your first leg is to windward, concentrate hard on sailing the boat as fast as possible close-hauled immediately after the start. This is when the fast boats often get away from the others, so work hard to stay in touch with the leaders. As well as sailing the boat as fast as possible, you also need to be able to spot windshifts. Most overtaking occurs on windward legs of the course and these are often due to the way competitors use each shift in the wind.

If you seem to be sailing more slowly than those around you, take a careful look at how the other boats are being sailed and how their sails are trimmed. Don't be afraid to experiment to find out the sail trim that gives you the best speed.

■ **Beware of arriving** *at the windward mark on port tack because you may find it very difficult to avoid other boats approaching on starboard tack.*

The windward legs

As you know, you have a choice of many different routes when sailing through the no-sail zone to a windward mark. You can choose to tack several times or only once, and, in a completely steady wind and no tide, there is no difference in the distance sailed. Once the wind starts to shift, however, you will sail the shortest distance if you tack each time you are headed by a new wind shift.

One of the best ways to gain a reasonable position in the fleet is to play it safe and avoid getting too far to one side of the course or the other. When sailing to windward, it is common to sail too far on one tack and end up a long way from the direct line between the start line and the windward mark. Try and get back to the middle of the course whenever a header gives you an opportunity to tack. In this way you will lose less if you miss a windshift and you may gain on boats that have picked the wrong side of the course and gone too far in that direction.

Checking for windshifts

Spotting windshifts is made easier if you have a compass, which enables you to constantly check the course you are achieving as you sail to windward. If the course changes you must check to see if you have been lifted or headed by the windshift. If you are sailing a two-man boat it often helps if your crew concentrates on spotting wind shifts and monitoring the other boats while you concentrate on sailing fast.

If you are lifted then you should continue on the same tack but if you are headed, by 5° or more, then you should tack.

Keep your eyes open

The strength of the wind often varies across the race course and gains can be made by seeking out areas of stronger wind. To spot changes in wind strength, keep an eye on the other boats, especially those sailing some distance away from you. If you see that there is more wind on one side of the course than the other, head for the stronger wind as soon as possible.

To start with, you will find it difficult to keep an eye on all the things you need to monitor as you race to windward. The trick is to regularly check each key performance indicator in turn. Watch the jib luff telltales for a few seconds to make sure you are sailing properly to windward. Look ahead of the boat for large waves that may slow the boat and check for signs of approaching gusts on the water. Check the telltales again and then look ahead of the boat for land or sea marks that can help you decide if you are being headed or lifted by a windshift. Use your compass, if you have one, to check the course. Now, look around the boat in all directions, to check the position of your competitors, and then look back at the telltales.

■ **As you approach the mark,** *tactics and precise boat handling will make all the difference as you change course and round the buoy, with the aim of retaining or improving your position in the race.*

Sailing for the windward mark

Make sure that you spot the windward mark as soon as possible after the start. Keep checking your position relative to the mark and aim to keep it in the area between your bow and the windward shroud. This is a simple means of ensuring that you sail toward the mark as much as possible and will help you avoid becoming confused by wind shifts.

Most courses are arranged so that boats leave the windward mark to port as they bear away onto the next leg of the course. Plan to approach the mark on a starboard tack, so that you have right of way at the mark. As you approach, prepare to adjust your centerboard, sails, and weight position as you bear away around the mark.

The downwind legs

The natural tendency is to relax on the downwind legs after all the effort of the windward leg but I'm afraid you need to keep concentrating! As soon as you have cleared the windward mark, check the course to the next mark. If the wind is aft of the beam and you have a spinnaker then it should be hoisted as quickly as possible.

At this stage, you are probably discovering that your boat-handling skills are not quite as good as you thought they were. The leading boats are probably some way ahead but you may have noticed that their spinnakers were hoisted and set almost as soon as the boats had rounded the mark. Make a mental note to spend some more time practicing your boat-handling and spinnaker techniques before your next race!

The second leg

The second leg of the course will probably be either a broad reach or a run. If it is a broad reach, hoist the spinnaker, then concentrate on steering straight for the mark and sailing the boat as fast as possible. Watch the boats up ahead and close by to check your boat speed and take the time to plan your next mark-rounding maneuver. You will probably have to jibe at the mark before heading on another reach to the leeward mark.

If your second leg is a run, you will need to hoist your spinnaker as quickly as possible at the windward mark and set the boat up for a run. How you sail this leg depends on the type of boat you sail and the strength of the wind.

Lighter boats sail much faster on a broad reach than on a run in all but very strong winds, and the extra speed more than makes up for the extra distance you have to sail. Heavier boats gain less extra speed when sailing on a broad reach but it can still be effective, especially when it is possible to plane on a broad reach but not on a run.

Watch how the leaders sail this leg and copy their techniques. Also be aware that wind shifts are just as important on the run as they are when sailing to windward, especially when you choose to sail a series of broad reaches rather than sailing a run dead downwind.

Imagine you are sailing on a broad reach on a starboard tack. If the wind shifts forward, this means that you can sail more directly for the next mark. If the wind shifts aft, however, you will need to head up to stay on a broad reach and will now be sailing further away from the mark. In this case, you should jibe and sail a broad reach on the other tack, which will allow you to sail more directly for the mark.

Rounding the leeward mark

Before you reach the leeward mark, prepare the boat for sailing close-hauled again. Get ready to lower the spinnaker and give yourself plenty of time to drop it before you reach the mark. Try to round the mark as smoothly as possible to keep your speed up, and remember that you will need your crew weight in position to balance the heeling force as soon as you turn to close-hauled.

You have now sailed around one lap of the course but there are probably still one or more laps to go. You may be well behind the fleet but don't give up. There is always a chance that you will catch up and even if you remain at the back of the fleet there is still much to learn. Make a mental note of the good and bad points of the race for discussion in the bar afterward, and try and watch how the good sailors deal with each of the situations you face.

Now you're hooked

You've finished your first race and maybe you haven't come in last. Even if you have trailed the fleet around the course and kept the race committee from the bar as they wait for you to finish, you should give yourself a pat on the back for completing the course safely. Your first race is over and perhaps you're already hooked.

When you get back to the clubhouse after the race, have a chat with the guys who did well and get their perspective on the race. Tell them about any problems you had and ask for their advice. Most sailors are happy to share their knowledge and to help you improve your own performance, but don't expect too many favors when you improve and start threatening their position!

A great way to learn more about racing techniques is to crew for an experienced racer. Try and find a crewing position in the type of boat that you want to sail, and spend a season racing as crew before buying your own boat. Another way to improve is to take a racing course at a good sailing school or club. This gives you the chance to sail different boats and to learn intensively over a period of a few days.

Joining a club

Now is the time to join a club if you haven't already done so. Sailing clubs cover the spectrum of types of sailing and social standing. Some are exclusively dedicated to dinghy sailing, while others embrace both dinghies and larger yachts. A few are exclusive social establishments, but most are friendly places where the novice can find opportunities to sail, meet other sailors, and learn more about the sport.

If you have your own boat and want to race, look for a club that has a strong fleet of the same class of boat. This will provide you with good racing and a group of like-minded sailors who can help you improve your skills and knowledge.

A simple summary

✓ Racing is fun and the best way to learn boat-handling skills.

✓ Watch the fast boats for clues about sailing your own boat fast.

✓ Remember to keep unnecessary weight out of your boat.

✓ Join a club that races your type of boat and ask experts for advice.

PART
FOUR

CRUISER SAILING IS VERY POPULAR

CRUISER SAILING SKILLS

NOW THAT YOU HAVE LEARNED TO SAIL, you may wish to move up to a *larger boat*. Cruising boats are bigger, heavier, and more complicated than their smaller cousins but, with good small boat skills, you should have no difficulty stepping up in size. When you start  to sail a cruiser, you will need to know how to handle the boat under *sail* and *power*, and how to adjust the sail area to suit light or strong winds.

In this section, I'll explain the crucial skills needed to handle your boat in confined spaces and how to bring it safely alongside, pick up a mooring, or drop anchor. If you *dream* of sailing over the blue horizon, you must first learn the skills of managing your boat at sea. Your new skills will include knowing *how to prepare* the boat and crew for a passage, and how to handle rough weather.

Chapter 15

Moving Up to Larger Boats

T HERE ARE MANY REASONS why you may want to sail a boat larger than a dinghy or a small keelboat. Perhaps you have a yearning to sail to foreign shores, or a growing family demands that you exchange the thrills of dinghy sailing for the more sedate pleasures of cruising. Whatever the reason, the step up to a larger boat is not difficult once you have mastered the basics of sailing aboard a dinghy or a small keelboat. The first step is to learn about the types of cruising boats available and to gain some experience aboard a variety of cruisers before you consider buying a boat of your own.

In this chapter...

✓ Types of cruisers

✓ Gaining experience

✓ Picking a cruiser

✓ Buying a cruiser

SAILING A CRUISER ALLOWS YOU TO EXPLORE DIFFERENT CRUISING AREAS

Types of cruisers

THE BASIC DIFFERENCE between a cruiser and a dinghy or small keelboat is that the former can stay at sea overnight or longer and has accommodation for the crew. Most cruisers are monohulls and have some form of weighted keel for stability, but there are also many multihull cruiser designs on the market that get their stability from their wide beam.

The term cruiser covers an enormous range of boats. At the smallest end of the scale are the trailer-sailers, which are small enough to fit onto a trailer and be towed behind a car. However, they offer only the most basic accommodation. Larger cruisers include a vast variety of traditional and modern craft that embrace every conceivable type of hull shape, construction material, rig design, and accommodation layout.

Boats can last a very long time so it is perfectly possible to find a yacht built as many as 100 years ago still going strong and providing its crew with fine sailing.

Once you have decided that you are interested in sailing a larger boat, you will undoubtedly spend many happy hours browsing the classified ads in sailing magazines or on the Web, and getting details from brokers. You will be confronted by a bewildering array of types, specifications, and sales claims. The first task is to understand the basic types of cruisers, which are defined by their design style, their hull type, and their rig.

Cruiser design

Cruising boat design has evolved over the years, but, unlike most other forms of transport, old boats often survive for a long time and comfortably share the seas alongside the most modern designs. Indeed, despite many improvements in design knowledge, materials, and equipment, an old design is often just as satisfactory a choice as one of its newer cousins.

If your desire is to enjoy extended ocean cruising, an older design can often prove to be as good as one of the many newer boats that are designed and built for coastal sailing rather than serious offshore passage making.

INTERNET

www.boats.com
www.boatforsale.org
www.ancasta.co.uk

Visit brokerage sites like these for used boats and to compare specifications and prices.

Race-boat development has always influenced the design of cruisers, and the gradual shift to longer, wider, and lighter boats has been mirrored in cruising yacht design. Today's yachts tend to be lighter and wider than older designs, and the overall length of the typical cruising yacht has increased over the years.

Starting big

As the buyers of cruising boats have become more affluent, the typical size of a first cruiser has increased. It is now not unusual for first-time cruiser sailors to start with a 35 ft (11 m) yacht, a size that would have been considered to be quite large only a few years ago. The interior volume of a modern cruiser is also far greater than that of an older design of the same length. This means that a modern cruiser offers the potential for far more accommodation than an older type, and today's buyers have come to expect new boats to be equipped to a very high standard of domestic luxury.

The emphasis on interior volume and on-board systems looks good in a sales brochure but can distract you from the other, more important attributes of a boat.

Comfort over performance

Some modern cruisers are designed more for comfort while tied alongside other boats in a marina than for serious offshore cruising. Boat manufacturers know that most boats are used essentially as floating holiday homes rather than for serious cruising. They may be used for only a few days or weeks every year. Many never go far offshore and rarely sail on overnight or longer passages. If this is the reality for most cruising boats, then it is understandable that manufacturers tend to focus on space and comfort as much as sailing performance and the ability to sail offshore in severe weather.

■ **A busy marina** *on a holiday weekend contains a wide variety of cruising yachts, sufficient to suit most tastes and requirements.*

As a potential sailor or buyer of a cruising yacht it will help if you recognize the various broad types and their key characteristics. Cruising boats are often described in terms of the type of hull and keel they have, their weight or *displacement*, and their rig type.

Hull types

If a boat is described as a traditional cruiser it means that the yacht is of a heavy-displacement type with a long keel. An older boat will be built of wood, but more recent types will be built of fiberglass or steel. Older designs are typically narrower and often deeper than modern cruisers and have less interior volume.

> **DEFINITION**
>
> **Displacement** *is the term used to describe the weight of a boat. For those of you who remember studying Archimedes' theory, it means the weight of water that is displaced by the boat. Boats are often characterized as light-, moderate-, or heavy-displacement types.*

Most modern cruisers are fiberglass with wider and shallower hull shapes than older designs. Many have moderate displacement, although lighter designs with a long waterline length and short overhangs at bow and stern are becoming increasingly popular.

Modern cruiser racers aim to combine the abilities of efficient cruising with performance suitable for club or regatta racing. These designs are usually lighter than a pure cruising yacht and are likely to have shorter overhangs, larger rigs, and more efficient keels and rudders. A good cruiser-racer design will offer fast, efficient cruising. Its popularity will also help to ensure large fleets and, therefore, good racing opportunities.

Keel types

A cruiser needs some form of keel to resist leeway and to provide stability. A traditional keel runs for half to three-quarters the length of the yacht and has the rudder attached at its trailing edge. Traditionally, a long keel was used to strengthen wooden vessels – it is used today only on heavy-displacement cruisers.

Most modern yachts use a fin keel that is much shorter (fore and aft) than traditional keel designs. Modern materials make this possible and allow designers to reduce the amount of surface area underwater while still providing an efficient keel shape.

Most cruisers have a moderately wide fin keel but racing boats often have very narrow keels. Some cruisers have fin keels with bulbs or wings at the tip to concentrate their weight as low as possible.

Yachts with fin keels have their rudders mounted separately. These are sometimes hung on the transom but they are more usually hung on a narrow skeg (a type of support) or cantilevered on their shafts – this type is known as a spade rudder.

Yachts that are designed to sail in shallow waters often use bilge keels or a centerboard. A centerboard works in the same way as in a dinghy but is often weighted to give extra stability. Bilge or twin keels are usually slightly less efficient than fin keels when sailing to windward, but they allow a yacht to be kept afloat in drying harbors and to sail in shallow waters.

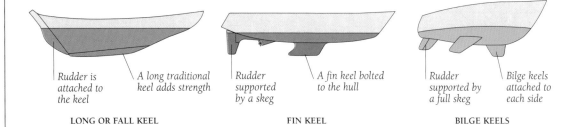

| Rudder is attached to the keel | A long traditional keel adds strength | Rudder supported by a skeg | A fin keel bolted to the hull | Rudder supported by a full skeg | Bilge keels attached to each side |

LONG OR FALL KEEL   **FIN KEEL**   **BILGE KEELS**

Rig types

A sailing boat's rig is characterized by the shape of its mainsail, the number of masts, and how many *headsails* it carries.

> **DEFINITION**
>
> A headsail is a sail carried on the forestay. A jib and a genoa are both types of headsail. A dinghy usually has only one headsail, either a jib or a genoa, but a cruiser often carries several different sizes of headsail.

A Bermudan mainsail, with three sides and corners, is the standard rig on modern boats of all sizes. A gaff mainsail has four sides and corners and is set on a shorter mast than the Bermudan sail. It has a boom at its foot and another boom, called a yard or gaff, along its head.

Early yachts carried a gaff rig because this had developed in working boats and was the best option given the materials of the day. As materials and rig engineering improved, the Bermudan rig was introduced and this has become by far the most common rig for yachts today.

Similarly, two-masted rigs used to be quite common as they allowed for smaller, more easily handled sails. Today, however, they are far less common and new sail materials and handling techniques have made sail handling much easier.

A sloop is the simplest and most common rig. It has one mast and carries a single headsail in addition to the mainsail, which could be either a gaff or a Bermudan.

A Bermudan sloop can be further classified as a fractional or masthead sloop. A fractional sloop has a smaller headsail set on a forestay that attaches to the mast some way down from the top. A masthead sloop has a larger headsail and the forestay attaches at the top of the mast. If you have already sailed a dinghy, you will recognize that most dinghies are rigged as fractional sloops, while many cruisers are rigged as masthead sloops. A cutter has one mast but carries two headsails, each on their own stay. A cutter can have either a gaff or Bermudan mainsail.

Boats with more than one mast are far less common today, but many older designs above 35 ft (11 m) can be found with either a ketch or yawl rig. In both types, a smaller mast – called a mizzen mast – is stepped aft of the main mast. A ketch has a taller mizzen mast than the yawl and it is stepped further forward. The schooner, another two-masted yacht, has the taller mainmast stepped aft with a smaller fore mast ahead of it.

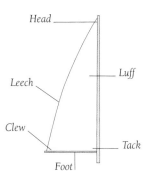

■ **The Bermudan mainsail** *is a three-sided mainsail, which will be familiar to you if you have sailed a dinghy.*

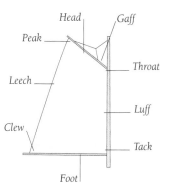

■ **The gaff mainsail** *is a traditional shape with four sides and corners and a top spar called a gaff to support the head.*

■ **The Bermudan sloop** *is a common rig with a single mast, a Bermudan mainsail, and a single headsail.*

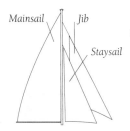

■ **The cutter** *is a popular rig for offshore cruising. It has two headsails – a jib, and a staysail.*

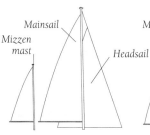

■ **The yawl** *is a two-masted rig with a smaller mizzen mast than the more popular ketch rig.*

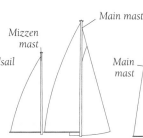

■ **The ketch** *is the most common two-masted rig. It may have a gaff or Bermudan mainsail.*

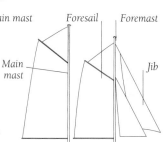

■ **The gaff schooner** *is not common today but is evocative of a bygone age when boats worked under sail.*

Gaining experience

BEFORE YOU CAN BEGIN TO MAKE A CHOICE *about what sort of cruising you want to do, or what type of boat will be most suitable, you have to gain some experience of sailing a cruiser.*

A good way to start is to sail on a friend's boat or to meet up with a skipper in need of crew through your sailing club or advertisements in magazines. Go for a few day sails and an overnight passage to help you decide if cruising really is for you and whether or not you want to learn more.

Do not sign up for a long cruise with a skipper you do not know. Go for a few short sails first to make sure that you can get along in the confines of a small boat.

When you have decided that you definitely want to go cruising, you should sign up for a cruising course at a recognized sailing school that offers cruising courses. If you can already sail competently aboard a dinghy or small keelboat, you will soon learn how to handle a larger yacht, but you also need to learn skills such as navigation, weather forecasting, and safety procedures before you take charge of a cruising yacht.

Learning at a sailing school will be the quickest and safest way to gain the skills you need and should also ensure that your certificates are recognized by your national sailing authority.

Rules and regulations

Although sailing has traditionally managed to avoid governmental regulation and sailors have been free to cruise without possessing licenses, there is now an increasing trend towards regulation and some countries require skippers of cruising boats to hold recognized certificates. At the same time, some governments are introducing certification of boats intended for offshore cruising. Check with your own national authority for the rules that apply in your area.

Remember that the most important thing is to go sailing as often as possible. If this can be aboard a range of boats in different waters and weather conditions, you will learn even faster.

Learning more

A good way to build your experience, especially after taking a cruising course, is to charter a yacht for weekend or holiday periods. This is a very cost-effective way of going cruising and also lets you get experience of different cruising areas and different boats. If you do not have the experience necessary to charter a yacht for unaccompanied sailing, start by booking a flotilla vacation or chartering a yacht with a skipper.

■ **Flotilla sailing** *can be a very good way to build experience aboard a cruising boat while having fun on vacation, first as a crew and later as a skipper.*

When you are not sailing, you can always read about cruising! There is a large number of books, magazines, and Web resources devoted to cruising in all its forms and they offer a great way to learn new skills and extend your knowledge. If you are dreaming of sailing off into the sunset there are many wonderful books of cruising tales that will fire your enthusiasm and provide an escape from cold winter evenings ashore.

Picking a cruiser

EVEN A SMALL CRUISER represents a considerable investment, both in purchase price and in maintenance and running costs. Despite this, it is amazing how many of us are tempted by unsuitable boats and delude ourselves into dreaming of a type of cruising we will never do. All cruising boats are a compromise and you need to be realistic in your ambitions when you set out to choose one for yourself.

If you plan to cruise, think about the area in which you expect to do most of your sailing and the type of cruising you hope to do. Most people can only manage weekend passages, with one or two longer cruises during vacations.

Occasional or vacation cruising does not require a blue-water cruiser equipped with every conceivable extra. The best choice of boat will be determined by the type of sailing that you plan to do and where you plan to do it. If you will be sailing in shallow-water areas, for instance, consider whether bilge keels or a centerboard would give you more scope in your cruising options.

All aboard

Consider how many people will be on board most of the time. Many cruising boats sail with a crew of only two or three and so, if this applies to you, you won't need a particularly large boat to enjoy good cruising. A smaller boat will be less expensive to buy and maintain, cheaper on mooring costs, and easier to handle.

If you want to go cruising but cannot afford the sort of boat you think you want, do not be put off. A small boat equipped with only the basic gear will be much cheaper to buy and run, but will deliver just as much, if not more, pleasure as a larger and more complex yacht. If the boat is simple, you are likely to spend much more time sailing it.

Most long-term voyagers cruise with just a couple of people on board, sometimes with their children or an occasional crew. This means that they are sailing short-handed most of the time, so a smaller boat has advantages in terms of boat handling as well as in cost of ownership. Many standard production cruisers are perfectly capable of undertaking long offshore voyages with little modification.

It is a myth to think that you need a large boat to go voyaging. The average size of boats cruising the world's oceans is about 35 ft (11 m), but many considerably smaller boats have taken their crews around the world.

Unless you are very experienced, you would be wise to select a well-built production boat from a reputable builder and to head offshore to gain experience of what works in practice before you start specifying changes or building your dream yacht.

Dreaming of the ocean

Many people dream of long-term voyaging but relatively few actually escape to sea full time. The reality for most of us is that our jobs and family ties prevent us from achieving more than a few weeks cruising every year, interspersed with weekend cruising or racing. So, if you are dreaming of heading off long-term, be realistic about the ties that hold you to the shore. If, however, you are one of the lucky ones that is free to sail away, there is a large number of boats available and capable of taking you long distances.

■ **New Zealand** *is a country that caters for boats, and many long-distance sailors are attracted to its wonderful cruising waters.*

Keeping it simple

With all types of cruising, it pays to keep the boat as simple as possible. This reduces the cost, makes the boat simpler to sail, and reduces the problems associated with gear failure in remote locations. Going with a simpler, smaller, and cheaper boat also means that you will be able to head off sooner than if you wait until you can afford your ideal dream yacht.

Once you have thought through these choices, you should draw up a list of attributes that you want your boat to have. Be realistic about what you can afford to buy and remember that you will be faced with running costs as well as the purchase price. Armed with your list you can then investigate suitable new or used boats advertized in the yachting press and on the internet.

Buying a cruiser

BEFORE YOU RUSH OUT TO BUY A CRUISER, *make certain that you really want to invest the considerable amount of money and time that buying and running it will entail. It is easy to underestimate the costs of owning your own boat and you should allow a budget for annual maintenance, mooring charges, and insurance. If you are considering buying an older wooden boat remember that it will require considerably more time and money spent on maintenance than a fiberglass yacht.*

One option for buying a larger boat that you would not otherwise be able to afford on your own is to enter into a partnership with one or more co-owners. This arrangement can work well and allows the sharing of costs and maintenance work, but make sure that you and your partners clearly define the details of the sharing agreement beforehand to avoid disagreements later on.

Make up a shortlist of boats that meet your criteria and arrange to have a test sail on each one. Do not buy a boat without a trial sail, unless it is a well-known type and you have been able to sail a sister ship.

Researching before you buy

Ask an experienced friend to come with you on the trial sail. If you are buying a new boat, visit the factory to take a look at boats at various stages of construction and to get an idea of the quality of work and equipment used in the construction of the boat.

New boats are sold by dealers and sometimes directly from manufacturers and you can find details in the yachting press. Make sure that you examine the small print of the inventory to make sure that all the equipment you see on the demonstrator is actually included in the sale price.

The value of a new boat can depreciate quickly but the most popular designs tend to hold their price well. If you have a choice, pick a popular type that you will be able to sell easily.

Always arrange to have a survey done when you buy a used boat. Make sure that your surveyor has professional qualifications and is a member of a recognized body. As the buyer, you will be responsible for the cost of the survey and the cost of hauling the boat out if necessary. Do not be tempted into having a survey done in the water, because it is important that the underwater surfaces and fittings are checked.

Most sales of used cruisers are handled through a yacht broker, although you may buy direct from the seller if you find your yacht through a classified advert. A broker earns a commission on the sale – paid by the seller – and a good broker should be able to assist the buyer in arranging a survey, finance, and insurance.

A simple summary

✔ It is not difficult to move up to a larger boat once you have mastered the basic skills in a dinghy or small keelboat.

✔ Learn to sail a cruiser and gain experience aboard several different types before you look for a boat of your own.

✔ Decide what type of sailing you want to do and how many people you want to sail with.

✔ If you are buying a used cruiser, always employ a surveyor to produce a full condition report.

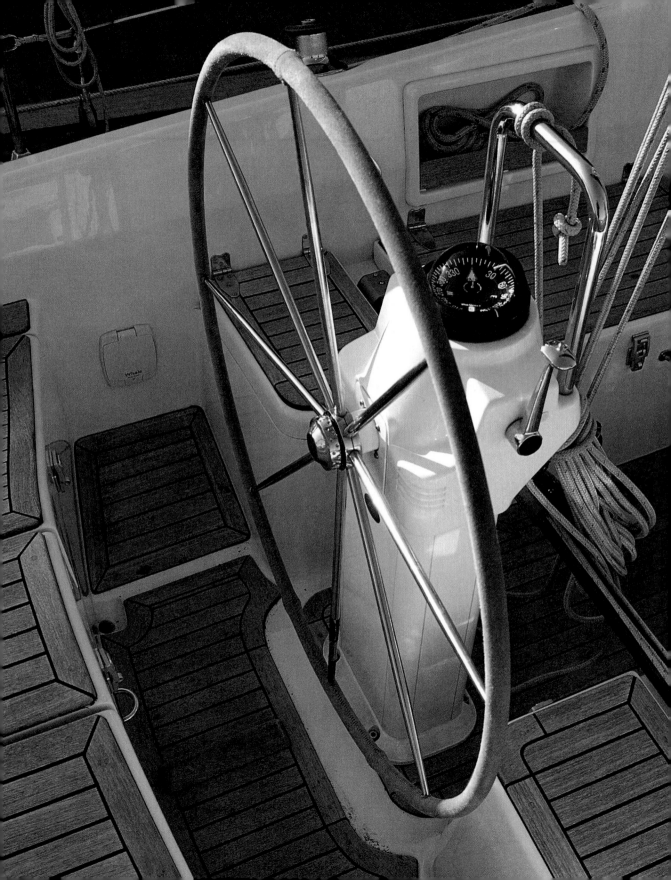

Chapter 16

Getting to Know a Cruiser

ONCE YOU HAVE LEARNED the principles of sailing in a small boat, it is not difficult to take those skills and apply them to sailing a cruiser. It will seem more daunting when you first start to sail one because of its greater size and weight, but it only requires practice for you to be handling the larger boat with ease. It is important that you get used to the more complex equipment found on board and that you learn to handle it safely. There are many aspects to sailing a cruiser beyond boat handling, but this is the important first step to becoming a good cruising crew and, eventually, a competent skipper.

In this chapter...

✓ Cruiser equipment

✓ Before you sail

✓ Handling under power

✓ Handling under sail

THERE WILL BE NEW TYPES OF GEAR TO GET USED TO ABOARD A LARGER BOAT

Cruiser equipment

YOU WILL RECOGNIZE much of the equipment on a cruiser if you have sailed a dinghy or small keelboat, but other gear will be new to you. Even the gear you do recognize will be much larger and heavier than you are used to. The equipment you find on a cruiser will depend on its size, the type of rig it uses, and whether it is fitted out simply or has more complex systems.

Because of the multitude of types of cruisers, there are many variations on the equipment used, both above and below decks. Until you gain much more experience, there will be new gear to examine – or a different way of doing something – every time you step aboard a different boat. While this can be confusing at first, it will be made simpler if you remember that most of this gear is designed to assist you in the basic tasks of sail and boat handling, and to enable you to handle a heavier boat with greater loads on sails and sheets.

All the skills and techniques you have learned still apply aboard a larger boat, you just have to remember that a larger boat responds more slowly than a smaller one, and the loads on the gear are usually higher than you can handle with muscle power alone.

The rig

The vast majority of new cruisers, and many older ones, are rigged as a Bermudan masthead sloop. This is the simplest and cheapest type of rig, so it is not surprising that manufacturers choose this above other options. It is also the most efficient rig for windward sailing, which is why racing boats all use this configuration. But windward performance need not be so critical for a cruiser, since most cruiser sailors try and avoid sailing to windward too often, preferring the more comfortable offwind points of sail.

Gaff rig and two-masted rigs can deliver good performance on reaching and downwind courses, and you may find you prefer sailing with one of these rigs as you get experience in a range of cruising boats.

A typical cruiser rig has a mast supported by an array of standing rigging. There will be a forestay from the mast to the bow. If the boat is a masthead sloop, the forestay will run from the bow fitting to the masthead, but in a fractional rig it will run to a point some way below the top of the mast.

A backstay, running from the top of the mast to the stern, will balance the pull of the forestay. It should have some form of adjustment so that the tension on the forestay can be varied. Between them, the forestay and backstay support the mast in a fore and aft direction.

A number of shrouds will support the mast in a sideways direction. The cap shrouds run from near the deck edges, over the spreader ends, and up to the masthead. Many cruisers have a single set of spreaders but some cruisers will have two sets. One or more lower shrouds each side run from the base of the spreaders to the deck. Often, they are arranged with one ahead, and one aft of the cap shroud on each side.

The sails

If your boat is a standard Bermudan sloop, it will have a mainsail and one or more headsails. The mainsail is usually left stowed on the boom when not sailing and is protected by a sail cover. Many cruisers use a roller-furling headsail that is left permanently stowed, rolled around the forestay. Other types of cruisers use a selection of headsails of different sizes to cope with a range of wind strengths.

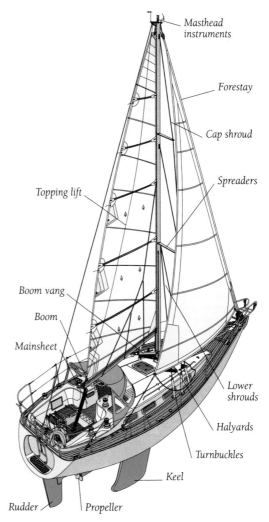

■ **Cruiser rigging** *is more complex, larger, and heavier than a dinghy's, but performs the same functions. Halyards are often led back to the cockpit.*

If a cruiser carries a range of headsails, it will usually include at least a large genoa for light winds, a working jib for medium winds, and a storm jib for strong winds. Sometimes other headsails will be carried to fill in the gaps between the basic headsails.

If several headsails are carried, these will be kept in sailbags when not in use and stowed down below or in a cockpit locker. Many cruisers also carry a spinnaker, or a type of asymmetric known as a cruising chute, to add sail area when sailing downwind. This is stowed below or in a cockpit locker until required.

On deck

Deck layouts vary between each different type of cruiser but all have common elements and certain types of equipment. Most cruisers have a raised area in the middle of the boat that is called the coach roof and provides headroom in the cabin below. A fore hatch is usually positioned at the front of the coach roof, and the main entrance – called the companionway – is situated at its aft end to allow access from the cockpit.

Take a stroll around the decks when you first step aboard a new cruiser and ask the skipper to explain any equipment with which you are not familiar.

The cockpit is the working area of the boat where the helmsman sits or stands and where the sheets, and sometimes halyards, are led for adjustment. The cockpit may be positioned in the middle of the boat, when it is known as a center cockpit, but is more often situated aft. Seats running around the cockpit usually contain cockpit lockers, where items like sails, ropes, and *fenders* are stowed.

> **DEFINITION**
>
> A fender *is a cushion, often cylindrical, that is hung over the side of a boat to prevent damage when alongside another boat or dock.*

> **DEFINITION**
>
> A stanchion *is an upright metal tube, usually made from aluminum or stainless steel, which fits into a socket bolted to the deck. The upper and lower lifelines run through holes in each stanchion and are fastened to metal frames at the bow (the pulpit) and stern (the pushpit).*

Sidedecks run around the edge of the boat between the coach roof and the gunwale, where *stanchions* support the lifelines that run around the perimeter of the deck. Tracks carrying the jib sheet fairleads usually run along each sidedeck, while cleats and fairleads for mooring ropes will be situated at the bow and stern, and sometimes in the middle of the boat.

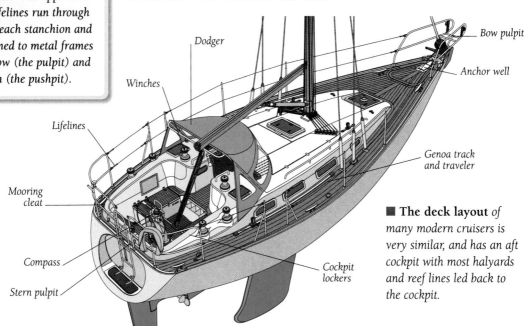

Dodger

Winches

Lifelines

Mooring cleat

Compass

Stern pulpit

Bow pulpit

Anchor well

Genoa track and traveler

Cockpit lockers

■ **The deck layout** of many modern cruisers is very similar, and has an aft cockpit with most halyards and reef lines led back to the cockpit.

The sidedecks, foredeck, and coach roof should all have a nonskid finish to prevent your feet from slipping when the decks are wet and the boat is heeled over. The cockpit floor and seats should also have a nonskid finish.

Down below

Most small and medium-sized cruising boats follow a fairly standard accommodation format since they are limited by the amount of space available and have to cater to use at sea and in port.

The accommodation is usually split between a forecabin and a main cabin, called the salon. The toilet compartment – called "the head" on a boat – is often between the two cabins, and the galley (the nautical kitchen) and chart table are located aft, near the companionway. Some modern boats have sufficient beam aft to have one or two sleeping cabins situated under the cockpit. Some very small boats only have enough room for a single cabin, head, and galley.

■ **A crash bar** *in front of the cooker in a cruising boat's galley will prevent you from falling into it when the boat heels.*

Take a good look around when you first go aboard a new cruiser and see how the accommodation has been arranged. Many modern cruisers are designed for comfort when in port and are far less useable when at sea, especially when the boat is heeled over.

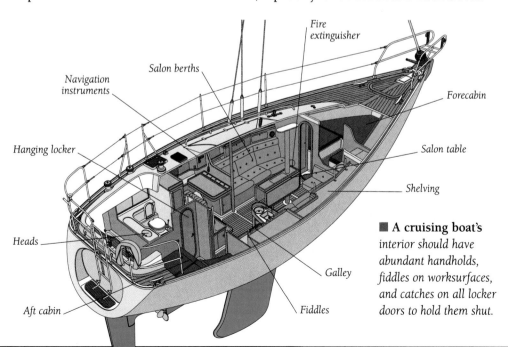

Fire extinguisher

Salon berths

Navigation instruments

Forecabin

Hanging locker

Salon table

Shelving

Heads

■ **A cruising boat's** *interior should have abundant handholds, fiddles on worksurfaces, and catches on all locker doors to hold them shut.*

Galley

Aft cabin

Fiddles

USING A WINCH

A winch is a drum-shaped mechanism that allows you to apply greater power to a rope than you could by pulling alone. There are two main types – self-tailing or standard. The standard winch is best used by two people, one to wind and the other to tail (or pull) on the rope coming off the winch. The self-tailing winch allows one person to wind while the mechanism on the top of the winch keeps the tension on the rope as it leaves the drum.

Before you can use a winch you must load it. This means wrapping enough rope around the drum to create sufficient friction to allow you to hold the load on the rope without it slipping. Always wrap the rope in the direction in which the drum rotates. This is nearly always clockwise but it is worth checking by turning the drum to see which way it spins freely.

Wind the handle as much as necessary, then secure the rope on the cleat near the winch and tidy up the rope tail.

With a self-tailing winch, you can lead the sheet or halyard into the jaws on the top of the drum after loading at least three turns. Now you can wind the handle without needing someone to tail the rope. Once you have finished winding, remove the handle and stow it so that it cannot slip overboard. Although the self-tailing mechanism should hold the rope, it is good practice to cleat it as well to ensure it doesn't slip out.

■ **When easing** *a rope out, ease the tension with one hand while using the other to control the rope as it slides around the drum.*

1 **Loading the winch**

You should wrap at least two or three turns of the rope around the drum.

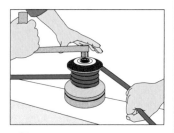

2 **Using the handle**

Put the handle into the socket on the top of the winch once the rope turns are on the drum.

3 **Winding in**

You can now wind the handle while another person tails the sheet or halyard.

Before you sail

BEFORE YOU SAIL ON A CRUISER *for the first time, take a few minutes to examine its layout above and below decks. Check to see how all the sheets and halyards are led and which winch is used for each sail control. If you find a piece of equipment that you haven't used before ask the skipper or another crew member to explain it to you.*

You should find out where the safety gear is stowed on your cruiser and how it should be used. This may seem excessive when you are only going out for a short sail on a summer's day, but it is always a sensible precaution and many good skippers will always conduct a short safety briefing when sailing with new crew.

When you have enough experience to skipper your own boat, always make a point of showing a new crew member around the boat and explain where essential equipment is stowed and how it is used.

Safety awareness

You should always have a safety harness and a lifejacket, which are often combined into one easily worn item. Take the time to try it on and adjust it for a comfortable fit even if you do not plan on wearing it. If the weather takes a turn for the worse, the skipper may ask everyone to wear their harnesses and it will be easier to adjust it now rather than later when you may need it quickly.

If you are a novice to cruiser sailing, it is a good idea to wear the harness and to clip on its safety line when outside the cockpit even in calm weather.

It takes only a moment's lack of care, or the lurch of an unexpected wave, to tip someone over the side if they are on deck and not secured to the boat. When clipping on the safety line, always attach it to a secure fitting. Look for a wire or webbing strap running the length of each sidedeck. These are called jackstays and are intended to provide a secure attachment point for your safety line while allowing you to move fore and aft along the sidedeck without having to reclip your safety line as you move about the boat. Never attach your safety line to a lifeline because these may not be strong enough to take the load. Look for D-shaped stainless steel rings bolted to the deck near the cockpit or use the jackstay.

The boat should be fitted with other safety gear including a liferaft, lifebuoys, fire extinguishers, flares (distress signals), and a first-aid kit. When you start a cruise in an unfamiliar boat, find out where each is stowed, and how and when they are to be used.

Before the boat leaves its berth, put on the clothes you expect to need and find out where to stow your other gear. Do not just put your bag on a settee or berth, as it may end up on the cabin sole (the floor).

HORSESHOE RING

FLARES

OVERBOARD POLE

Handling under power

MOST CRUISERS ARE FITTED WITH AN ENGINE

to help them get in and out of harbor and to get them home when the wind drops. How a cruiser handles under power depends on the size of the engine, the shape of the hull, keel, and rudder, and the amount of windage of the rig.

A traditional-type cruiser with a long keel will not handle as easily under power as a more modern type with a shallower hull shape, fin keel, and a skeg or spade rudder. The older boat is likely to have a less powerful engine than a modern boat, and its hull shape will make it more difficult to handle when backing up or when turning.

Because of the differences in the way various designs handle under power it is useful if you can get experience in handling as many different types as possible. Of course, it is easier to learn on a modern boat that handles well under power, but an older design will teach you a subtlety of touch and the ability to anticipate a boat's behavior. When you first start to learn to handle a cruiser under power, make sure that you pick a practice area that is well away from other boats or obstructions.

Propeller effects

The key to understanding how a boat behaves under power is to learn about the propeller effect, called prop walk. As well as pushing the boat forward or backward, the propeller also tends to push the stern to one side or the other. When a boat is moving ahead, most propellers rotate clockwise (when viewed from behind). This rotation causes the stern to move to starboard as the boat moves ahead. With a standard gearbox and propeller arrangement, the direction of rotation is reversed when you go astern. This means that the propeller now rotates anticlockwise when viewed from behind and the rotation causes the stern to move to port as the boat backs up.

Forward and backward

When you motor forward, the rudder works as soon as the boat is moving at a reasonable speed and it is easy to resist the sideways prop walk and keep the boat on a straight course. When moving backward, however, the rudder is far less efficient and the boat is usually moving slowly so prop walk has a much larger effect. In some cases, prop walk can be so severe that it is impossible to steer the boat in a straight line in reverse.

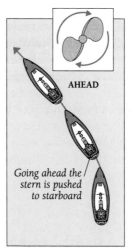

AHEAD

Going ahead the stern is pushed to starboard

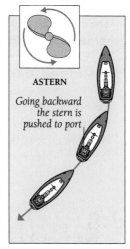

ASTERN

Going backward the stern is pushed to port

■ **The propeller** is *more efficient when the boat is going ahead but prop walk will still have an effect when you are starting off.*

■ **Conventional** *propellers are less efficient in reverse, so prop walk astern has a greater effect, especially at slow speed.*

WHEEL OR TILLER

Many cruisers of 35 ft (11 m) or larger are fitted with wheel steering. When you use a wheel for the first time, remember that when the boat is moving forward it will turn in the same direction as you turn the wheel. So, if you turn the wheel to port the bow will swing to port. Remember that when you reverse (go backward), the stern will move in the same direction as you turn the wheel. Wheel steering is less sensitive than a tiller and gives less feedback. You will need to experiment to find out how rapidly the boat turns as you turn the wheel.

If your boat is fitted with a tiller be careful when backing up, especially if you are steering a modern cruiser with a spade or skeg rudder. The load on the tiller can be very large and you may not be able to hold it if you turn the tiller too far off the centerline. Many years ago, I found myself pinned at the back of a cockpit by a tiller I had moved too far to one side when the boat was motoring quickly in reverse. The force on the rudder was far greater than I could hold on the tiller and I was lucky to reach the throttle with my foot or it could have been rather embarrassing!

Anticipating prop walk

You can check the direction of prop walk before you leave the dock if, with the boat tied up securely, you put the engine in reverse at about half throttle. Look over each side by the cockpit and find the disturbed water coming off the propeller. If the disturbance is to starboard, the prop walk will move the stern to port when going astern. If you sail a traditional type of cruiser with a long keel, you can expect the effect of prop walk to be far more apparent than a modern fin-keeled cruiser. In all boats it will have most effect when the boat is moving slowly and the throttle is opened sharply. In this case, prop walk will occur before the boat has started moving forward or backward quickly enough for the rudder to take effect. Minimize prop walk by opening the throttle gently to build up speed and gain steerage way.

Steering under power

Handling a cruiser at slow speed under power is an important skill because you need to be able to maneuver safely in confined spaces such as in a marina. In these situations, much damage can be done if you mishandle the boat so it is important that you practice maneuvering under power away from any obstructions.

Try backing up and see if you can keep the boat moving in a straight line and whether you can steer it against the prop walk. Now experiment by backing up into the wind, away from the wind, and across the wind. You will probably find that the boat will go backward in a straight line when the wind is astern since the windage of the mast will help hold the bow downwind and keep the boat straight. It may be much more difficult to keep a straight course when the wind is from ahead or on one side as the windage of the mast will try and push the bow downwind. Now try motoring ahead at various speeds and see how tight a turning circle you can achieve. This will be vital when you need to be able to turn in a narrow channel.

Fortunately, the prop walk effect can be utilized to assist you when you need to make a very tight turn.

The direction in which you can make the tightest turn is determined by the direction of prop walk in your boat when going astern. If your boat walks its stern to port in reverse, start your turn to starboard.

Turning tightly

With the boat traveling at slow speed, put the tiller or wheel hard over and use the throttle to give a short burst ahead to start the boat turning. Put the throttle in neutral and keep the tiller or wheel hard over while you give a strong burst of reverse power. Prop walk will push the stern to port as the reverse power stops the boat's forward motion. As soon as the boat starts moving backward, shift into forward gear and give another burst of power. By using alternative bursts of forward and reverse power and letting prop walk help turn the boat, you can turn most boats in little more than their own length. Each boat has different characteristics but time spent practicing boat handling under power will teach you how to handle your boat safely in close-quarter situations.

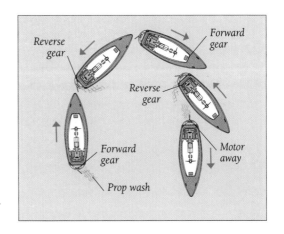

■ **In forward under power**, *the prop wash hits the rudder which is hard over and swings the stern. In reverse, prop walk swings the stern to port.*

Handling under sail

HOW A CRUISER HANDLES under sail depends on its hull and keel shape and the type of rig it carries. While you are learning to sail a cruiser, keep in mind the basic skills you learned in a dinghy or small keelboat. All the same principles apply, but you have to learn how the size and weight of a larger cruiser determine how it must be handled through each maneuver.

It is not hard to sail a cruiser efficiently in open water and at normal speed, but it is much more difficult to do so at slow speed and in confined water. When you first start to practice, find a stretch of clear water where you will be free to experiment without any risk of collision.

Trivia...
When you're handling your modern boat under sail or power, spare a thought for the sailors who handled large sailing ships and yachts without the help of engines or modern sail-handling equipment. Their achievements and the subtlety of their skills are a useful reminder of how easy we have it today.

The first step is to practice the same maneuvers you learned in a dinghy. Sail on a beam reach and get used to using the sheet winches to trim the jib. Practice bearing away and luffing up to courses between close-hauled and a run, adjusting the sail trim for each course change.

You will find that a cruiser turns more slowly than a dinghy and it also takes longer to sheet the sails in or out.

Cruiser crew

The number of crew on a cruiser can range from the lone sailor, up to a full-crewed cruiser racer with perhaps eight or more people on board. Obviously, the speed with which you can hoist, lower, and trim sails will depend on how many willing and skilled hands you have available.

However many crew you have, it is important that you work as a team with the skipper directing operations by giving clear instructions. The loads on sheets and halyards can be very high and can cause injury if the equipment is not handled properly.

The skipper must make sure that the crew members are warned about each maneuver before it happens and that they are prepared and in a safe position before it is started.

■ **The heavier gear** *aboard a cruiser means you should sheet the boom into the middle before a jibe, then ease it out under control when it has jibed.*

Once you have gotten used to steering the boat and trimming the sails, you can try tacking and jibing. Tacking will take longer in a cruiser than in a dinghy because the boat is heavier and turns more slowly. The sails are also larger and more work is involved in sheeting the jib or genoa to the new side. When tacking, your aim should be to turn the boat smoothly through the tack with the minimum loss of speed.

The speed of the tack must be adjusted to suit the speed with which the crew can handle the jib sheets. If you turn the boat too quickly through the tack, your crew will be unable to get the new jib sheet onto its winch and wind the sheet in before the sail fills with wind. As helmsman, you can help your crew a great deal if you slow down the turn once the bow has passed through head-to-wind. This gives the crew more time to sheet in the jib before it fills with wind and makes their task much easier.

INTERNET

www.rival-bowman.co.uk

This UK company, Rival Bowman Yachts, makes the Starlight and Bowman range of cruising yachts, including the Starlight 35.

How to jibe

Jibing a cruiser is like jibing a dinghy except that you must allow for the heavier gear and greater loads on the equipment. When jibing a dinghy, you can allow the boom to swing freely, but the weight of a cruiser's boom means that you can only do this in very light winds. At other times, you should sheet in the mainsail before you jibe so that the boom has less distance to travel when it swings across.

If your mainsheet runs on a traveler across the cockpit, lock the traveler in the middle before the jibe and then sheet in the mainsail until the boom is over the quarter. Cleat the mainsheet and then jibe the boat. In medium and strong winds, the boat will try to turn to windward as the boom swings over and you should correct this with the tiller to keep the boat on a run or broad reach. Once the boom has swung across, you can ease the mainsheet to let it out to its correct position for the new course. On many cruisers, other than the smallest, it is easiest if a crew member handles the mainsheet, rather than the helmsman trying to do this and steer simultaneously.

■ **If you slow down the turn** *when the boat has passed through head-to-wind, your crew will have an easier job of sheeting the jib.*

A simple summary

✔ Cruiser equipment varies from one boat to another but you will soon understand the purpose of the basic gear and learn to recognize variations.

✔ Take time to explore a new boat's layout and find out where the safety equipment is stowed.

✔ Handling at low speed under power is easier once you understand prop walk.

✔ A cruiser sails in exactly the same way as a dinghy, but you must get used to handling larger sails and steering a heavier boat that turns more slowly.

✔ Good teamwork is needed when sailing a larger boat with several crew.

✔ Practice tacking, jibing, and sailing on different courses in open water, free of obstructions.

Chapter 17

Adjusting Sail Area

IN ORDER TO BE EFFICIENT across a broad range of wind strengths, a cruiser's sails need to be adjustable in size. In light airs, the mainsail and jib will lack drive, especially downwind, and the sail area needs to be increased if speed is to be maintained. Conversely, in stronger winds the working sails will be too large and it will be necessary to reduce the size of the sails to keep the boat under control. When you sail a cruiser, you will need to know when to increase or reduce sail area and you must become familiar with the equipment and techniques needed to carry out the changes quickly and safely.

In this chapter...

✓ Large sails for light winds

✓ Adding downwind sail area

✓ When to reduce sail

✓ Small sails for strong winds

213

A SPINNAKER IS A GREAT SAIL FOR DOWNWIND SAILING IN LIGHT CONDITIONS

Large sails for light winds

IN LIGHT WINDS, the working sails (the mainsail and the jib) of the typical Bermudan sloop will not generate enough power to sail at hull speed so larger sails are needed if you want to sail faster. Obviously you cannot increase the area of the mainsail, which is limited by the length of the mast and boom, but you can increase the sail area in front of the mast.

When sailing close-hauled in light winds, your performance can be improved by changing the working jib (a jib used in moderate winds that doesn't overlap the mast) for a large genoa. This will increase the sail area considerably. The genoa will set better in light winds because it is made of a lighter cloth than a sail designed for heavier winds.

This is easily accomplished if your cruiser has a selection of sails that can be hanked to the forestay and hoisted, but it is less easily achieved if your boat has a roller-furling genoa that is more or less permanently attached to the forestay.

Roller-furling/reefing genoas

Roller-reefing genoas are made of fairly heavy cloth and are not as large as genoas designed for light winds. On some boats it is possible to lower the roller genoa and replace it with a larger and lighter genoa, but it is often more practical to roll away the genoa on the forestay and hoist a lighter sail – a *reacher* – that is designed to allow it to be set flying. You may not be able to point as close to the wind with this sail as you would be able to with one hanked to the forestay, but it will still increase your speed considerably in light wind.

A reacher is set flying by attaching its tack to the bow fitting and hoisting it with a genoa halyard, or with a spinnaker halyard if you have one.

Adding downwind sail area

THE NEED FOR ADDITIONAL SAIL AREA *in light winds is increased the further off the wind you sail. When you are sailing close-hauled, your boat's speed increases the apparent wind speed felt by the sails, but as you bear away to courses further off the wind, the apparent wind speed drops.*

By the time you are sailing on a broad reach or run, the apparent wind speed will have dropped considerably and your boat's speed will be significantly reduced. The simplest way to increase sail area when sailing downwind is to wing-out your largest jib or genoa by poling it out to windward with a whisker pole, just as you learned to do in a dinghy. If you have a reacher, this can be poled out instead of a genoa but it will require a longer pole to extend it properly.

A poled-out genoa or reacher will increase your speed on a broad reach or run, but you will get extra drive still from a spinnaker or a gennaker.

A conventional cruiser spinnaker is exactly the same as a dinghy's spinnaker except that it is bigger, more powerful, and will be made from heavier nylon sailcloth. A gennaker, sometimes called a cruising chute, is similar to the asymmetric spinnaker used on many high-performance dinghies, but it is smaller and easier to handle. The cruising gennaker has its tack attached at the bow rather than at the end of a long bowsprit.

A gennaker is easier to set and handle than a spinnaker, but it is not as efficient when sailing on a run because it falls into the disturbed air behind the mainsail, whereas a spinnaker is held clear by the spinnaker pole.

You can use a spinnaker pole to hold the clew of the gennaker to windward when sailing on a run, just as you would pole out a genoa. However, if you have to handle a pole, you may as well use a spinnaker, because it is a more effective sail.

■ **Cruiser racers** *usually use a spinnaker because it is the best all-round downwind sail for racing and cruising.*

Equipment

The equipment needed to set a spinnaker on a cruising boat is much the same as on a dinghy, but the gear is larger and therefore extra care should be taken. The spinnaker pole fits onto a bracket on the front of the mast and is controlled and adjusted by an uphaul (or topping lift) and a downhaul (or foreguy). The way these are arranged will vary from boat to boat but the principle is the same – you use them both to hold the pole in a horizontal position.

Small cruisers often use the same sheeting system as a dinghy, with a single sheet and guy to control the spinnaker. On larger cruisers, it is easier to jibe the spinnaker if you use twin sheets and guys – with one of each being rigged on either side of the boat.

Only one sheet and one guy are used at the same time, but having twin sheets and guys makes it much easier to move the pole from one side of the boat to the other during a gybe. Each guy is led through a block on the gunwale at the point of maximum beam while each sheet runs through a block near the stern, before being lead to a winch. Always put a spinnaker sheet or guy on a winch before it comes under load, as the force on it will be far higher than you can directly hold.

SPINNAKER SOCKS

A really good alternative for hoisting a spinnaker or gennaker – to help avoid twisting, and preventing the sail from filling before it is fully hoisted – is to use a spinnaker sock. The sock is also the best way to hoist these sails when sailing short-handed. To hoist the sail, the halyard is attached to the top of the sock and the sheets are attached to the clews. The sail is hoisted in its sock, and when the halyard is secured, the mouth is pulled up to the top of the sail by a light line that runs up through a block on the top and runs down to the deck. The mouth gathers the sock above it and the bundle sits above the sail until you want to lower the sail. When the time comes to drop it, simply release the guy to collapse the sail and use the light line to pull the mouth down over the sail. Finally, lower the sock complete with the sail.

■ **A sock is a long** *nylon tube with a fiberglass, bell-shaped mouth at the bottom. The head of the sail is fed up through the tube and attached to its top.*

Handling spinnakers

Unless you use a spinnaker sock, a cruiser's spinnaker is usually hoisted direct from its bag (sometimes called a turtle). The key to getting the sail up and set without any twists in it is to make sure it is packed properly in its bag. If you are uncertain about how the sail has been packed, repack it before it is hoisted.

To do this, find the head of the sail and lay it to one side. Run your hands down one of the edges leading from the head, making sure it is not twisted, until you come to one of the bottom corners. Lay it to one side and run your hands along the foot until you reach the other bottom corner. Now, with the three corners separated, bundle the middle of the sail into the bag until only the three corners poke out of the top.

Once the bag is packed properly, it has to be fastened on the leeward side of the boat, near the bow. The best places are either in the pulpit or attached to the leeward lifelines. The bag should have clips or straps on one side or the bottom to allow it to be tied in position. Don't forget to tie it on or you will lose the bag when you hoist the spinnaker.

Hoisting a spinnaker

Attach the halyard to the head of the sail, and the sheet and the guy to their respective corners. Make sure that all three arrive at the bag along the same path – the halyard should lead around the back of the jib, under the foot, and over the top lifeline; the sheet and guy should lead outside everything else and arrive at the bag over the top lifeline. As one crew member hoists the sail, another should pull on the guy to get the tack of the sail to the pole end fitting.

Once the sail is ready to hoist, steer onto a broad reach or run. This is important because the sail can then be hoisted in the lee (wind shadow) of the mainsail and will not fill with wind before you are ready and it is fully hoisted.

■ **As the spinnaker** *is being hoisted, the guy is pulled to bring the tack to the pole end. When the sail is hoisted fully, the pole will be pulled aft to set the pole square to the wind.*

Once the sail is fully hoisted and the halyard cleated, the helmsman can steer to the desired course. When on course, pull the guy back to set the pole at right angles to the apparent wind. Cleat the guy and trim the sheet to fill the sail. Now that the sail is up and full, drop the jib and tie it down or, if you have roller furling, roll it away.

Don't drop the jib before you hoist, even if the mainsail is blanketing it. Having the jib up helps prevent the spinnaker wrapping itself around the forestay during the hoist.

Hoisting a gennaker

Because a gennaker does not need a pole, except if you choose to use one when sailing dead downwind, it is less complicated to rig and hoist. Pack the sail in the same way as a spinnaker and then fasten the bag at the bow. Attach the tack of

TRIMMING A SPINNAKER OR GENNAKER

When you're cruising, you won't want to spend all your time trimming the spinnaker or gennaker. Fortunately, if you don't mind compromising your performance, you don't have to. However, you will need to concentrate on steering to keep the apparent wind at a fairly constant angle.

Trimming techniques

For a cruising trim, set the pole angle just forward of a right angle to the apparent wind, adjust the pole height to get the tack level with the clew, and cleat the guy. Trim the sail until it has a slight curl at the luff and then trim it harder so that the curl disappears. Cleat the sheet and steer to keep the sail full. If it collapses, bear away until it fills and then luff up back to the original angle to the wind.

If you are feeling energetic and want a bit more performance, trim the spinnaker in the same way as you would in a dinghy. Adjust the pole with the guy to match changes in apparent wind, and keep trimming the sheet to keep the luff on the edge of curling.

It is easier to trim a gennaker because you do not have a pole to adjust. You can treat the sheet in exactly the same way as for a spinnaker – over-trim it and cleat it off if you're feeling lazy, or trim it for speed.

the sail to the bow fitting, fasten the halyard to the head, and tie the two sheets to the clew – the sail is then ready to hoist. Remember to lead the windward sheet around the outside of the forestay, rather than between it and the mast, and attach the tack to the bow fitting outside the pulpit (rather than inside) so that the sail can fly freely around the bow. Both sheets lead through blocks near the stern and then to a winch.

JIBING

In principle, jibing a cruiser spinnaker is exactly the same as jibing a dinghy spinnaker, but the size of the sail and the need to move a heavier pole to the opposite side of the boat mean that you must take extra care. On small cruisers, you can use the dinghy technique of an end-for-end jibe, but on larger cruisers the dip pole method is better.

Start by steering onto a run and setting the spinnaker square across the boat by pulling the pole back and easing the sheet. Pull in the mainsheet to bring the boom inboard and cleat it. While the helmsman steers carefully on the run, you can focus on changing the pole to the new windward side.

1 Before the jibe

A crew member releases the pole from the guy and eases the topping lift to drop the outer end. He pulls the foreguy at the same time so that the pole end swings down and forward.

2 During the jibe

When the pole end is low enough to reach, a crew member drops the new guy into the pole end fitting. The pole is raised again on the new windward side, the guy tightened, and the old sheet eased.

3 After the jibe

On the new course, the guy is set and the sail trimmed with the new sheet. At any time during this process, the mainsail can be jibed and eased out to its proper position for the new course.

Jibing a gennaker is easier because there is no pole. Bear away to a run, jibe the main, and ease out on the old sheet while pulling in the new one to jibe the gennaker.

Dropping spinnakers and gennakers

Hoist the jib before you drop the spinnaker and have the helmsman bear off to a run or broad reach so that the spinnaker can be dropped in the wind shadow behind the mainsail. Once the boat is on a run, have one person stand by the halyard and another grasp the lazy guy (to leeward) or, if a single sheet system is used, the sheet. The next step is to collapse the sail behind the mainsail.

One way to collapse the spinnaker is to let out the guy. If twin sheets and guys are used, it usually helps if you release the sail from the guy at the pole end.

Snap shackles that are used to attach the sheets and guys to the sail are designed for quick release, and "tripping" the guy from the sail will allow the spinnaker to fly free of the guy and windward sheet, held only by the leeward sheet and guy, and the halyard. Always duck below the pole when releasing the sail because the pole will spring back to windward when the sail blows free.

Once the sail has collapsed behind the mainsail, it is pulled in under the boom by pulling on the lazy guy or the sheet. The person tending the halyard lowers the sail as the cockpit crew gathers it in. It is usually easiest to bundle the sail below, through the companionway, before repacking it in its bag. The person lowering the halyard must only drop the sail as fast as the cockpit crew can pull it in, or it will end up in the water and will be much harder to recover. Once the sail is safely below, tidy up the sheets and guys and stow the spinnaker pole.

The technique for dropping the gennaker is the same. Just release the tack from the bow, pull on the sheet, and recover the sail under the boom. Bear away to a run first so that the sail can be dropped safely in the mainsail's wind shadow.

INTERNET

www.seldenmast.com

Seldén Masts supply rigs and all the ancillary parts for most yachts, from dinghies to cruisers. They also offer a useful guide to handling a spinnaker on a cruising boat.

■ **With the spinnaker pole** *eased forward and lowered within reach, a crew member can trip the sheet and guy from the sail to allow it to blow free and collapse behind the mainsail.*

When to reduce sail

IT'S FAIRLY OBVIOUS – at least I hope it is by now – that a good time to reduce the sail area is when it gets windy and the boat starts to heel too much. But how much heel is too much?

Dinghies should be sailed as upright as possible, but keelboats are designed to sail with some heel to allow the keel to develop useful righting leverage. A keelboat or cruiser's hull shape helps determine the maximum angle of heel you should allow. Boats with wide, shallow hulls need to be sailed more upright than narrower, deeper designs. Expect a keelboat to sail at its best at heel angles within a range of 10–25°.

Heeling is never comfortable below deck and it gets harder to live with at angles above 15°. If you are cruising, you may want to sacrifice a bit of speed for greater comfort by reducing sail earlier than you would do if you were racing or on a short sail.

Dealing with strong winds

Until you gain experience, do your best to avoid windy weather. Gain experience in stronger winds gradually if you can, preferably with an experienced friend or instructor on board. At any time that you feel the wind is stronger than you are used to, or that the boat is becoming harder to steer or control, think about using smaller sails. Don't worry if other boats are still carrying full sail: If you feel that you are not fully in control, reduce your sail area for a more comfortable ride.

Maintaining balance

When reducing sail, it is important to maintain the sail balance to avoid creating excessive weather helm or, even worse, lee helm. This is why dropping one sail or the other is often not a desirable option. Under mainsail there will usually be considerable weather helm, especially when sailing upwind or on a reach. With a jib, the opposite is the case. Lee helm makes it difficult or impossible to sail upwind or even on a beam reach. Unless you are sailing downwind, try to reduce the size of both jib and mainsail to maintain the balance between the two and avoid creating weather or lee helm.

Optimizing sail setting

Before you reduce the sail, think about whether the sails are set properly for the wind strength. Badly set sails will cause the boat to heel more than it should and make more leeway, but you can rectify this easily as long as your sails are not too old and stretched. As the wind increases, flatten your sails to reduce the drag and heeling forces. Tighten the clew outhaul on the mainsail as much as possible, and tighten the halyard or the Cunningham control (if you have one fitted). Use the vang to set some twist in the sail and tighten the backstay if you have an adjustable one. If your boat has a mainsheet traveler, drop it to leeward on its track.

Tightening the backstay will bend the mast on most boats, helping to flatten the mainsail, and will also tighten the forestay, which has the effect of flattening the jib. Finally, move the jib sheet fairleads aft a bit. This will tighten the foot and ease the leach, flattening the lower part of the jib and allowing the top to twist off and spill some wind.

Adjustments help flatten the sail and create a shape that is better suited for strong winds, because drag and heeling force are minimized.

Small sails for strong winds

WHEN YOU DECIDE THAT *the time has come to reduce the sail area, you have a number of options – these depend on how your boat is rigged.*

One option is to simply lower the jib or the mainsail completely. If you are sailing downwind, you could drop either sail and still make reasonable progress. However, the boat may not handle so well if you want to sail on a reach. Most cruisers do not sail to windward very well under mainsail alone and many will not sail above a reach with just a jib. It is important to get to know how your boat behaves under either sail alone, and when drifting with no sail set. Experiment in medium-strength winds at first to find out how your boat reacts with only one sail set.

When sailing to windward in rough weather, one option is to motorsail with a reefed mainsail. If you drop the jib, reef the main, and sheet it in tight, you can use the engine to help you power to windward. The reefed mainsail provides some drive and also steadies the boat and prevents the rolling that occurs under engine alone. The secret to this technique is to steer at a closer angle to the wind than you would if you were sailing normally, and to avoid letting the boat heel much. Many engines are limited to a small heel angle if they are to work properly, and there is also a danger of the cooling water intake coming out of the water if the boat heels too much.

Reducing headsail size

When you are sailing a Bermudan sloop, the first step in reducing sail is to reduce the size of the headsail, especially when you are carrying an overlapping genoa.

If you sail with a roller-furling headsail, it is simply a matter of taking a few rolls in the sail by easing the sheet and pulling in on the furling line. When sufficient sail has been rolled away, the furling line is cleated and the sail sheeted in again. The only problem with this seemingly simple system is that it rarely results in a well-setting sail once a few rolls have been taken in. Roller-reefed headsails usually develop a baggy shape that makes them very inefficient for sailing to windward and adds to the heeling force – the opposite of what is required. Nevertheless, many coastal cruising sailors choose to sail with this equipment because of the ease with which the sail can be reefed and furled.

> ### Trivia...
> One of the oldest rig designs is the Chinese junk rig, which has an unstayed mast. The mast, which is usually made of wood, supports a single mainsail and no jib. The mainsail is fully battened and can be reefed easily by lowering the halyard, with the battens self-stacking on top of the boom.

If you plan to sail offshore or expect to have to deal with rough weather on a regular basis, another alternative to a roller-reefing headsail is to have a range of headsails of different sizes that can be changed to suit the conditions. Another option that makes sense is to have a removable inner forestay on which a jib called a staysail can be set to replace the roller genoa in strong winds.

Changing headsails

If you sail with hanked on headsails, you will have a number of them in your sail locker from which to choose. To change the headsail, the old sail is lowered, unhanked, and the sheets removed. The old sail is stowed away in its bag and the new sail is attached and hoisted in the normal way. This task requires at least one crew member to go and work on the foredeck, which will be wet and moving violently in rough weather.

If you are sailing upwind, slow the boat down by easing the sails or heaving-to before you send someone forward – this will make the task safer. Foredeck conditions can also be made much more acceptable by bearing away downwind during the headsail change. The foredeck will be more stable and the headsail will be blanketed by the mainsail, which will make dropping it easier.

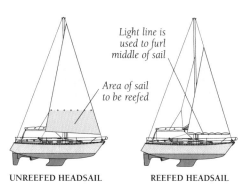

Light line is used to furl middle of sail

Area of sail to be reefed

UNREEFED HEADSAIL   REEFED HEADSAIL

The crew going forward should always move along the windward sidedeck and be clipped on. When moving a heavy sail bag, drag it rather than carry it and don't be afraid to move on your hands and knees if the motion is difficult. Once on the foredeck, brace yourself in a secure position before starting the job. Some jibs designed for heavy weather have a row of reef points so that they can be reduced in size quickly and easily if the wind increases further. To reduce the area, the sail is partly lowered and the new tack fitting attached to the bow. The sheets are moved to the new clew and a light line is used to furl up the middle of the sail.

Reefing the mainsail

Once the headsail size has been reduced, the usual next step in reducing sail is to reef the mainsail. The most common type of mainsail reefing is called slab reefing. If the reefing gear is properly organized, it is a quick and easy operation that can be done, in many boats, from the security of the cockpit. The first step is to ease the mainsheet (in order to spill wind from the sail), ease the boom vang, and take the weight of the boom on the topping lift – unless you have a solid vang that will support the boom. Then ease the halyard to bring the first reef to boom level.

While slab reefing is the most common mainsail reefing system, there are other systems that roll the mainsail away inside the mast, or inside or around the boom. All rely on more mechanical equipment than the slab-reefing method – they usually do not give such a good reefed sail shape, and are unnecessary on most medium-sized cruisers.

USING A TRISAIL

Most cruiser mainsails have two or three slab reefs so that the sail can be reduced in size in stages. By the time you are forced to resort to the third reef, the wind will be blowing very hard, but what happens if the wind increases even further? One option is to drop the mainsail entirely, but, if this is not desirable, you can resort to replacing it with a trisail if you have one aboard. A trisail is a small, battenless sail that is strongly built and designed for severe wind strengths. Once the mainsail has been stowed on the boom, the trisail is hoisted on the main halyard. Its tack is fastened to a downhaul or tied to the gooseneck, and it is usually set loose-footed – with twin sheets from the clew led to blocks on the quarters and then to the headsail sheet winches.

Pull the cringle (ring) in the luff down to the boom using a reef line or by hooking it under a ramshorn (hook at the boom), and then hoist the halyard back up until the luff is tight. Now pull or winch the leech reef line to pull the leech cringle down and out toward the boom end.

Cleat the leech reef line, ease the topping lift, and trim the mainsheet, before tightening the vang. There is now a fold of sail hanging down along the length of the boom. This can be left free or, if you prefer, can be tidied into a neat roll and secured by a light line or shockcord led through the reef cringles from leech to luff. Leaving it loose is fine on a typical, short-footed mainsail, but on a traditional design with a long boom you should tie up the loose sail.

■ **To reef the mainsail,** *the halyard has been lowered so the luff cringle can be pulled down to the boom. The leech reef line is being pulled in to complete the reef.*

A simple summary

✔ The average Bermudan sloop is underpowered in light winds unless lighter, larger sails are used.

✔ Using a spinnaker or gennaker downwind is fun and adds considerably to performance.

✔ A gennaker is more convenient on a cruiser than a spinnaker but is less effective on a run.

✔ Reduce sail area to reduce heel and maintain control, safety, and comfort in strong winds.

✔ Slow the boat or turn downwind when changing a jib to make it safer for the foredeck crew.

✔ Slab reefing is the most common system for reefing a mainsail, but other types are available.

Chapter 18

The Problem of Parking!

SAILING PURISTS HATE THE TERM PARKING because one does not "park" one's boat, does one? The trouble is that there are a lot of ways to secure the boat by attaching it to the land, and a lot of terms used to describe them. It is more common today to tie a boat up to a floating dock in a marina than to use the traditional methods of lying alongside a quay wall, anchoring, or picking up a mooring. However, you may be faced with any one of these procedures, depending on where you sail, so you should prepare yourself by learning a few simple rules.

In this chapter...

✓ Learning slow-speed handling

✓ Securing your boat alongside

✓ To and from a berth

✓ Using moorings

✓ Anchoring – a lost art?

SAFELY SECURED ALONGSIDE, AND YOU CAN BREATHE A SIGH OF RELIEF!

Learning slow-speed handling

BEING ABLE TO CONTROL your boat at slow speeds and in confined spaces is crucial to hassle-free parking. Naturally, you should practice slow-speed maneuvers in open water before attempting them in tight situations.

How your boat drifts

You will usually use your engine when approaching or leaving a *berth*, but you should also know how to sail in or out. Not only is it very rewarding to carry out the maneuvers under sail, but you may also find that you have no choice if your engine fails. The key to handling your boat at slow speed is to understand its drifting characteristics.

Once a boat loses steerageway (sufficient motion to enable it to be steered), it is at the mercy of wind and tide. The way it reacts will depend on its weight, underwater shape, and *windage*. You must practice with your boat so that you understand how it will behave when it is moving slowly or when it is stopped in the water.

Practice stopping the boat at different angles to the wind and observing how quickly the bow swings downwind. Under engine, steer into the wind and then shift into neutral to see how quickly the boat stops from different starting speeds. Find out if you can steer the boat downwind under the windage of the rig alone without sails.

Wind direction and strength are important considerations, particularly at slow speeds. Your boat will tend to turn its bow downwind once it loses steerageway, due to the windage on the mast. You need to ascertain how quickly this will happen.

Practicing maneuvers

Under power, make sure you understand prop walk and can turn your boat in the tightest possible turning circle. Learn to control the boat when going astern and take note of how the strength of the wind affects the boat at slow speed under power.

Practice maneuvers under mainsail and jib alone. Find out how slowly you can sail before losing control, and how quickly you can regain steerageway once stopped.

■ **Practice sailing** *a cruiser under jib alone and mainsail alone to check its handling.*

If you sail in tidal waters or areas of strong currents, you must learn to use the tide or current to assist your slow-speed handling maneuvers. Whenever you are parking, you must aim to stop your boat as you arrive in the berth.

If a tide or current is flowing, you can only stop the boat safely if you approach into the tide or current. Do not try to enter a berth or mooring downtide under sail or power.

The best way to learn boat-handling skills is with an experienced sailor on board. Spend a day taking your boat into and out of different berths and you will quickly learn how to judge and control your speed.

Securing your boat alongside

WHENEVER YOU WANT TO *lie alongside another boat, dock, or quay wall, you must know how to tie up your boat so that it is secure and safe from damage. Ropes called mooring lines are used to secure the boat, and knowing how to arrange and handle mooring lines is an essential part of cruiser handling.*

The size of mooring lines depends on the size and, most importantly, the weight of your boat. Nylon is the best rope material for mooring lines because it is strong. It stretches well to help absorb shock loading and reduce loads on fairleads and cleats.

Ropes and lines

Lines should always be neatly coiled when not in use, and stored, preferably by hanging them up, in a locker from where they can be easily retrieved.

Several lines are needed to hold the boat safely alongside and to prevent it swinging back and forth and causing damage. The precise arrangement depends on whether you are tied to a quay wall and have to allow for the rise and fall of a tide. If you are tied to another boat or floating dock, remember that these will also move up and down in response to changes in tidal height.

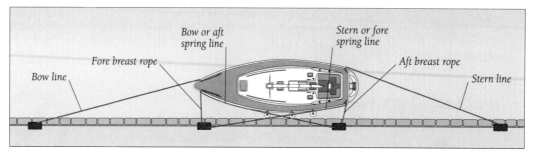

Bow or aft spring line

Stern or fore spring line

Fore breast rope

Aft breast rope

Bow line

Stern line

■ **When securing a boat** *alongside a quay wall in tidal waters, you will need to adjust the springs and breast ropes as the boat rises or falls, but long bow and stern lines need less adjustment.*

Each mooring line has a different function – and may take a new name such as rope or line, depending on its purpose. The bow line (or head rope) and stern lines position the boat and must be strong enough to take the main load. They need to be long enough to allow for any rise and fall of tide and are typically at least the length of the boat. If you are berthed alongside a quay wall, the lines should be taken as far fore and aft of the yacht as possible so that they will need little adjustment as the tide rises and falls.

The bow and stern spring lines (sometimes called the fore and aft spring lines) prevent the boat moving ahead or astern. They are not usually as long as the bow and stern lines and will need more adjustment as tidal height changes. Fore and aft breast ropes are sometimes used in addition to the four main lines to hold the boat close alongside. Breasts and spring lines may be used alone, without bow and stern lines, when you are lying alongside a dock.

Lying alongside

If you are lying alongside another boat, you should rig breast ropes and springs to your neighbor, and bow and stern lines to the shore or dock so that your neighbor's lines do not take any extra load because of your yacht.

If you are lying alongside in tidal waters, don't run the springs out under the lifelines. Lead them through fairleads at bow and stern, otherwise you may damage your rails when the boat falls on the tide.

If you leave your boat alongside for any length of time in tidal waters, make sure that there is sufficient slack in the lines to allow for the lowest level of tide, otherwise the boat will end up hanging from its lines and something will break. The best way to avoid problems when mooring with lines is always to have one rope for each job and to tie them up on their own cleats. Trying to use one rope for two tasks, say a bow line and a bow spring line, is a sure recipe for problems, as is tying up two ropes on the same cleat.

Always tie up the end of a line to a cleat ashore or on the dock or neighboring boat. Bring the rest of the line back aboard where it can be cleated and neatly stowed. This avoids leaving rope ashore and makes it easy to adjust lines from on board.

Protecting your equipment

All lines should be led through fairleads so that they cannot chafe on the deck edge or other obstructions. Lines are particularly susceptible to chafe where they are led through fairleads or across the edges of quay walls. Protect them by threading them through short lengths of plastic tubing, which should be positioned at likely points of chafe.

Always use fenders to prevent your boat touching the neighboring yacht, dock, or quay wall. Use at least four fenders when lying alongside and have one or two spare in case someone berths alongside without sufficient fenders to protect both craft.

You do not need to position your fenders at equal intervals along the boat. Concentrate them near the point of maximum beam and adjust your mooring lines to keep the boat parallel to whatever it is secured to.

Fenders should not be tied to the lifelines, if possible, as constant movement leads to damage to the lifelines, stanchions, and fittings.

Fenders can be tied to the handrails on the coach roof or to the toerails. The constant movement of fenders can lead to wear on the gelcoat or paint finish on the hull. This can be avoided by using a fender skirt, which is hung between hull and fenders. Sometimes, when mooring alongside an uneven quay wall, it can be very difficult to keep the fenders in position. A fender board (a long plank) can be carried to hang outboard of the fenders to help solve this problem.

■ **Long cylindrical fenders** *are the easiest to stow and they are the most adaptable in use. They can be hung vertically or horizontally over the sides of your boat as the need dictates.*

To and from a berth

YOU WILL BE CONFRONTED with many different situations when approaching or leaving a berth (or slip), and only experience will equip you with all the skills necessary to handle the more complex ones. However, you can deal with most of them by remembering a few key steps:

1. In the absence of tide or current, make your final approach to a berth as near head-to-wind as possible, and leave in the same way. If a tidal stream or current is running, make your approach and departure pointing into the stream.

2. Always examine the situation beforehand and check the direction of wind and tide relative to the boat and the berth.

3. Always choose a leeward berth if possible, allowing for possible windshifts. A windward berth is more difficult to approach, less comfortable to be in, and more difficult to leave under power – and often impossible under sail.

4. If you are berthed stern-to-wind or -tide and need to turn the boat to leave, use the mooring lines to turn the boat around in its berth.

5. Plan to have an escape route when approaching a berth so that you can return to safe water if you need to abort the maneuver at the last minute.

6. Brief your crew carefully about the maneuver before you start, explain their individual jobs, and give them time to prepare any equipment you need such as mooring lines and fenders. Make sure a boathook is on deck and that the decks are clear of unnecessary equipment.

7. If you are approaching a berth, make a dummy run to assess the approach and to make a final check on wind and tide at the berth.

8. Give clear orders to your crew during the maneuver and use pre-agreed hand signals if there is a danger of an order not being heard.

9. Go slowly when arriving and leaving but don't let the boat lose steerageway.

Arriving under power

Drop the sails well clear of the berth and stow them neatly. Make absolutely sure that there are no ropes hanging over the side. A rope wrapped around the propeller at this stage would be a serious embarrassment, to say the least.

Take a careful look at the berth and check the direction of wind and tide, if any. Decide your direction of approach and confirm which side will be next to the dock. If possible, berth on the side to which prop walk will pull the stern when you put the boat in reverse. This will make the final approach much easier.

Once the crew have prepared the lines and fenders on the correct side, make your final approach to the berth as slowly as possible while heading into the wind or current. Steer into the berth and put the engine in neutral, allowing the boat to coast in on its own momentum and using the wind or tide to stop the boat. Just before the boat stops, give a short burst of reverse and then prop walk will pull the stern in towards the berth. If you do this correctly, the boat will stop parallel to the berth and settle gently against her fenders as your crew take the lines ashore.

If you have to berth on the side away from the reverse prop walk, make your approach at a shallower angle and try to coast into a stop without using the reverse gear if possible.

Leaving under power

Before you prepare to leave, start the engine and let it warm up while you decide on your exit route. Check the direction of wind and tide and aim to leave facing into the strongest element. If necessary, turn the boat in its berth using mooring lines so that you can leave bow first, or, if your boat handles well in reverse, plan to leave stern first. Make sure that your exit route will take you clear of other boats, with no danger of drifting into them under the effects of wind or tide.

Assuming that you are pointing into wind or tide and will be leaving forward, you must prepare your lines for release. The trick is to release first the lines that are not taking any load. If you are lying bow-to-wind or -tide, the fore spring line and bow line are the most important ropes holding the boat, but you can safely release the back spring and stern lines just before you leave. If these two ropes are taking any load, reassess your views on the wind and tide situation.

Once you have briefed the crew, you are ready to leave. Remember that the stern of the boat swings out when you turn so if you simply cast off (release the lines) and motor out while steering away from the dock, the stern will swing in and collide with it. The solution is to move the bow out before you motor away in a straight line. In a small cruiser, this can often be achieved by casting off and then pushing the bow off manually, using a boathook from the foredeck.

INTERNET

www.setsail.com

This is a great site for anyone interested in long-distance cruising. It has lots of practical advice on boat handling, cruising matters, and weather forecasting.

In a larger cruiser, it is easier to use a spring line to turn the boat before leaving the berth:

(1) If you are leaving bow first, rig the bow line and the fore spring line as slip lines by leading the line around the cleat ashore and back aboard. With both ends of a line on board, a crew member can cast off and recover it from the boat.

(2) Cast off and coil the stern line and aft spring. Position a fender between the dock and boat near the stern.

(3) Motor gently back against the fore spring line and have a crew member ease the bow line. The bow will start to swing outward as the stern, held by the fore spring line, swings in toward the dock. Gently increase the throttle if the bow is slow to swing out. Cast off one end of the bow line and recover the line by pulling steadily on the other end.

(4) Once the bow has swung out sufficiently, put the engine into neutral and then motor ahead, cast off and recover the fore spring line, and steer out of the berth.

Arriving under sail

Docking a cruiser under sail, especially in a confined space, requires skill and good judgment. Make a point of practicing these skills with an instructor before you attempt them on your own in a cruiser. When you are practicing, and whenever you are berthing for real, it is handy to have the engine running in neutral in case you get into any difficulties. If you don't have an engine, be sure to pick your berth with care and avoid difficult situations.

Always plan your approach carefully and work out an escape route in case the wind shifts or changes in strength. The success of the maneuver depends on your knowledge of your boat's slow-speed handling characteristics and on having an efficient crew who can respond quickly to instructions. The choice of approach is much the same as when approaching under power. Always head into the strongest element of wind or tide so that you can use it to stop you when you reach the berth.

If there is no tide, always approach into the wind, preferably under mainsail alone. In a tide or current, head into the stream to stop, and pick the sail to use depending on the angle of the wind to the boat.

If, when you approach head-to-tide, the wind will be from ahead of the beam, make your approach under mainsail alone. Use a jib with the mainsail only if your boat does not handle well under mainsail alone, or if the wind is so light you need the extra power. If possible drop the jib first, because it will make the job easier for the foredeck crew. If the wind will be on or aft of the beam, come in under jib alone.

Reducing speed

If you are approaching too fast in the final stages, slow down by getting your crew to "back" the mainsail if you're approaching into the wind. This is done by the crew pushing the boom to one side as far as possible, while being ready to let go and duck if the wind proves too strong. Do not attempt this in a large boat or in a strong wind. If you're approaching downwind, lower the headsail, either fully or partly. The crew will need to hold the leech of a partly lowered headsail to keep it drawing.

Always try and come in on the leeward side of the berth. Don't choose a berth that has the wind blowing onto it unless absolutely necessary and then approach under power if possible. You will not be able to sail off if the wind stays in this direction and it is a very difficult approach to make under sail with no escape route available. The only way is to approach downwind under headsail alone, turning into the tide to stop to windward of the berth so that the boat blows sideways into its berth. Stop the boat with the bow pointing slightly upwind to allow for it drifting faster downwind than the stern. Lower the headsail and get the lines ashore.

If you are moving too fast in the final stages of docking, swing the boat hard one way for about 15° and then the other way for the same amount. The boat will swing through an S-shaped course, losing speed as it side-slips in the turns. Warn the crew to hang on to something secure before starting this maneuver.

Leaving under sail

It is often possible to leave a berth under sail, but if the wind is light and the tide strong, you will have reduced control and it will be easier to leave under power. If the wind is blowing onto the berth, however, you won't be able to sail off and you will have to use an engine or lines, or, if necessary, row out an anchor to get yourself out of the berth. If there is a tide present, it is best to leave bow into tide to give greater control. If the boat is lying with the stern facing the tide, you should turn it using mooring lines before you attempt to sail off. If the wind is from directly ahead you will have to hoist and back the headsail to push the bow off.

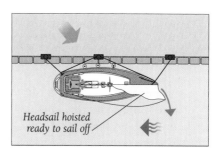

Headsail hoisted ready to sail off

OFFSHORE WIND AFT OF BEAM

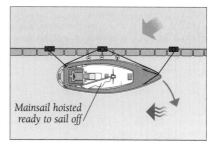

Mainsail hoisted ready to sail off

OFFSHORE WIND AHEAD

■ **Once you are lying** *head-to-tide, sail off under jib only if the wind is on or aft of the beam. If the wind is from ahead, sail off under mainsail alone, or mainsail and headsail together if the wind is light.*

Using moorings

WHEN YOU VISIT A HARBOR with visitors' mooring buoys, your first task is to choose a suitable mooring. You must ensure that the mooring is strong enough for your boat, that it is laid in water deep enough so that you will still float at low tide, and that there is room for the boat to swing. You should also consider how sheltered the mooring is, from both wind and swell, especially if you plan an overnight stop.

Before the approach

Other important points to consider are how easily you will be able to approach and leave the mooring under power or sail, and its proximity to other boats or the shore. Be careful not to pick up a local's permanent mooring because the owner may return at any time and claim his buoy. If you do have to pick up someone else's mooring, never leave the boat unattended in case the owner does appear. If possible, ask the harbor master or an experienced local sailor for advice about a suitable mooring.

It is much simpler to pick up a mooring than to come into a dock, but there is still some preparation to be done before the mooring is approached. You should brief one or two crew to pick up the mooring and they should have a mooring line and boathook ready. Make a dummy run to check the approach route and to make a close inspection of the mooring and its particular pick-up arrangement.

Handling moorings

On larger cruisers, the bow may be quite high out of the water. This makes it difficult to pick up the buoy or thread the mooring line through the ring on top of the buoy. In this case, consider coming alongside the buoy with it just forward of the shrouds where the freeboard is usually less than at the bow. As the boat makes its final approach to the buoy, the foredeck crew should indicate its position and distance by hand signals because the helmsman may lose sight of it in the last few yards.

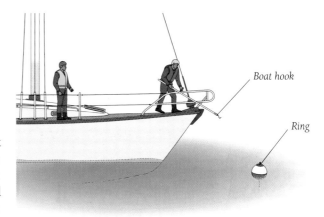

Boat hook

Ring

■ **If the buoy** has a ring on top of it, you can grab it with a boathook and hold it while a mooring line is tied to the ring. If not, hook the line under the buoy.

Once the buoy is alongside, the foredeck crew should either pull the pick-up buoy on board, or tie the mooring line to the ring on the main buoy or to the chain under the buoy – preferably using a round turn and a bowline. If there is a pick-up buoy to be pulled aboard, check the condition of the rope or chain between it and the main riser. If it looks at all suspect, tie-up to the main chain with your mooring line. Make sure any mooring line is led through a fairlead to prevent chafing.

To leave a mooring, the foredeck crew must prepare to drop it immediately on the skipper's order. If a pick-up buoy has been brought aboard, its line should be uncleated and then held with a turn around the cleat. If a mooring line has been tied to the buoy or chain, it should be reled as a slip line with both ends on board. On the skipper's command, one end can easily be released and the line recovered. When the buoy has been dropped, make sure that the skipper knows it has gone and is clear of the boat.

Approaching a mooring under power

It is important to decide whether the wind or tide will have the most significant effect on the boat and then make your final approach heading into the stronger element. Look at other boats anchored or moored to see which direction they are pointing, especially boats of a similar type to yours that will be affected by wind or tide in a similar way.

It is important to approach a mooring into the strongest element in order to have maximum control and to be able to stop at your chosen spot.

Plan your course to clear other boats and obstructions and, once you have decided on an approach route, fully brief the crew and give them time to prepare a line and boathook. Always try and have an escape route planned in case of an unforeseen circumstance. Approach slowly under power, aiming to use the wind or tide to slow the boat until it stops at the mooring. If you lose sight of the buoy in the last boat length or so, have a foredeck crew indicate its direction with arm movements.

Leaving a mooring under power

Leaving under power requires you to plan your route and brief the crew. The boat will be pointing toward the wind or tide, whichever is strongest, and, for maximum control, you will normally leave initially in that direction, unless an obstruction requires you to turn to another course. When maneuvering room is limited, you can help the boat turn quickly as you leave by having the foredeck crew walk the mooring buoy or the mooring line back along a sidedeck. To turn to starboard as you leave the mooring, walk it back along the port side, and vice versa. Make certain you keep the mooring well away from your propeller.

Approaching a mooring under sail

Check how other boats are lying and decide if the wind or tide will have the strongest effect on the boat. The secret is always to approach into the strongest element to retain control and be able to stop. If you are in any doubt, approach into the tide.

You must decide whether to make your final approach under mainsail or headsail alone. As with docking, the rules are:

- If the wind is forward of the beam for your final approach use the mainsail only
- If the wind is on the beam or further aft, then approach under headsail only

If the mainsail is used with the wind on or aft of the beam, you won't be able to let it out far enough to spill all the wind so you won't be able to stop!

With the wind forward of the beam, approach under mainsail alone to keep the foredeck clear of a flapping headsail. Approach on a close reach, easing or trimming the mainsail to control your speed. Let the sail flap in your final approach to allow the boat to stop. When the mooring buoy is secured, drop the mainsail and stow it.

If the wind is aft of the beam, sail upwind of the mooring, lower the mainsail, and sail slowly toward the spot under headsail alone. Ease or trim the sheet to control your speed. In strong winds, you may have to lower or furl the sail and proceed under bare poles if the boat is moving too fast even with the sheet eased. Use the S-curve technique described earlier to reduce excess speed.

Leaving a mooring under sail

The same rules apply to leaving under sail. If the wind is from ahead of the beam, you should leave under mainsail only, or mainsail and headsail together. If it is on or abaft the beam, leave under headsail alone.

When the wind is forward of the beam, hoist the mainsail and prepare the headsail. In light winds, or if your boat doesn't handle well under mainsail alone, you may need to use both sails. Otherwise, leave the headsail lowered and ready for immediate hoisting, or furled if you have a furling system. When you are ready to leave, get your crew to pull the mooring buoy aft along the windward sidedeck to give the boat steerageway and turn it in the desired direction. When the wind is aft of the beam, hoist the headsail when you are ready to drop the mooring, sheet in, and sail off. Get into clear water before turning head-to-wind to hoist the mainsail.

Trivia...

A berthing or mooring situation is one occasion when a roller-furling headsail system does make life easier. It is easy to partly or fully furl the headsail when you need to, and it avoids cluttering the foredeck with a lowered headsail.

Anchoring – a lost art?

ANCHORING IS A FUNDAMENTAL TECHNIQUE for a sailor to learn, although it is used less in areas where marinas are plentiful. Nevertheless, anchoring is a vital skill that allows you to choose a remote place for a quiet stop, or to take a temporary rest if you need to wait out a foul tide or ride out a gale in shelter. You need to be aware of the correct procedures.

The approach to an anchoring spot is handled in exactly the same way as if you were picking up a mooring, but obviously you do not need to be quite so exact with the positioning of your boat. Before you can anchor you have to make sure that you have the right equipment at hand and that you know how to use it.

Equipment

All yachts should carry at least two suitably sized anchors together with appropriate lengths of chain or rope rode. Your choice of anchor and your decision about whether to use chain or rope will depend on the type of boat and the area in which you normally sail.

A typical arrangement will include a main anchor and a lighter anchor – a kedge – for short stops in good weather or for pulling the boat off after running aground.

■ **If you cruise** *widely, your anchors will have to work in a variety of different terrains, ranging from coral to sand, mud, and rock.*

The Bruce, CQR, Danforth, and Fortress anchors are all good anchors designed to bury themselves in the seabed. They work very well in sand, mud or shingle, but the traditional, heavy Fisherman's anchor still performs better than most when anchoring in rock or weed.

The Bruce is a popular choice for the main anchor, with an aluminum Fortress a good option as a kedge.

Anchor specifications

The best choice of rode is chain which, although much heavier than rope, is stronger and does not suffer from chafe from underwater obstructions. A nylon rope rode is appropriate for the kedge, which may have to be used from the tender where the light rope will make the job much easier. Even here, though, there should be a short length of chain between anchor and rope to take the chafe from the seabed.

An anchor's holding power is very dependent on the amount of rode you can pay out; this will depend on the amount you can carry and the depth of water you are in.

The absolute minimum scope for anchoring in good conditions is a ratio of chain against depth of water of 3:1, and a ratio of rope against depth of water of 5:1, but it is much better to increase these ratios to 5:1 and 8:1 respectively, if you have sufficient rode.

In rough conditions in an exposed anchorage, you may well have to pay out chain or rope up to ten or more times the depth of water to avoid the anchor dragging. Don't forget to allow for the rise of tide if you anchor at low tide.

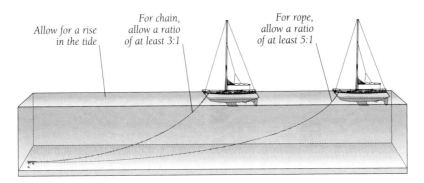

Allow for a rise in the tide

For chain, allow a ratio of at least 3:1

For rope, allow a ratio of at least 5:1

■ **The amount** of rode you need to let out depends on the depth of water, the height of any waves, and the type of seabed. If in doubt, let more out.

Choosing an anchorage

When choosing an anchorage, you need to consider the amount of shelter from wind and waves, the depth of water, the type of seabed, and the ease with which you can approach and leave the chosen spot under sail or power.

An anchorage that may be sheltered from the wind direction in which you anchor may become untenable if the wind swings and the anchorage becomes exposed. The same may happen if a tidal current changes direction and causes a change in the sea state. Consider the weather forecast before you anchor and take into account any predicted changes in wind direction or strength.

Tidal effects

Check the tide charts and tide tables to see if any changes will affect your anchorage. In shallow water, check that there will be sufficient water at low tide to keep you afloat and allow you to leave if necessary. Check the chart or local sailing directions for a description of the type of seabed.

Be careful when anchoring on rock, weed, or coral covered by thin sand because these bottoms provide poor holding for most anchors. If possible, pick a spot with sand or firm mud.

LAYING TWO ANCHORS

Sometimes two anchors are used, either to reduce the swinging room in a crowded or restricted anchorage, or for extra security.

To restrict the swing to wind or tide in a crowded anchorage, two anchors can be laid ahead and astern. The main anchor is dropped and the boat reversed while twice the needed length of cable is let out. The kedge is then dropped and the main rode pulled in while the kedge rode is let out to position the boat midway between the anchors. The two rodes are then joined and both let out. They are then made fast on cleats. The boat will now swing around a much smaller radius than if they were secured to one anchor.

To provide extra security, two anchors can be laid in tandem (in-line) on one rode or at an angle of about 45° using two separate rodes. If the latter arrangement is used, be prepared to relay your anchors if there is a major wind shift and don't use this arrangement when the boat will have to swing to a tide change.

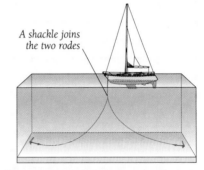

A shackle joins the two rodes

■ **Arranging one** *anchor ahead and one behind allows you to limit the amount the boat will swing.*

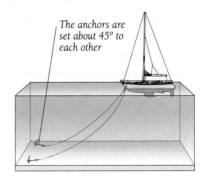

The anchors are set about 45° to each other

■ **Two anchors** *can be attached to one rode or to two separate rodes, to give extra holding power.*

Finally, consider any other yachts in the anchorage and the route you would use to approach and leave. Allow plenty of room between you and other boats, leaving enough space to swing clear of others if the wind or tide change direction. Try and anchor with boats of a similar type and size to your own, as they will react in much the same way as your boat to the effects of wind and tide, and changes in their strength or direction.

Dropping anchor

Get the anchor and rode ready before you make your final approach to the chosen spot. The anchor should be stowed in its bow roller and any lashings or securing pins released, but make sure that it cannot drop before you are ready. Tell the foredeck crew how much rode will be required and ask them to prepare it on deck so that it is ready to run without snagging. Cleat the rode at this point.

When the boat reaches the chosen spot and has stopped moving through the water, or better still is moving astern, give the order to let go. The anchor should be lowered, not dropped free, into the water and the rode allowed to run out under control until the anchor reaches the bottom. The rest of the rode is let out as the boat drifts away from the anchor.

If you have made your approach under power, it is easy to use the engine to move the boat astern to set (dig in) the anchor. Under sail it is more difficult, at least in light winds, but if you have approached under mainsail alone you may be able to back the mainsail to sail backward.

When the strain comes on the rode, the skipper should take a series of bearings with a hand bearing compass on two or more points on shore in order to make sure that the boat is stationary and not dragging its anchor. If the anchor is dragging, you can try letting out more rode and if this doesn't work, haul the anchor up and try another spot.

Weighing anchor

No, I don't want you to put the anchor on the scales – weighing means recovering the anchor! The first step is to bring the boat above the position of the anchor. This can be done by hand in light weather or a small boat, but you will need the help of a windlass (a mechanical device for winding rope or chain), the engine, or the sails in stronger conditions or on a larger boat.

When the boat is over the anchor and the chain is "up and down" (vertical) the crew must signal to the skipper so that he knows the anchor is ready to break out. The rode is then hauled by hand or windlass until the anchor breaks out of the seabed. At this point you should motor or sail slowly until the foredeck crew have gotten the anchor and rode stowed. If the anchor cannot be broken out by hand or with the windlass, it may be necessary to haul the rode as tight as possible and then cleat it and use the power of the engine or sails to break out the anchor.

If you intend to go long-distance cruising, you will encounter many different types of anchorages, and the security of your boat will depend on the quality of your anchoring gear (ground tackle). Carry sufficient stout anchors, chain, and rope to deal with any eventuality.

■ **Some cruisers** *have an anchor well set into the foredeck. This is used to stow the chain and sometimes incorporates an anchor windlass (winch). The anchor may be stowed in a well or on a roller in the stemhead fitting.*

A simple summary

✔ Parking the boat may involve coming alongside a berth, picking up a mooring, or dropping an anchor.

✔ The ability to handle the boat at slow speed in confined spaces, under both power and sail, is crucial to success.

✔ The boat must be secured properly using the right type and size of mooring lines.

✔ Always approach into the strongest element of wind or tide so that you can stop the boat when and where you want to.

✔ The boat must be secured in such a way as to prevent it from damaging itself or its neighbors.

✔ The direction of wind and tide are the main factors that determine how you approach each situation.

Chapter 19

Over the Blue Horizon

By THE TIME YOU HAVE LEARNED how to handle your cruiser, you will be itching to head off and experience the thrill of a well-executed passage and a safe arrival at a new port. But first you need to know how to prepare and plan your passage. Before you sail out of sight of land, or even a few miles along a seemingly benevolent coastline, prepare yourself for sailing at night and the possibility of dealing with bad weather. Build your experience with short trips, graduate to an overnight passage and longer cruises, and you will soon be ready to cruise to far-off shores.

In this chapter...

✓ Preparing boat and crew

✓ Making a passage plan

✓ What happens at night?

✓ Dealing with rough weather

✓ Reducing the terrors of fog

THE DREAM OF SAILING OVER THE HORIZON IS WITHIN YOUR REACH

Preparing boat and crew

WHEN YOU ASSUME THE ROLE OF SKIPPER, *you also accept that the safety and welfare of the boat and crew are your responsibility, so be cautious about undertaking passages in weather conditions beyond your level of experience.*

■ **Keep the cockpit** *and deck clear of rope by coiling and tidying up loose rope ends.*

Planning ahead

Making a passage will be easier if at least some of your crew have passage-making experience. Don't attempt an ambitious cruise with a weak crew. If you can't find an experienced sailor to come with you, adjust your plans to suit your crew's ability.

Before a passage, take the time to check all important parts of the rig and equipment. Use a defects log so that you can keep track of the maintenance you need to do and can monitor the state of your equipment. You need to be sure that all parts of the boat are in good order. Check the engine oil level and cooling system and visually check all wiring and control connections. Pump the bilge and tidy away all loose gear so that nothing can come loose.

Making preparations

Make sure that you have sufficient food, water, and fuel for the expected passage time, and carry an extra supply of each to allow for any delays due to bad weather or an emergency situation. Remember that however short or simple the passage or however benign the conditions may promise to be, the sea and weather pay no respect to human plans and you must be prepared to deal with the unexpected.

Brief your crew in advance about your passage plan and any gear that they will need aboard. Once they arrive, take them through the yacht, showing each of them which bunk to use and where to stow their personal gear. Explain the layout of the yacht and where all the important equipment is stowed. Make certain they all know the location of all the safety equipment and how to use it, and that they understand the procedures required if someone falls overboard.

When passage making, it is essential that all members of the crew, including you, get sufficient rest so that you can all continue to perform at your optimum level of efficiency.

Keeping watch

When setting out on a passage of more than a few hours, you should operate a *watch system* that allows all crew members to have time off watch for rest and sleep. A traditional watch system has one watch on duty for 4 hours followed by 4 hours off-watch. To prevent each watch having the same periods on duty each day, the watches are staggered by two "dog watches" of 2 hours each in the late afternoon and early evening, during which everyone is usually awake.

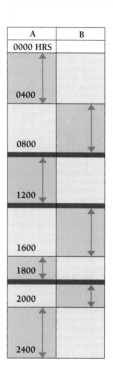

A	B
0000 HRS	
0400	
0800	
1200	
1600	
1800	
2000	
2400	

It is not necessary to use the traditional watch system. Many skippers devise their own system to suit the particular needs of their crew and the length of the passage.

It is very important for everyone to get sufficient rest and that light and noise are kept to a minimum below deck when the off-watch crew is trying to sleep. Novices are often reluctant to go below deck and rest during the day but it is important to do so in order to stay awake and be efficient during night watches. Make sure that everyone understands the importance of being on time for his or her watch. In the confines of a small yacht, when people are tired, it is very easy for tempers to fray if the watch on deck is not relieved on time because the new watch has overslept!

■ **The traditional watch** *system runs from midnight to midnight. It has five watches of 4 hours and two watches of 2 hours. You can adapt the system to suit your needs.*

KEY

ON WATCH

RESTING

MEALTIMES

DEFINITION

A watch system divides the crew into two or more watches, one of which is responsible for sailing the yacht while the other rests or prepares meals.

Turning green

Seasickness is another issue that you have to consider. Most of us have suffered from seasickness at one time or another and it can be a very debilitating condition. Fortunately, most people who suffer from it do so for only a few hours and soon establish their "sea legs."

A few people are chronic seasickness sufferers and do not recover quickly. In severe cases, the only cure is to get ashore as soon as possible. You will find out how you react as you increase your cruising experience. If you do suffer from seasickness there are many preventatives available. Discuss the problem with your physician or pharmacist and take the medication they recommend a few hours before you set sail.

Making a passage plan

YOU SHOULD START PLANNING for a cruise or passage some time before the day of departure. The first task is to prepare a navigation plan – which we will learn about in Chapter 22 – and from this you will be able to estimate how long the passage will take and whether it will involve sailing at night. You should also create an alternative plan to allow for changes in the weather or other factors that may cause you to change your itinerary.

When you are planning a cruise made up of a number of passages, remember to build in some spare days for rest and recreation ashore. This is especially important if you are sailing with children, who will usually enjoy the cruise more if passages are kept short and time is built in for exploration.

Getting your papers in order

Using the passage plan, you will be able to work out your fuel, food, and water requirements and allow for stops to replenish stores if necessary. Check your yacht's insurance details to make certain that you are covered for the passage and, if you are going to be sailing in foreign waters, make sure that your crew bring their passports and make any visa arrangements that may be necessary. Make sure that your yacht's registration papers are on board and that you have your certificate of competence with you. Many countries now require a small boat skipper to possess certification, so check that you have all the necessary paperwork with you.

INTERNET

www.sailmakers.com
www.yourguide.net/
boating/

Check out these sites for information on sail manufacturers.

In many countries, a Coastguard Service is responsible for managing rescue operations at sea. Many coastguards operate a system that allows you to inform them of your passage plan, destination, and estimated date and time of arrival. On reaching your destination, you must notify the coastguard of your safe arrival. If you do not arrive, the coastguard has details of your yacht and its crew and they can begin a search and rescue operation if you are significantly overdue.

If the coastguard in your sailing area operates a system of contact for yachtsmen, it is wise to take advantage of it, but make certain that you remember to inform the coastguard on arrival or if your plans change, otherwise they may launch an unnecessary and expensive search operation.

What happens at night?

ON SEVERAL OCCASIONS, I have met non-sailors who imagine that all yachts and ships stop for the night, dropping anchor while the crew gets a good night's sleep! Of course, when you are coastal cruising, you will often stop for the night in a marina or anchorage, but on longer passages you will need to sail through the hours of darkness.

In fact, sailing at night can be a wonderful experience in good conditions and there is nothing quite like sailing across a sea made silver by moonlight, or experiencing the magic of phosphorescence sparkling in your bow wave and wake. But to fully enjoy the experience, you and your crew need to be well prepared for night sailing.

Sensible precautions

For your first night-time passage, try and have on board at least one crew member with experience in night sailing and make thorough preparations. It is important that all crew members who work on deck are familiar with the equipment and can find and use it in the dark. Make sure that the crew understand the watch system and stick to it so that they get sufficient rest. Retaining night vision is important and this is made easier if red lights, or at least very dim white ones, are used below decks.

■ **Sailing at night** *can be magical, but be prepared before the onset of darkness.*

Before it gets dark, there are a number of preparations you should make:

- Prepare and eat a hot meal, and wash up and stow all loose gear below
- Check the deck and stow any unnecessary equipment
- Make sure the on-watch crew dresses warmly and wears foul-weather gear if necessary
- Insist on safety harnesses being worn and clipped on when in the cockpit or on deck, even in calm weather
- Switch on and check the navigation lights at dusk, update your position on the chart, and complete any passage planning necessary to cover the hours of darkness
- Write instructions for the on-watch crew – such as course to steer or lights expected to be seen – in the log book or on a deck slate, and make sure that one or two torches are at hand in the cockpit

RECOGNIZING LIGHTS

At night, all vessels must display navigation lights according to their size and type. The International Regulations for Preventing Collisions at Sea (often referred to as the Col Regs) specify the type, size, layout, arc, and distance of visibility of lights to be used by all types of vessel. Various combinations indicate whether a boat is anchored or under way, under sail or power, fishing or trawling, or many other possibilities. You should have a detailed reference book on board. Make sure that you know all the common arrangements of lights and check that your boat's lights conform to the regulations. Always display the correct lights.

BASIC NAVIGATION LIGHTS

■ **Boats under** 23 ft (7 m) must show a white light if under sail or oars. If motoring, you need a fixed all-around light, unless your boat does over 7 knots, when you need the full lights below.

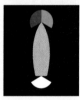

■ **Sailing boats** over 23 ft (7 m) must show red and green sidelights (over an arc of 112.5°) and a stern light (covering 135°). Under 65 ft (20 m), one tricolor light may be used at the masthead.

STEAMING LIGHTS

■ **Power boats** show the same side and stern lights as sailing boats plus a steaming light. A sailing boat under power must show a steaming light and may not use a tricolor light.

■ **Large power craft** show separate sidelights, a stern light, and two steaming lights, with the aft one higher than the forward one.

EXTRA ALL-AROUND LIGHTS

■ **A vessel trawling** shows these extra all-around lights on the mast.

■ **A vessel constrained** by her draught shows these additional all-around lights on the mast.

■ **A vessel fishing** shows these all-around lights on the mast.

■ **A vessel** minesweeping shows these additional all-around lights on the mast.

■ **A pilot vessel** on duty shows these additional lights on the mast.

■ **A vessel restricted** in its ability to maneuver shows these all-around lights on the mast.

Consider whether a sail change is needed and do this before darkness falls. It can be helpful to change to a smaller headsail, or roll away part of a rolling headsail to improve visibility, but don't sail undercanvassed in light weather.

Only an experienced crew should sail with a spinnaker at night, as it can be difficult to take it down in the dark. Plan to change to a poled-out headsail before nightfall.

The effects of darkness

At night, your perception of the boat's behavior may change. It may feel rougher than it is and it will be difficult to judge distances. Inexperienced crew may feel nervous and should be paired with an experienced crew. Keep a good lookout all around the boat, including immediately astern because ships can appear suddenly. Check the set of the sails by shining a flashlight on their luffs periodically, but do not wave the flashlight around or shine it in someone's eyes, as this will ruin their night vision.

Dealing with rough weather

THE BEST WAY TO DEAL WITH DIFFICULT CONDITIONS, especially when you are inexperienced, is to avoid them as much as possible. Sailing in rough weather can be fun and exciting but it also brings increased risk of gear failure and other accidents. Try to increase your experience of rough weather gradually and with an experienced sailor or instructor on board.

This may be easier said than done however, and it is always possible to be caught by bad weather that has not been accurately forecast. There is no strict rule for what constitutes heavy weather – a weak crew in a small cruiser may have a rough ride upwind in Force 5, while an experienced crew in a larger yacht would be comfortable in much stronger winds.

How you react to rough weather depends more on the size, type, and strength of your boat, the state of the sea, and whether you are sailing up- or downwind than it does on the strength of the wind.

Seeking shelter

The ideal situation is to reach a sheltered harbor before bad weather arrives but this may not be possible and it may even be dangerous to try to reach port. Don't head for harbor unless you are absolutely certain that the harbor is safe to enter in strong winds, with no off-lying shoals or other navigational dangers, and with no risk that you could end up on a lee shore if it is not possible to enter the harbor.

■ **Sailing this close to a lee shore** *in a fairly strong wind may be an acceptable risk when you are racing, but it could be dangerous.*

Avoid lee shores in heavy weather at all costs. A windward shore, even without a harbor but with a sheltered anchorage, can offer some protection while the bad weather passes.
However, you must be certain that the wind will not shift to turn the windward shore into a lee shore.

If you have any doubt about entering harbor, don't – stay at sea. Head offshore as quickly as possible and get as much sea room as possible between you and any potential lee shore.

Staying at sea

If you have to, or choose to, stay at sea you must prepare for the arrival of bad weather before conditions start to deteriorate. Assume that you will have to deal with heavy seas and take the following steps to prepare the boat to cope with them:

- Clear the decks of any loose and unnecessary gear, and double check the lashings on any equipment stowed on deck, such as a dinghy
- Close all ventilators that may leak, and fit the door boards in the companionway
- Ensure that everything is stowed securely down below
- Bring the logbook up to date and plot the latest position on the chart because navigation will get harder once rough weather arrives
- Study the chart and pilot book to examine your options, check on any dangers nearby, and plan your best course of action
- Pump the bilges before bad weather arrives and then at regular intervals
- If you don't have a permanent radar reflector, rig a removable one to increase your visibility to shipping
- Turn on your navigation lights if visibility deteriorates

As the wind increases, you should reef the mainsail and change or reef the headsail to keep the boat moving fast but comfortably without excessive heel. Keep the boat sailing fast before the bad weather arrives, especially if you are making for shelter.

Don't reduce sail to suit a forecast wind strength, but adjust the sail area on the basis of the wind you are actually experiencing.

Looking after the crew

The majority of cruising boats will take far more bad weather than most crews can cope with comfortably. Rough weather, high winds, and large waves can be frightening and the increased motion will be tiring. If your crew is to continue to perform well it is vital that they are kept warm, dry, and well fed and that they are given an active role in getting through the bad weather. Your crew should prepare by adding warm layers as necessary and donning foul-weather gear and boots.

Everyone on board must wear a safety harness. Check that these are properly adjusted and insist that the crew clip on whenever they are in the cockpit or on deck.

If possible, cook a hot meal before the bad weather arrives and prepare thermoses of soup and hot drinks, together with easy-to-eat but nutritious snacks, to sustain the crew once the motion makes it too difficult to cook. Make sure that anyone who needs an anti-seasickness tablet takes one as soon as bad weather is anticipated.

Bad-weather tactics

As skipper, you are responsible for determining the best course of action. You may choose to make for a safe harbor, anchor under a windward shore, or seek open water to ride out the bad weather well clear of the shore.

If your destination is downwind and there is no risk of arriving at a lee shore before the weather moderates, you can continue on course, reducing sail to suit the strength of the wind. A common tactic is to drop the mainsail completely and sail under a small jib. If the wind gets really strong and the boat starts to become difficult to control even under its smallest jib, you may end up sailing under bare poles. Many modern, shallow-hulled, fin-keeled cruisers will surf downwind quickly and comfortably in this way under the control of an experienced helmsman, but a less skillful person may have trouble steering accurately enough.

Heavier boat designs do not respond well to being driven fast downwind and you may lose control if the boat surfs on waves. In this case, you must slow the boat down.

Use your longest lines (joining them if necessary) and secure their ends to your headsail winches and cleats before dropping the bight over the stern. Tying an anchor to the middle of the bight can add weight and effectiveness. This arrangement should slow the boat down considerably and will help hold the boat in line with seas approaching from behind. Commercially made parachute drogues (parachute-shaped sea anchors made of a strong material) can be purchased to do a similar job.

Hove-to and lying a-hull

If your destination is upwind or across the wind, you must slow the boat down once it becomes too rough to continue sailing. The standard first step is to heave-to under a deeply reefed mainsail and storm jib. Most cruisers will lie at an angle of about 60–70° to the wind when hove-to. The motion will be eased considerably and the boat will rise to the seas while drifting slowly to leeward.

At some point, depending on the size and type of boat, the wind strength, and the wave height, it may become too uncomfortable or dangerous to stay hove-to. If you have plenty of sea room to leeward, you can consider running before the wind but otherwise you could decide to lie a-hull.

This means lowering all sails and lashing the tiller to leeward. Most boats will lie approximately beam-on to the seas and will be fairly comfortable as long as the seas aren't breaking. Once the waves start to break, there is a danger of the boat being knocked down or rolled. At this point, lying a-hull becomes dangerous and you will be forced to run downwind unless you can use your engine to help you.

If your engine is powerful enough, you can consider motorsailing on a close-hauled course with a deep-reefed main. Use the engine to provide sufficient steerageway so that you can point very close to the wind. The reefed mainsail will give some drive and will reduce the rolling motion. As each wave crest approaches, head up to point straight into it and then bear away a bit once the bow has gone through the crest. In very large and breaking seas, this may be the only option if you do not have sufficient sea room to run off downwind.

Reducing the terrors of fog

FOG CAN BE A GREATER DANGER *to a small boat than rough weather. When fog arrives, it reduces your visibility, possibly to near zero, and makes you vulnerable to collision, either with other craft or with the shore or other navigational hazard.*

If fog falls before you leave harbor, the best action is to stay put. Don't put to sea unless you are sure that conditions are clearing.

If fog is forecast, consider your options carefully. Putting to sea in busy coastal waters when fog is expected can be extremely hazardous.

SOUND SIGNALS

In fog, vessels indicate their presence by using sound signals, some of which are shown below. Many navigational aids, such as buoys and lighthouses, are also fitted with sound-signal equipment to help you identify them. Their signals are marked on charts and in pilot books. Sound can be distorted by fog so don't assume a direction for the sound; stop and listen to check, and proceed with caution.

KEY

▬▬ ▪ ▪ FOG HORN

○ GONG   ▲ BELL

▲▼▲▼ RAPID BELL-RINGING

■ **Under sail** (*and some other craft*), *use one long and two short blasts on the foghorn every 2 minutes.*

■ **Making way** *under power – the signal is one long blast on the foghorn every 2 minutes.*

■ **Under way** *but not making way (stopped in the water), use two long blasts every 2 minutes.*

■ **Aground** – *under 100 m (330 ft), use three bells, rapid ringing, three bells at 1-minute intervals.*

■ **Aground** – *over 330 ft (100 m), use three bells, rapid ringing, three bells, and a gong every minute.*

■ **At anchor** – *under 330 ft (100 m), use rapid ringing of the bell forward in the boat every minute.*

■ **At anchor** – *over 330 ft (100 m), use a rapid bell rung forward and a gong sounded aft at 1-minute intervals.*

■ **Pilot boat** *on duty uses four short blasts (after under way or making way) every 2 minutes.*

Immediate actions

If you are at sea when fog appears, immediately plot the boat's present position (see Chapter 23), plan a course of action, and hoist a radar reflector as high as possible (unless you have one permanently fitted).

All commercial vessels and many yachts use radar as a primary means of collision avoidance. It is in your best interest to ensure that you help them see you by using an effective reflector.

1. Turn on the yacht's navigation lights and delegate a member of the crew to make the appropriate sound signal with the foghorn.

2. Station extra lookouts with one on the foredeck. If you are motoring, the lookout on the foredeck should be as far away as possible from the noise of your engine so they can hear the sound of another boat's engine.

3. Make sure that all the crew put on lifejackets because there will be no time to find them if a collision should occur.

4. Check that the liferaft is ready for instant release if needed, and have some red and white hand flares available.

5. If the weather is calm, consider putting the dinghy over the side and towing it astern so that it is immediately available in the event of a collision.

6. If your yacht is fitted with radar, make sure it is turned on as soon as visibility deteriorates, and station a crew member with experience of reading a radar screen to monitor it. Don't rely on radar; you must still have lookouts on deck.

Recovery of a man overboard is likely to be impossible in fog, but think carefully before allowing the crew to clip on safety harnesses. Crew members down below should wear lifejackets and remain fully clothed so that they can get on deck instantly if necessary.

In the event of a collision, the crew must be able to jump clear, but if the weather is rough, the danger of falling overboard should be weighed up against the danger of wearing a harness.

Tactics in fog

Your choice of tactics will depend on whether you are close to land, in a busy shipping area, or well out to sea. In the latter case, you will continue on course, keeping a good lookout and making the appropriate sound signals.

If you are in or near a busy shipping lane, your first priority will be to get clear of it as quickly as possible. Plot a course (Chapter 23) to take you into shallow water, where large vessels won't be encountered. If you have to cross a shipping channel, do it at right angles as quickly as possible. Once in shallow water, you can either heave-to or anchor until the fog lifts. Remember that other small yachts may have the same idea.

Where possible, proceed under sail because the noise of an engine will prevent you from hearing other boats. If it is calm and you have to motor, do so at a reasonable speed so that you have good steerageway and can turn quickly if necessary. Stop the engine at regular intervals so that you can listen for the sound of other vessels or navigation aids. Keep the mainsail hoisted as this will make you more visible to another vessel.

If a harbor with a safe entrance is close at hand, you could consider making for it but you need to be confident in your navigation. You should not rely solely on a single electronic aid such as GPS to ensure your safe entry (see Chapter 21).

If, despite your best efforts, a large ship appears out of the fog and is heading straight for you, the first thing you'll probably see will be its white bow wave. In such a case, turn parallel to the ship's course (end on to the ship) and you'll have the best chance of the bow wave hurling the boat clear.

A simple summary

✔ Make sure that you have sufficiently experienced crew for the passage you are planning, and check all important parts of the boat before you sail.

✔ Set a watch system if the passage includes an overnight sail.

✔ Make sure you have sufficient food, water, and fuel on board for the expected length of the passage plus a margin for safety and unexpected developments.

✔ Before nightfall, prepare the boat and crew for sailing at night.

✔ Get used to dealing with rough weather with an experienced sailor or instructor to guide you.

✔ Don't leave harbor in a thick fog and, if possible, head for shallow water when you encounter fog at sea.

✔ Remember to make the appropriate sound signals in fog.

PART FIVE

USING NAVIGATION INSTRUMENTS

FINDING YOUR WAY

ONCE YOU START SAILING a cruiser in coastal waters or offshore, you need to be able to *find your way* across the sea just as navigators have done for centuries. Today, modern navigation aids make life much easier but the *essential skills* of reading a chart and fixing your position must still be learned. You will find out how to use charts and the magnetic compass, together with the *simple tools* used for working on a chart.

Most cruisers have a range of electronic instruments used to measure speed, depth, and wind speed and direction, together with position-fixing devices such as radar and GPS sets. As a proficient navigator you must be familiar with these tools, but you need to be able to do without them, if the technology fails.

Chapter 20

The Indispensable Chart

WHY INDISPENSABLE? Because whenever you need to find your way at sea, you can only do so safely with the aid of a chart. Whenever you sail beyond familiar local waters, it is essential that you have a selection of charts of various scales that cover the area and any harbors you may visit. Charts are produced by the hydrographic agencies of most maritime countries and by a number of commercial publishers in popular sailing areas. You can buy charts at most chandleries (marine stores) and you should make sure you have the most up-to-date version available. In addition to paper charts, you can also buy electronic chart systems.

In this chapter...

✓ Chart information

✓ Reading a chart

✓ Buoys to guide you

✓ Using a chart

✓ Electronic charts

STUDYING A NEW CHART OFFERS THE THRILL OF EXPLORATION AND NEW CRUISING ADVENTURES

Chart information

A KEY REQUIREMENT OF NAVIGATION is avoiding a close encounter of the hard kind, so one of the most important items of information on a chart is the position of the land. Modern charts usually use a color to indicate land above high water and other colors to indicate shallow areas, deep water, and land that is uncovered at low tide. Make sure you understand what the colors mean on the charts you use.

> **DEFINITION**
>
> *A chart is a nautical map. It is a representation of the surface of the globe on a flat sheet of paper. It concentrates on coastlines, the depth of water, and other physical features of interest to sailors.*

Depth and height

The depth of water is usually measured in meters (m) and tenths of a meter, but you may encounter some charts that use feet (ft) and fathoms (fm). A fathom is 6 ft (1.8 m). The chart's title information will also tell you what reference point – called chart datum – the depth measurements are taken from. The datum used, like the measurement units, may vary depending on the chart issuer, but is usually the lowest astronomical tide (LAT). This is the lowest level to which the tide is ever expected to fall. In most situations, the actual depth of water will be higher than shown on the chart because the tide rarely falls to its lowest level.

> *On a chart, the units used for measuring depth will be clearly shown, usually as part of the title information and also in the margins.*

Some objects marked on the chart, such as lighthouses, chimneys, mountain peaks, and rocks that are never covered by the tide have their heights marked alongside them. These heights are measured from the level of the water at mean high water spring tides (MHWS) – the average level of high water at spring tides – and are shown in feet or meters depending on the chart.

Objects that are periodically uncovered when the tide falls, such as rocks and wrecks, also have their heights marked against them on the chart, but the heights of these objects are measured from chart datum not from MHWS. The height on the chart will be underlined to show that it is a drying height.

> **INTERNET**
>
> **www.noaa.gov**
>
> *The National Oceanographic and Atmospheric Administration celebrated its 30th year of service in 2000. The official site includes the charts for US waters.*

Direction

The compass rose is one of the most obvious features on a chart, because it is prominent and repeated several times. It consists of two circles, one inside the other, marked in degrees – 0° to 360° – clockwise from north (north is indicated by 0° and 360°). Direction is measured in a clockwise direction relative to north using the 360° notation.

The direction that your boat is sailing in is called a heading. The direction of an object from your boat, or between two objects is called a bearing.

The meaning of "north"

The term "north" can have three meanings. Lines of longitude run north–south between the north and south geographic poles and because of this, charts are orientated to "true" north (°T). The outer compass rose is also orientated to true north.

We normally measure direction using a magnetic compass and this points to magnetic north (°M). Unfortunately, the magnetic north and south poles are not in the same place as the geographic poles and actually move over time, but their positions are known. The compass roses allow you to measure direction on the chart. The outer circle uses true north as its reference point, while the inner circle refers to magnetic north. There is a third type of north – compass north (°C) – but it is different for every compass! Although a compass should point to magnetic north, the presence of a magnetic object or an electrical current close to the compass will cause it to deviate to one side or other of magnetic north. This error is called deviation.

Most navigators use directions relative to magnetic north for chart work but some use true north. Always show which reference system you are using by appending a T or M to directions you write in the log book or on the chart – such as 180°T or 180°M.

Position

Horizontal and vertical lines run across a chart at regular intervals to form a grid. These are lines of latitude and longitude. The latitude lines run across the chart horizontally, east to west, and are called parallels of latitude. The longitude lines run vertically up and down the chart, north to south, and are called meridians of longitude.

■ **Only simple instruments** *are needed to work on the chart. A pencil, plotting instrument, and a pair of dividers are the items you will use most often.*

Latitude and longitude are measured in degrees (°), minutes ('), and tenths of a minute. There are 60' in 1°. The angle of a parallel of latitude is measured north or south from the equator, which is designated 0° latitude. The angle of a meridian of longitude is measured east or west of the prime meridian (0°), which runs through Greenwich in the United Kingdom and is often called the Greenwich meridian.

Thanks to latitude and longitude, we can describe the position of any point on the surface of the earth by giving its latitude and longitude. However, while lat and long – the commonly used abbreviations – are incredibly useful for defining position, it is often more convenient, when coastal sailing, to give a position with reference to a fixed land- or seamark using a direction and distance. For instance, if I was sailing in the Solent just off Cowes, England and wanted to give my position to someone, I could describe it as 180°M from South Bramble buoy, distance half a mile.

Reading a chart

WHEN YOU FIRST EXAMINE a chart, look at the title information and check the printing date to see how old it is. Always try to use the latest chart edition because some features may have changed. While coastlines do not change very often, man-made features alter frequently.

Keeping up to date

Because charts are expensive, whether in paper or electronic form, most of us tend to put off buying new ones. However, it is possible to update your old charts. Chart authorities issue lists of corrections, often on a weekly basis, that enable you to correct your charts. You can also return them to a chart agent for correction. To be frank, this is a worthy task but one that somehow I – and, I suspect, most sailors – rarely or never get around to. Use other references to double-check the chart information and always remain alert to the possibility of recent changes.

A chart is potentially out of date from the moment you buy it, so always treat information with caution.

Scale

Charts are published in a range of scales. Small-scale charts cover whole seas or oceans and are used for passage planning and plotting your position on long passages. Medium-scale charts are typically used to cover sections of coastline and are useful for giving coastal and offshore detail around your departure point and destination. Large-scale charts cover small areas in great detail and are essential when you are entering a strange harbor or navigating a difficult stretch of water. The scale of the chart is shown close to its title.

When entering harbor or navigating close to a difficult coastline, always use the largest scale chart available. Smaller-scale charts may not show some information that can be crucial when you are navigating close to dangers.

SYMBOLS

Charts supply a huge amount of information in a very small space – they do this by using symbols to represent items of interest and potential dangers. If you have the right sort of memory for this type of information, you may be able to learn many of the hundreds that can be found on the chart. However, if you are like me, you'll need to use a reference chart. Each chart publisher produces a reference chart – such as the US chart No. 1 – which carries an explanation for every symbol used by the publishing authority. Make sure that you have the appropriate reference chart on board because it is an indispensable aid.

 ■ **A limiting** *danger line marks the edge of the danger area.*

 ■ **Eddies** *show some water disturbance.*

 ■ **Obstruction** *of a known depth.*

 ■ **Obstruction** *swept to depth shown.*

■ **Overall** *tide rips with water surface disturbed.*

 ■ **Rock awash** *at chart datum.*

 ■ **Rock ledge** *with exact depth unknown.*

 ■ **Traffic-separation** *scheme indicates one-way traffic lanes.*

 ■ **Wreck** *with depth taken by sounding.*

 ■ **Wreck** *with depth unknown; thought to be safe.*

 ■ **Wreck** *swept by dredge to depth shown on chart.*

 ■ **Wreck** *showing part of its structure above chart datum.*

 ■ **Wreck** *that is considered dangerous to shipping.*

 ■ **Wreck** *that is not considered dangerous to shipping.*

Distance and speed

Distances at sea are measured in units called nautical miles. A nautical mile is defined as one minute (1') of latitude and can be measured using the latitude scale at the side of the chart nearest to your position.

Never use the longitude scale to measure distance because the meridians are not parallel — they curve in to meet at the poles. Therefore, 1' of longitude varies from 1 nautical mile at the equator, to zero at the poles.

Always measure distance on the latitude scale at the same level as your position on the chart, because the actual length of a nautical mile varies slightly. This is because the earth is not a perfect sphere and so 1' of latitude is slightly shorter at the equator and slightly longer at the poles. The length of a nautical mile has been standardized for ease of use by international agreement at 6,076 ft (1,852 m) – a bit longer than a standard mile. A nautical mile is subdivided into 10 cables, written as tenths of a mile, each cable being approximately 600 ft (183 m). When writing distances on the chart or in the logbook, use the abbreviation "M" for a nautical mile and "ca" for a cable.

Speed in knots

As you may remember from your school math, speed means distance covered in a certain time period. When we are on land, we describe our speed in terms of miles per hour or kilometers per hour. At sea, we describe our speed in terms of nautical miles per hour, but we have a special name for this unit – the knot. When writing speed on the chart or in the logbook we use the symbol "kn" for the knot.

Beginners often make the mistake of describing speed as knots per hour, but this immediately shows their lack of knowledge so please avoid this and remember that a knot is 1 nautical mile per hour.

Trivia...

Most cruising yachts use an electronic speedometer – called a knotmeter – which has a sensor – called a transducer – fitted through the hull. Don't be misled by the apparent accuracy of a digital readout. Unless the instrument is calibrated properly, it will not be as accurate as it appears.

Buoys to guide you

THE SYSTEM OF NAVIGATIONAL AIDS that marks hazards and safe water around our coasts and harbors is an invaluable asset to seamen. These sea- and land-based signposts have developed over centuries from local systems that used their own choice of shapes and colors, into a standardized system agreed by international convention. In practice, there are two systems in use.

The International Association of Lighthouse Authorities governs the two systems; IALA system A, which is used in Europe, Africa, India, Australia, and most of Asia, and IALA system B, which is used in North, Central and South America, Japan, Korea, and the Philippines.

The two navigational aid systems differ only in that IALA A uses red port and green starboard lateral marks, while in IALA B the colors are reversed.

Lateral marks

The edges of channels are indicated by buoys called lateral marks. Channels are marked according to the direction of buoyage which, in the case of rivers and estuaries, is usually in the direction of harbor from seaward.

Around coastlines, buoyage is typically arranged in a clockwise direction, but where the direction of buoyage is not obvious it is always marked on charts. Buoys are often numbered, starting from seaward with even numbers on red marks and odd numbers on green marks (in the IALA B system). In the US, the rule "red light returning" usually applies.

If a light is fitted to a lateral mark it will be red for a starboard-hand mark or green for a port-hand mark (in IALA B).

IALA A lateral marks

■ **Port-hand marks** *are usually can shaped but a spar (pole) may be used. A topmark, if fitted, will be can shaped.*

■ **Starboard-hand marks** *are usually conical but a spar may be used. A topmark, if fitted, will also be conical or triangular.*

IALA B lateral marks

■ **Port-hand marks** *are conical but a spar may also be used. Topmarks, if used, are conical or triangular.*

■ **Starboard-hand marks** *are can or spar shaped and a topmark, if fitted, will also be can shaped.*

Night-time navigation

Navigation at night is made easier by the use of lights to identify buoys, shore beacons, and lighthouses. Buoys have short-range lights with a range of about 2 miles (3 km). Larger light floats or shore beacons have a 3- to 10-mile (5- to 16-km) range, and lighthouses have long-range lights that are visible for about 20 miles (32 km).

Understanding light sequences

Each kind of buoy is lit differently, and the characteristic of each light is marked on nautical charts and in books called sailing directions. The main colors are white, red, green, and yellow, but purple, blue, and orange lights are also used.

In addition, a flashing pattern is used to assist in identification. The main light sequences are shown in the diagram on the right. "Occulting" means that the dark periods are shorter than the flashes of light, while "isophase" means that the periods of light and darkness in the sequence are of equal length.

The abbreviations feature on charts and you should become familiar with them. The number in brackets after a light sequence abbreviation indicates the number of flashes in that sequence. If the letter "s" appears after a number, this relates to the number of seconds that dictates the frequency of the sequence. For example, "FL VQ (9) 10s" means "Very quick flashing nine times, every 10 seconds."

For accuracy, use a stopwatch to check the timing of a light sequence and time it through three full sequences.

When you approach a harbor at night against a backdrop of shore lights, it can be difficult to pick out a particular buoy. Always double-check to be certain. When you are close to a buoy, check the chart for the bearing to the next one and then look along the bearing using a hand bearing compass.

Common light sequences

⊢―――――⊣ *Period of light sequence*

OC: OCCULTING

OC(2): GROUP OCCULTING

OC(2+3): COMPOSITE GROUP OCCULTING

ISO: ISOPHASE

FL: FLASHING

L FL: LONG FLASH

FL(3): GROUP FLASHING

FL(2+1): COMPOSITE GROUP FLASHING

Q: QUICK FLASHING

Q(3): GROUP QUICK FLASHING

IQ: INTERRUPTED QUICK FLASHING

VQ: VERY QUICK FLASHING

VQ(3): GROUP VERY QUICK FLASHING

IVQ: INTERRUPTED VERY QUICK

UQ: ULTRA QUICK FLASHING

IUQ: INTERRUPTED ULTRA QUICK FLASHING

Cardinal marks

Cardinal marks are used to mark isolated or individual dangers and are named according to the direction that they are placed in relation to the danger they mark. A north cardinal mark is placed to the north of the danger and you should keep to the north of the mark. Keep to the south of a south cardinal, and so on.

The cardinal marks all use two black cone topmarks placed one above the other. At night, sequences of white lights are used to indicate which quadrant the buoy is in.

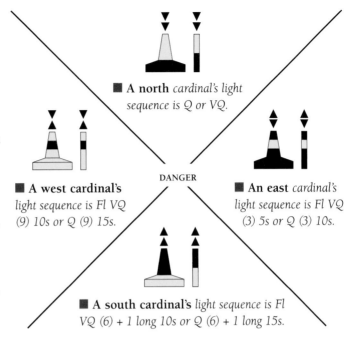

■ **A north** *cardinal's light sequence is Q or VQ.*

■ **A west cardinal's** *light sequence is Fl VQ (9) 10s or Q (9) 15s.*

DANGER

■ **An east** *cardinal's light sequence is Fl VQ (3) 5s or Q (3) 10s.*

■ **A south cardinal's** *light sequence is Fl VQ (6) + 1 long 10s or Q (6) + 1 long 15s.*

■ **Cardinal marks** *are pillar or spar shaped and are painted black and yellow – color combinations and topmark arrangements vary according to their position relative to the danger they are marking. At night, cardinal marks are identifiable by white light sequences.*

■ **An isolated danger mark** *[white light, Fl (2)] is used to mark a small, solitary danger that is surrounded by safe water.*

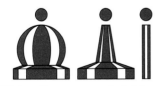

■ **A safe water mark** *[white light, Iso, Oc, or long Fl 10s] is used to mark the middle of wide channels or as a landfall mark.*

Other marks

While the lateral and cardinal marks are the most common buoys, there are others that are used to mark isolated dangers, safe water, and junctions in channels. Special marks are used to indicate certain designated areas, such as water-ski areas or military-exercise areas. They are not primarily intended to assist navigation but where a can, conical, or spherical shape is used it is intended to indicate the side on which you should pass.

Aids to navigation also include land-based signposts, the most prominent of which are the lighthouses that mark many headlands and other dangerous sections of coast. Lighthouses, and some other beacons, use colored sector lights to indicate safe and dangerous areas. The details of the colors and sector angles of these lights will be given on the chart.

Using a chart

THE BEST PLACE TO WORK ON A CHART *is on a proper chart table, but you can use the salon table if you wish or any other convenient flat surface. Most chart tables are not large enough to take a full chart, so fold the chart if necessary, making sure that you can still see one of the latitude scales at the edge of the chart and a compass rose.*

Arrange the chart on the chart table with the lines of longitude pointing straight up. It is less confusing for most people to work on the chart with north upward, although some people like to turn it so that their course points upward.

Don't be afraid to write on the chart, but make sure that you only use a soft pencil so that your notes and markings can be easily erased after each passage.

Have a number of soft pencils close to the chart table, together with a good-quality eraser and a pencil sharpener.

An important use of the chart is to measure direction and distance. To do this, you will use the latitude scale and the compass rose together with some simple tools called plotting instruments.

Using a chart on deck

Sometimes you want to use a chart on deck, especially when entering or leaving harbor, or during a tricky passage among rocks or shallow water. This avoids having to run backward and forward between the chart table and the cockpit but means that you need to control and protect the chart. If there is any wind, the chart may be blown overboard, and any rain or spray will reduce it to a soggy mess in no time. You can avoid losing or ruining an important chart if you use a plastic cover to protect it. If the cover has a hard back, it will be easier to use the chart on your knees in the cockpit.

■ **When racing, especially in small boats,** *there is sometimes no choice but to use a chart on deck. Protect it with a cover or the chart will be ruined very quickly.*

Electronic charts

YOU CAN BUY ELECTRONIC CHARTS to use with an instrument called a chart plotter or with chart-plotting software. They allow you to navigate on screen and to combine electronic information with the detail on the chart.

Chart plotters display chart information on screen and allow you to identify positions, courses, and distances. You can zoom in or out to alter the area covered, and can overlay data from a GPS set (Global Positioning System) or radar – which we will meet in the next chapter – on the electronic chart. The position shown by your GPS set can be shown directly on the chart, or the radar image can be compared to the details on the chart. The best systems have different types of chart information on different layers and you can turn layers on or off to display just the information you require on screen.

Using electronic systems with care

Many of these systems offer useful features, but they are also relatively costly and are vulnerable to power failure, especially in small yachts. If you choose one of these systems, be prepared to learn to use it properly. Although digital systems give the impression of great accuracy, this should not be assumed unless information can be checked using another source. Using these systems is not an alternative to learning to navigate with simple manual tools and techniques. Paper charts must always be on-board as a back-up in the event of equipment failure.

A compromise between an electronic chart and a paper chart is a digitizing pad used under a conventional paper chart. This allows you to use an electronic mouse or puck on the paper chart to measure directions and distances electronically.

A simple summary

✓ Always have the proper charts on board for the passage you are planning.

✓ Study your charts, familiarize yourself with the symbols, and get used to the key features.

✓ Use a soft pencil to write on charts and protect the chart if you have to use it in the cockpit.

✓ Electronic charts offer useful features, but they are not as fail-safe as paper charts.

Chapter 21

Basic Navigation Tools

DESPITE ALL THE HYPE ABOUT ELECTRONIC SYSTEMS, it is good to know that only the most basic tools are actually required for navigation. The introduction of the Global Positioning System (GPS) has simplified navigation and contributed greatly to safety, but there are times when you may be forced to do without this aid, and you should have the skills necessary to revert to traditional navigation techniques that have guided sailors for centuries. Once you have learned them, you will have a better understanding of how to use the electronic tools and will have the skills to remain safe when, not if, these tools fail.

In this chapter...

✓ The compass guides your way

✓ Equipment for chart work

✓ Navigation instruments

273

USING A HAND BEARING COMPASS TO FIX YOUR POSITION IS A SATISFYING SKILL TO LEARN

The compass guides your way

THE COMPASS IS *your most important navigation instrument. You use a compass to steer a course and to take bearings of shore objects and navigational marks when you need to check your position. You can also use it to check the bearing of another vessel to avoid a collision.*

Compass types

Most yachts need two types of compass: a steering compass for steering a course, and a hand bearing compass for taking bearings of objects and other vessels. A steering compass may be mounted on a *binnacle* or on the bulkhead between the cockpit and cabin.

To read a steering compass, check the course against a reference mark, called a lubber line. It is important that the compass is mounted with the lubber line on, or parallel to, the boat's fore and aft line so that the course can be read accurately.

■ **A binnacle compass** *is read from above by reading the course against the lubber line.*

When you use a hand bearing compass, hold the compass up to the eye or at arm's length (depending on the type) and read the bearing on the card against the lubber line. The way a compass card is marked varies with the size and design of the compass, but usually there is a clear mark every 5° and the appropriate number every 10°. Depending on its design, the card will be marked on its top surface, its edge, or both.

Electronic fluxgate compass

Another type of compass found on yachts is an electronic fluxgate compass. This uses an electronic circuit to sense the lines of magnetic force. The reading is displayed as a digital readout to the nearest degree. The apparent high accuracy implied by this readout should be treated with some scepticism. Fluxgate compasses are sensitive to being aligned horizontally in both directions, otherwise significant errors can arise that are not apparent from the readout. Fluxgate compasses are available for both steering and hand bearing uses and are also used to deliver course information to other electronic instruments such as an autopilot, chart plotters, GPS, and radar sets.

Magnetic variation

A compass shows the direction of magnetic north – not true north to which charts are oriented. The position of magnetic north is known, however, as is the amount by which it moves annually, so directions can be converted between true and magnetic north.

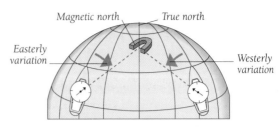

■ **The amount and direction** *of magnetic variation depends on the boat's position.*

The angular difference between magnetic and true north is called variation and its amount and direction – either east or west – depends on where you are located on the earth. The amount of local variation and its rate of change is marked on the chart's compass rose. When you have to convert between true and magnetic bearings, use the compass rose or addition or subtraction.

To convert from °T to °M ADD westerly variation and SUBTRACT easterly variation. To convert from °M to °T ADD easterly variation and SUBTRACT westerly variation.

Magnetic deviation

Compasses are affected by the close presence of ferrous metal (such as the engine) and electrical equipment, which put out magnetic fields. The result of this interference can deflect the compass card from magnetic north. This error is called deviation and can be measured and compensated for.

Deviation is either east or west of magnetic north depending on the boat's heading. Deviation varies depending on the relative positions of the source of interference, the compass, and magnetic north.

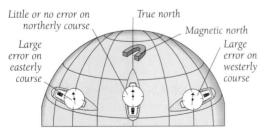

■ **Deviation** *here is caused by the closeness of the engine to the compass and varies with the course.*

If your steering compass is mounted well away from any sources of interference, you may have zero deviation. One way to check deviation is to have the helmsman steer an accurate course of due north (000°C) and use a hand bearing compass to sight along the centerline of the boat, while standing clear of any possible interference – behind the helmsman is usually best.

Note the course steered and the reading from the hand bearing compass. Turn to 030°C and repeat. Continue recording bearings every 30° until you have completed a full 360°.

Now plot the results on graph paper. This is your deviation card, which is used to convert between the course shown by your compass and the magnetic bearing. The required figure can be read off the deviation curve or arrived at by simple arithmetic:

To convert from °M to °C ADD westerly deviation and SUBTRACT easterly deviation. To convert from °C to °M ADD easterly deviation and SUBTRACT westerly deviation

Steering a compass course

Steering a compass course can cause confusion. There is a simple rule to follow:

- If the number on the compass is higher than the required course, turn to port
- If the number on the compass is lower than the required course, turn to starboard

Equipment for chart work

YOU NEED ONLY A FEW TOOLS to work on a paper chart. Use soft pencils to avoid permanently marking the chart. The 2B type produces a dark line that is easily erased. Hexagonal pencils resist rolling off the chart table when the boat heels. You will also need a pencil sharpener and a soft eraser.

DRAWING COMPASSES   DIVIDERS

PLOTTER

■ **Chart instruments** *include drawing compasses, a pair of dividers, and a plotter.*

You will frequently need to measure the direction between two points or to draw a line on the chart to indicate a course to steer or a bearing of an object. This is achieved by using a traditional instrument called a parallel ruler, or with a more modern instrument called a plotter. Another common requirement is to measure the distance between two points. This is usually achieved by using dividers, which have two adjustable metal arms. Buy dividers that are at least 6 inches (15 cm) long so that you can measure a reasonable span on the chart.

INTERNET

www.raymarine.com
www.greenham-regis.com

These sites are good starting points when looking for electronic instruments.

Measuring direction

A parallel ruler consists of two rulers held by two hinged arms that allow the rulers to be "walked" across the chart. Imagine that you wish to measure the direction between two points:

● Lay the parallel rulers on the chart so that one edge touches the two points
● Hold one of the rulers firmly and slide the other toward the nearest compass rose
● When the hinged arms are fully extended, hold the ruler you have just moved so that it cannot move further, and slide the other toward it
● Repeat the process of "walking" the rulers across the chart towards the compass rose
● When one ruler reaches the compass rose, align its edge with the center of the rose and read off the direction against the inner, magnetic rose or the outer, true rose
● If the rulers slipped, start the process again

If you want to transfer a direction from the compass rose to another part of the chart, use the same technique but start at the compass rose by aligning the rulers on the true or magnetic direction you require. Then walk the ruler across the chart until one edge is aligned with the point from which you wish to draw the direction line. A plotter achieves the same result, but it is easier and more accurate for most people to use on a small boat's chart table because it does not have to be moved across the chart. There are several different makes of plotter with variations on the same theme but the Breton, Hurst, and Portland plotters are among the most popular. Different instruments are used in slightly different ways, so study the instructions for the one you buy.

Plotters are used in conjunction with the grid of latitude and longitude lines marked on the chart, rather than with the compass roses. The plotter is engraved with its own compass rose and a square grid of lines, any of which can be lined up with a line of latitude or longitude on the chart to orientate the plotter to true north. Once the plotter has been aligned with a line of latitude or longitude, its straight edge is then lined up with the required bearing to be measured and the bearing is read off from the plotter's compass rose.

Measuring distance

In order to measure distance on a chart, you need to be able to compare the distance between two points with the latitude scale on the side of the chart. Use the dividers to measure distance by transferring the length to be measured to the latitude scale at the side of the chart.

Singlehanded dividers, with a bowed shape at the top, are much easier to use than the straight type that require two hands for opening and closing.

Another way to measure distance is to use the ruler scale on the edge of a parallel ruler or plotter. Measure the distance using the scale on the ruler and then move the ruler to the latitude scale to find the distance. Sometimes you may need to be able to draw an arc of a circle at a certain radius on the chart. Keep a simple pair of drawing compasses at the chart table for this purpose.

Keeping a logbook

One item that is essential is a logbook. This is used to record time, position, course, distance run, and other important information that you may need to record. Whenever you head out on a longer passage or if the visibility threatens to close in, you should update the logbook at regular intervals. In fact, it is a requirement of maritime law that you keep a log and you could be required to produce yours in the event of an incident at sea.

The format you use for your logbook is entirely up to you. It is not necessary to buy a commercially produced logbook, and many experienced navigators make their own by simply ruling a few columns in a cheap notebook or on loose-leaf sheets inserted into a ring binder. Try and keep your entries as neat as possible because you may need to refer back to them on passage. Be disciplined about recording the key information at half-hourly or hourly intervals when cruising close to shore, or at less frequent intervals when well offshore.

A rough notebook is handy for calculations and notes, and some skippers use a deck log for use by the crew on watch, with the information transferred at intervals to the main logbook.

Other equipment

Reading the symbols on a chart can be difficult, especially at night, and you may find it useful to have a magnifying glass on hand. You should also have a light source situated where it can illuminate the chart without spreading light too widely and interfering with the off-watch crew, who may be trying to sleep.

Reference books are needed to supplement the information contained on charts. Your main reference book should be a current nautical almanac that covers your sailing area. You may need other publications depending on your cruising area. Various types of pilot books or sailing directions are available, and these give you useful information on passage making, anchorages, or harbors you may wish to use, and ports of refuge.

Although tidal information will be shown on your charts, you may prefer to carry a tidal atlas for your sailing area. This will show the direction and rate of tidal currents in pictorial form, which can be easier to interpret than the information on charts.

Navigation instruments

DESPITE THE MASS of electronic navigation aids that are available for small boats, there are only a few instruments that are essential for successful navigation. You need some means to measure distance sailed, which together with your compass will provide all the essential information.

A depth sounder is a prudent addition, although even this can be replaced by a simple hand lead line for measuring depth in shallow water. Most sailors, however, choose to add extra instruments that provide more information for performance enhancement, position fixing, and collision avoidance.

SPEED

DEPTH

WIND

■ **Performance instruments** *typically used on many yachts include an electronic log to show speed and distance covered, a depth sounder, and a wind speed and direction instrument.*

Electronic aids don't remove the need to learn and use the basic skills. You should never rely on them exclusively as all are liable to fail at some time.

Distance and speed

Distance sailed is measured by an instrument called a log. Electronic instruments show speed as well, but this is not necessary other than for interest, performance monitoring, and for predicting the distance that will be sailed in the next hour.

Most yachts are fitted with some form of electronic log that uses a small paddle wheel impeller mounted through the hull and connected to the electronics in the display head. The impellers are usually retractable so they can be cleared of weed when necessary.

Depth

The simplest form of depth sounder is a lead line – a light line tied to a piece of lead or other weight. You should always carry one as a back-up and for measuring depth in shallow water. A lead line is traditionally marked with specific types and colors of material but you can devise any marking system that suits you. A 50-ft (15-m) length of line marked with knots will suffice. The traditional lead has a hollowed bottom that can be armed (filled) with tallow or grease, to enable you to collect a sample of the seabed.

Most yachts use an electronic depth sounder that works by sending out pulses of sound toward the bottom and measuring the time taken for them to be reflected back.

Most electronic depth sounders can display depth in meters, feet, or fathoms and many have deep and shallow water alarm settings.

■ **GPS instruments** *can be bought as a stand-alone set or incorporated into a powerful chart plotter.*

Position finding

The Global Positioning System (GPS) is the US military's satellite-based positioning system that has revolutionized navigation at sea and on land. GPS sets and their antennae are small and are available in hand-held units. They receive signals from a network of 24 satellites and can show your position to an accuracy of within 100 ft (30 m) or better.

GPS receivers provide a digital readout of position in latitude and longitude or as a bearing and distance from a chosen position. The latter is often easier to use for plotting position.

Receivers can be programmed with 100 or more waypoints – positions of charted objects or turning marks on your course. GPS units also offer several other functions. These include showing course and speed over the ground.

Trivia...
Before the advent of GPS, two other systems, Decca and Loran, were used to provide position fixes. These land-based-radio position-finding systems have been superseded by the popular worldwide use of GPS.

A man overboard function is usually available. On pressing a "panic button," the unit will store the current position and show a course back to that spot. If you have to use this emergency facility, remember that the man overboard will drift with the tide or current from the position shown.

Radar is another electronic system that can be used for position fixing, as well as its main function – collision avoidance. A radar set consists of an antenna that transmits signals and receives reflections from the shore, buoys, or other vessels, and a display unit usually mounted at the chart table. Today's sets are small enough and sufficiently frugal with power to be fitted to most yachts over about 35 ft (11 m).

Radar provides a bearing and range (distance) between the yacht and any objects displayed by the radar. If the object is marked on a chart you can use the range and bearing to plot your position. Radar's accuracy is far better at determining range than bearing however, so the best sort of radar fix uses three ranges of charted objects.

If the object is another vessel, you can determine its course and speed and whether or not it represents a collision risk. This feature is particularly useful in restricted visibility or in crowded shipping lanes.

In my opinion, a radar set is potentially the most useful electronic tool aboard a yacht.

■ **A radar reflector** *should be used by every yacht sailing in coastal or offshore waters to help increase the yacht's visibility to ships' radar sets.*

When a chart plotter is connected to a GPS set, the boat's position can be displayed directly onto the electronic chart. Hook a radar set into the system and the radar image can be superimposed on the chart, either on the plotter's display or the radar display. The system can even be connected to an electronic autopilot to automatically steer the boat between waypoints on the electronic chart (using GPS information to keep the boat on track) and manage any required course alterations.

A simple summary

✔ A compass is the most important navigation instrument.

✔ Only a few simple tools are required for working on a chart.

✔ Pick from a range of reference books to find the ones you need for your cruising area.

✔ There are many electronic navigation instruments available, but the essential one is the basic log that measures distance sailed.

✔ If you choose to fit more sophisticated instruments, a GPS and radar set are the most useful tools aboard a cruising boat.

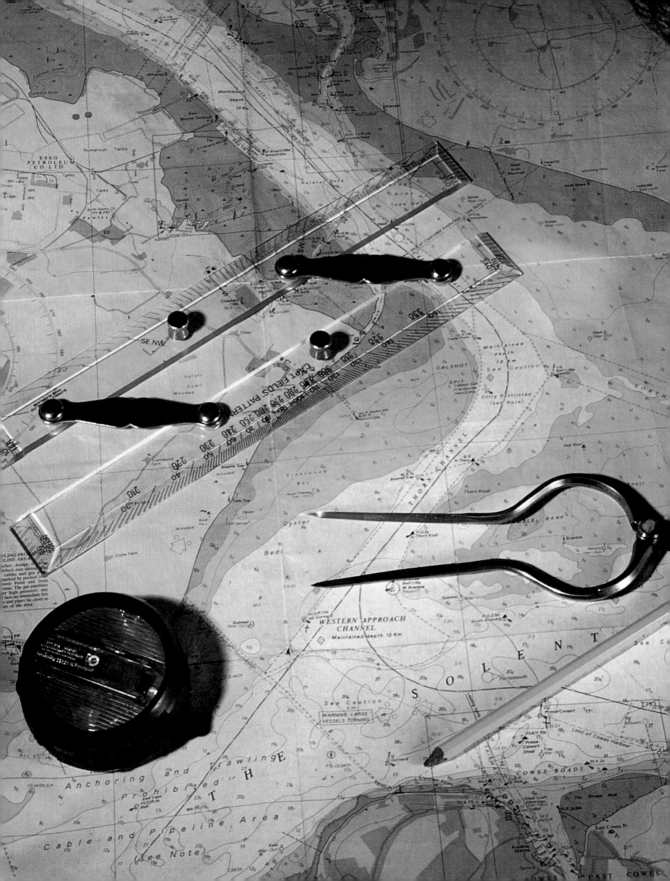

Chapter 22

In and Out of Harbor

GETTING SAFELY IN AND OUT OF HARBOR can be one of the hardest parts of navigating a yacht on passage. These are the times when you will be closest to the hazards of the shore, shallow water, and other shipping. Before you start a passage, remember the six Ps – Perfect Planning Prevents Pitifully Poor Performance. Do your homework and identify as much of the information you need as possible before you head off.

In this chapter...

✓ Plan your passage

✓ Know the height of tide

✓ The art of pilotage

✓ Using the depth sounder

✓ Making a landfall

SAFE PILOTAGE REQUIRES ONLY A CHART, SIMPLE INSTRUMENTS, AND A FEW REFERENCE BOOKS

Plan your passage

THE BEST TIME TO START *planning a passage is well before the actual trip. The worst time is as you drop the mooring and head out of the harbor! Take your charts and reference books home with you, and spend a few pleasant evenings planning your next cruise and extracting all the information you will need for each passage.*

Plotting waypoints

To start planning a passage, use a chart of a scale small enough to show both the departure point and destination. Use a pencil to draw the track (the course you want to follow) and then write down the latitude and longitude of any point where you will need to make a course alteration – called a waypoint. If you have a GPS, you can enter the waypoints into the set and it will calculate the course and distance between each waypoint. Pick your own waypoints, suitably chosen to be clear of hazards, and double-check their latitude and longitude before you program them into your electronic aids.

Don't use waypoints published in pilot books or the almanac. Occasionally, publishing errors will cause the wrong latitude or longitude to be printed, but, more likely, other small boat navigators will use the published waypoints and may all be converging on the same point!

Checking for hazards

Carefully check along the track between each waypoint to make sure it is clear of any dangers en route. Adjust it, if necessary, to give you the appropriate searoom. If the weather is rough, you may want to change your route to give you greater searoom from a coastline or areas of rough water. Make a note of any traffic scheme for shipping near your track, and if you have to cross one, plan to do so at right angles to the lane.

When you're happy with the track, measure the total distance and the distance between turning points or waypoints. Keep notes that you can refer to later. A GPS set can fail and it is a good idea to have notes on paper if you have to navigate without the GPS. It is worth writing up passage notes before the trip, including track bearings and distances between waypoints, and details of navigation marks that you expect to see along the track. Note down the times and heights of low and high water for the days you will be sailing and mark up the tidal atlas with the correct times on each page, starting at the page for high water. Aim to know all the details of the passage well before you start.

Know the height of tide

IF YOU SAIL ON TIDAL WATERS, you will need to be able to find out what the height of the tide is at various times or to find out what time the tide will reach a certain height. You can get this information from a number of sources. Most harbors issue their own tide tables with tidal information given for every day of the year, but the most useful information will be found in a nautical almanac. This will usually include some tidal information on every port in the area covered by the almanac.

The information provided for each major port (known as a standard port) usually includes the time and height of high and low water for every day of the year. To help you find out the depth at any time between high and low water, the almanac often has a graphical tidal curve that allows you to calculate easily the information you need.

It is often impractical for an almanac to include tidal curves for every harbor in its area of coverage. In this case, the information for the smaller ports (known as secondary ports) is found by applying a set of corrections, called tidal differences, to the time or height figures for the closest standard port. Different almanacs may use slightly different systems for finding tidal time and height information, so read the instructions in your almanac carefully and practice with a few examples before using it for real.

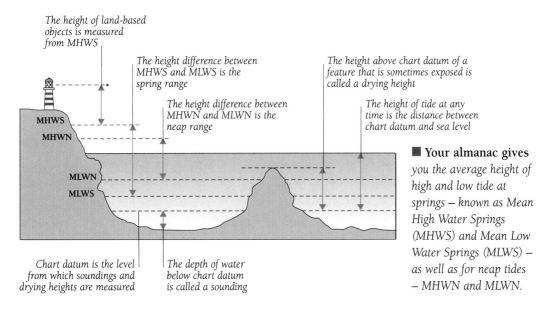

The height of land-based objects is measured from MHWS

The height difference between MHWS and MLWS is the spring range

The height difference between MHWN and MLWN is the neap range

The height above chart datum of a feature that is sometimes exposed is called a drying height

The height of tide at any time is the distance between chart datum and sea level

MHWS
MHWN
MLWN
MLWS

Chart datum is the level from which soundings and drying heights are measured

The depth of water below chart datum is called a sounding

■ **Your almanac gives** *you the average height of high and low tide at springs – known as Mean High Water Springs (MHWS) and Mean Low Water Springs (MLWS) – as well as for neap tides – MHWN and MLWN.*

To find the depth of water at a particular spot, you must add the height of tide to the depth at chart datum shown for that spot.

TIDES						
0000 Dover; ML3.7; Duration 0505; Zone 0 (UT)						

Standard port DOVER

Times						
High Water	Low water		MHWS	MHWN	MLWN	MLWS
0000 0600	0100 0700		6.8	5.3	2.1	0.8
1200 1800	1300 1900					

Differences DEAL

+0010 +0020	+0010 +0005	-0.6	-0.3	0.0	0.0

■ **Here, the time** *of high and low water at Deal, in the UK, together with the heights of high and low water at spring and neap tides can be found from the standard port Dover.*

Rule of Twelfths

If you are sailing in an area where the tide rises and falls in a symmetrical way over a 6-hour period, you can use a rough guide, known as the Rule of Twelfths, to obtain height or time information. This is suitable for many areas and where high accuracy is not required, but it should be used with caution.

First, find the range by subtracting the height of low water from the height of high water, then divide the range by 12. The rule says the tide will rise or fall:

- 1st hour $\frac{1}{12}$ of the range
- 2nd hour $\frac{2}{12}$ of the range
- 3rd hour $\frac{3}{12}$ of the range
- 4th hour $\frac{3}{12}$ of the range
- 5th hour $\frac{2}{12}$ of the range
- 6th hour $\frac{1}{12}$ of the range

If the times and heights of HW and LW from the tide tables are: HW = 0015, 6.2 m, LW = 0620, 1.4 m, then the range = 4.8 m (6.2 – 1.4).

What height of tide will there be at 0415, or 4 hours after HW? By the rule of twelfths, the tide will drop one-twelfth of 4.8 m (0.4 m) in the first hour, two-twelfths of 4.8m (0.8 m) in the second hour, and three-twelfths of 4.8 m (1.2 m) in both the third and fourth hours. Therefore, the tide will fall 3.6 m (0.4 + 0.8 + 1.2 + 1.2) from high water by 1515 so the height of tide (above chart datum) will be 6.2 m – 3.6 m = 2.6 m

Now that you understand how to calculate the height of tide at any time (or the time for a given height), you can use this skill to check the depth of water at any point on your track, or when entering or leaving harbor.

The art of pilotage

PILOTAGE IS AN ART because it involves a creative approach to finding your way using just your eyes, a chart, and a compass. You use pilotage techniques when within sight of land such as when negotiating harbors. At these times, you need to be on deck rather than at the chart table. You don't have time to plot fixes on the chart, and tidal current data isn't accurate enough in a situation where a small error can be the difference between safe water and a hazard.

A chart plotter can be handy in these circumstances but only if you can see it clearly from the helm. Even then, you should still be using pilotage techniques as confirmation. Your aim is to determine a series of safe tracks that will take you between hazards to your destination. You need to be able to confirm at any time that your boat is on or close to these tracks, without having to plot a position on the chart. Two types of bearing are useful for pilotage. The first is the bearing of the safe track between hazards and the other is a clearing line. The bearing of a safe track or a clearing line can be measured by compass or, more simply and effectively, with a *transit* (also called a range).

TRANSITS

Transits are often constructed to mark "leading lines" that identify the safe passage into and out of a harbor. Natural transits are more numerous, and examination of the chart will often identify several prominent land- or seamarks that you can use as transits along your track. Transits don't have to line up exactly to be useful.

■ **To clear** *the rocks at the entrance, the lighthouse and rock should be kept in transit or closed until you turn into the cove.*

CLOSED
TRANSIT

IN
TRANSIT

OPEN
TRANSIT

A clearing line is used to keep you to one side or other of a hazard. Stay on the correct side of the clearing line and you are certain to be in safe water.

You can measure a compass bearing with the hand bearing or steering compasses. If the boat can be pointed at the object, the steering compass can be used but otherwise the hand bearing compass must usually be used.

Check the chart carefully to identify useful transits along your track and use these as clearing lines or to mark the safe track wherever possible.

Study the chart and harbor plans to determine the safe track and identify suitable transits near your course. Identify all the navigation marks you expect to see on the route and check for dangers close to your course. Don't trust your memory, but use a notebook to jot down all the key details.

Note down all the land- or seamarks or other significant features you expect to see. Include their distance from the track and note the bearings of any clearing lines. If you're piloting at night, write down the light characteristics of all lit marks in the area.

Try and avoid using the chart on deck. It is difficult to keep under control in a breeze and will be ruined quickly in the cockpit. If your course is from north to south, it can be difficult to interpret the chart upside down.

Prepare a pilotage plan for use on deck. The way you do this is a matter of personal choice, but your plan should include courses to steer for each leg of the course with distances between turning points and navigation marks.

Sticking to the plan

Once you are under way and following your passage plan, cross off each feature on your note plan as you pass it and concentrate on knowing where you are in relation to the safe track. Aim to move from one safe position to another, and be careful to double-check each observation you make, by eye or compass. It is easy to get complacent and make false assumptions, especially when you are tired, so be careful to avoid making your observations fit your expectations.

INTERNET

www.fijiyachting.com/ nav.html

There are many resources on the Web that can help you when passage planning, such as this site describing navigation in Fiji.

Using the depth sounder

THE DEPTH SOUNDER IS A VERY USEFUL navigation tool, but it is often overlooked by inexperienced navigators. A depth sounding, or a series of soundings, can often be used to check other information or to obtain a position line directly.

For instance, if your safe track takes you across a significant deep patch of water, you can use the depth sounder to tell you when you have reached that spot and thus confirm your distance along your track.

Remember that before you can use the depth sounder in this way, you must know the height of tide accurately above chart datum. Your depth sounder will read the total depth of water at that time so, to compare it with the depth marked on the chart, you must deduct the height of tide above chart datum from the echo sounder reading. This process is called a reduction to soundings and it is important to carry it out whenever you are using the depth sounder to check or fix your position.

Make sure that you know whether the depth sounder reads the depth from the surface, the bottom of the keel, or from the transducer. The unit can be calibrated to read from any of these, but it helps to avoid confusion if it shows the depth from the surface.

■ **Keep an eye on the depth** *whenever you are sailing close to the shore or in an area of shallow water. Most depth sounders have an adjustable alarm that can be used to warn you of shallow water.*

Making a landfall

LEAVING A HARBOR IS USUALLY SIMPLER *than approaching one,
especially if you haven't visited it before. Identifying land- or seamarks as you
approach a coast can be difficult, even in good conditions, and in restricted
visibility it can be impossible without taking unacceptable risks.*

With GPS and the increased use of radar on small boats, it is far less stressful
approaching an unfamiliar coast or harbor than it used to be, but you should
always be able to take over with traditional methods if the electronics fail.

*Remember the adage "use it or lose it" – keep using and
practicing your manual navigation and pilotage skills.*

If you are approaching a coastline in tidal waters, set your final
waypoint uptide of your destination. In the absence of tide set it
upwind. This allows you to head off downtide or downwind for the final
approach and gives you a margin for error. There is nothing worse than being in
sight of your destination and struggling to reach it against the wind or tide.

Approaching by night

It is often easier to approach a coastline at night, at least in an area that has some lit
land- and seamarks. You can usually identify the approach buoys by their light
characteristics from further away than you could in daylight. Ideally, you would
approach just before dawn when lights are visible, and enter the harbor in daylight.

If there is a lighthouse near your destination, you will see its light from miles away at
night in good conditions. By taking a bearing on it you can get a position line. A useful
trick when approaching a coastline at night is to note the time that a lighthouse first
appears over the horizon and take a bearing on it.

*Because of the curve of the earth, your height of eye and the height of
an object on the horizon determine your visual horizon. Your almanac
contains a table for calculating the distance to (off) an object as long
as you know your height of eye and the object's height above sea level.*

You can estimate your height of eye above the sea, and the height of
lighthouses is marked alongside their symbol on the chart. Remember that this is
the height above mean high water spring tide, so you must calculate the height of tide
to discover the actual height of the light above the water at that time.

You do this in the same way as described earlier, but remember to deduct the actual height of tide from the level given in the almanac for MHWS and add that to the charted height of the lighthouse.

A bearing of the lighthouse combined with a distance off provides you with a position fix for the final approach. There are many other ways of fixing your position, which we will investigate in the next chapter.

As you approach the coast or harbor, aim to get an accurate landfall fix before getting close to any dangers. Once you know exactly where you are, you can begin the final approach using your pilotage skills and pre-prepared pilotage plan.

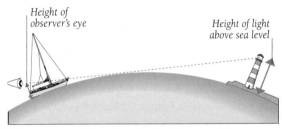

Height of observer's eye

Height of light above sea level

■ **Distance off** *can be calculated from a table in your almanac, but you need to know the height of your eye above the sea and the height of the lighthouse.*

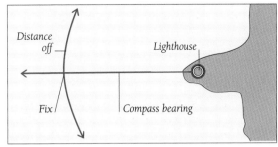

Distance off

Lighthouse

Fix

Compass bearing

■ **To get a position fix,** *take a bearing of the lighthouse with your compass when you first see it, and combine it with the distance off.*

A simple summary

✔ Planning your passage and the departure and arrival stages is a vital ingredient of a trouble-free cruise.

✔ You can work out the height of tide at any time by using the information in your nautical almanac. Remember to add the depth shown on the chart to the height of tide to get the total depth.

✔ Transits are the easiest and most accurate way of obtaining a position line.

✔ Remember that the depth sounder has more uses than helping you avoid grounding.

✔ When planning to approach the shore, aim to get an accurate position fix before approaching any dangers.

Chapter 23

Starting to Navigate

ONCE YOU ARE SAILING ALONG a coast or heading offshore, it is time to switch from pilotage to navigating. Now, you will use the chart and your navigation instruments to fix your position, set a course, and compensate for tidal streams or currents. You will need to maintain a log of your journey and to periodically plot your position, using the information from the log to provide an estimated position in between fixes or to confirm the accuracy of a fix. Don't worry if at first these navigational tasks seem daunting. They are quite simple to do in practice and once you have got the hang of the techniques, you will not have to spend much time at the chart table.

In this chapter...

✓ Fixing your position

✓ Plotting a course

✓ Allowing for tidal streams

✓ Plotting a position

293

A COMFORTABLE, WELL-LAID-OUT NAVIGATION AREA MAKES THE JOB MUCH EASIER

Fixing your position

MODERN NAVIGATION TECHNOLOGY *allows us to know our exact location at any time but this is a relatively new luxury. For centuries, sailors navigated the oceans without knowing their exact position for most of the time. Before the introduction of GPS and its earlier cousins, sailors estimated their position based on the course and speed that they had achieved since their last known position. Whenever possible, they confirmed their estimate by fixing their position.*

Today, we can use GPS and radar to provide a fix, but the traditional methods are still vitally important. You should practice as many methods as possible so that you can cope with all eventualities.

The simplest way of fixing your position is to sail close by a charted sea- or landmark and to fix your position by eye. An entry in the logbook such as, "1215 hours, abeam Fairway Buoy, 50 yards to port," will be perfectly adequate to fix your position.

Fixing position by eye can also be accurate enough even when you are further away from a charted feature. Sailing along a coastline with good visibility and no off-lying dangers, it could be sufficient to log your position as abeam a particular headland, approximately 1½ miles (2.5 km) off, together with the time and log reading. This level of accuracy, particularly when the fix is compared with your estimated position, is all that is needed in such conditions. If visibility is poor, however, or the coastline has off-lying dangers, you will need a more accurate fix. Similarly, if the fix is to mark a departure point from which you will plot a new course, the more accurate it is the better. Accurate fixes require the creation of position lines.

Position lines

A single position line, such as a transit of the sort we use for pilotage, shows that your position is somewhere along the line, but it cannot tell you exactly where you are. It can still be useful if the position line is parallel to your track, showing you are on course, or at right angles to the track, showing how far along it you are.

To know exactly where you are requires at least two position lines. Since you must be on both lines, your actual position is where the two lines cross. When you draw the two lines on a chart, your position is clearly marked by their intersection. In practice, of course, there is a degree of error, depending on how accurately you can measure each line of position. If you happen to be on two transits at the same time, you will get a very accurate fix but most other position lines are less accurate than transits.

You can make your fix more accurate by using three or more lines of position. Ideally, these would all intersect at one point, but in practice they will form a small triangle, called a "cocked hat," on the chart. Your position is inside this triangle.

The size of the triangle formed by three lines of position is a good indication of the accuracy of the fix. An accurate fix will give a small triangle, so beware of any fixes that result in a large triangle of position.

You can obtain a position line by measuring either the bearing or the distance off a charted object and plotting the resultant line on the chart. If you measure the bearing of an object, you will get a straight position line. If you measure the distance off an object, you will get a circular position line.

Once you understand the principles of position lines, you have learned the basics by which all position fixing systems work. It doesn't matter whether you use a GPS, radar, sextant, compass, depth sounder, or your own eyes to create a fix – all work by identifying lines of position.

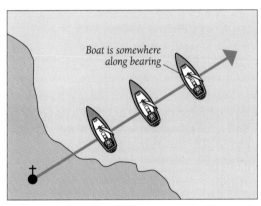

■ **If you take a bearing** *of a charted object and plot the line on the chart, your boat must be somewhere along that single position line.*

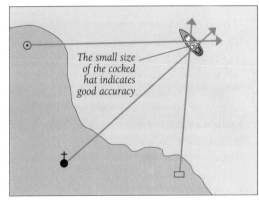

■ **In a three-point fix,** *three position lines plotted on the chart produce a small triangle, or "cocked hat," the size of which is a good guide to accuracy.*

Compass bearings

Using a hand bearing compass to take bearings on land- or seamarks is a simple skill that every cruising sailor should have. If your electronics fail you can still fix your position when within sight of land- or seamarks as long as you have a compass and chart. Practice taking compass bearings and comparing the fix they provide with your GPS position. Challenge yourself to improve your accuracy and you will soon be confident enough to navigate with the basic tools and to enjoy the satisfaction it brings.

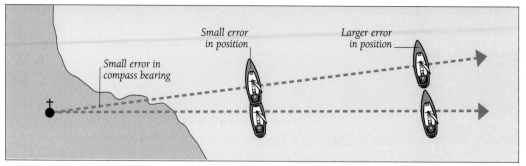

Small error
in position

Larger error
in position

Small error in
compass bearing

■ **Be as accurate as possible** *when taking compass bearings. A small error in bearing will lead to a larger error in position the further away you are from the object you are using for the bearing.*

The first step is to identify two or three sea- or landmarks within sight that are shown on the chart. If you can only find two, they will give a more accurate fix if they are about 90° apart. If you have three marks available, try to choose ones about 60° apart.

Beware of using two position lines that cross at a shallow angle since this will exaggerate any errors in measuring the bearings.

It helps accuracy if the mark is close to the boat. A typical error of just 3° in the bearing will give a significant positional error if you are a long way from the mark, but will be much less if you are close to it.

Make sure that you identify the correct marks on the chart or your fix will be worthless. Take bearings of each mark with the hand bearing compass from a point on the boat known to be free of deviation. Brace yourself in a secure position and take three bearings on each mark using the average bearing to plot the position line. It helps if there is someone who can write down the bearings as you take them.

Draw the position lines on the chart and check the size of the cocked hat where they intersect to estimate the accuracy. If you are happy with the result, draw a circle around the triangle and label it with the time and log reading. Job done!

Using GPS

Yacht navigation has been revolutionized by the use of GPS thanks to its accuracy and the fact that a fix is available virtually whenever the navigator needs one. This seemingly constant availability can tempt the navigator into relying exclusively on the system and, as an inherently lazy person, I am as tempted as anyone to sit back and let the GPS show the way. However, I have experienced too many failures of electronic systems to ever feel totally comfortable relying on a single source of information.

I use the GPS as my main information source, but I also check it regularly using other methods. If the two sources do not agree for any reason, I sit up and take notice and look for a third or fourth way to confirm my position.

A GPS set calculates its position by working out how far it is from a number of satellites orbiting the earth. By calculating the distance from a satellite, the GPS receiver creates a curved line of position – just like a distance off from a lighthouse. The receiver calculates the fix by identifying the intersection of the curved position lines from a number of satellites. The more satellites there are in range of the receiver the better, because it will select the best ones to use for an accurate fix.

The set will normally display the boat's position in degrees, minutes, and tenths of a minute of latitude and longitude but this is not usually the best form for the small boat navigator. Plotting a latitude and longitude position on a paper chart can be awkward and may lead to errors.

A better way is to find a suitable land- or seamark near the track and program its latitude and longitude into the GPS as a waypoint. Set the GPS to display the boat's position as a bearing and distance from the waypoint. This is much easier to plot on the chart. Once you have plotted the fix by GPS, mark it with the time and log reading, note the depth as a rough check of position, and compare the fix with an estimated position. If there is a significant discrepancy, try and double-check by using another source.

Using radar

If you have a radar set on board, it gives you the ability to measure bearings and distances of features that can be seen by the radar and that you can find on the chart. Using radar effectively requires skill and experience and you should consider attending a short course to make the best use of your set. Identifying objects displayed on the screen can be difficult because radar reflections from coastlines can be confusing and those from buoys may be difficult to separate from "clutter" caused by a rough sea.

INTERNET

www.capjack.com
www.powercruising.
com/macnaut.html

Many Internet sites such as these offer software navigation tools.

If the objects can be clearly identified, the radar can be used to show the bearing of the object and its distance (range) away from the boat. A radar bearing is not as accurate as a radar range, so, for the most accurate radar fix, try and measure the distance off two or preferably three objects. Use a pair of compasses to draw the position lines on the chart and create a cocked hat.

Practice using the radar for navigation in your home waters and in good visibility until you are confident in your abilities.

Plotting a course

IN ORDER TO NAVIGATE on a passage, you need to be able to set a course to steer that will take you safely to your destination. This process is known as plotting a course and it is an essential skill for navigating offshore, even if your boat is equipped with a GPS and chart plotter.

The first step is to draw a line on a chart, joining your departure point and your destination, or the next turning point. This line is called the ground track. Check along the track to make sure that it does not pass over or near shallows, overfalls, or other hazards or restricted areas. Measure the distance using dividers and the latitude scale at the side of the chart. Divide the distance by your anticipated speed to find the expected duration of the passage and an estimated time of arrival (ETA).

In the absence of current, tidal stream, or leeway the track marked on the chart is the course to steer. Measure its direction on the chart using a parallel ruler or plotter. Whether you measure the direction in °T or °M is a matter of personal preference, but be consistent and make sure that others involved in chart work know your preference.

Allowing for leeway

As you know, all sailing boats slide sideways to some extent when they are sailing close-hauled or on a reach and this leeway must be allowed for if the wind is on or ahead of the beam on your course.

Let's assume that your course means that you will be sailing on a reach. To allow for leeway you must adjust the bearing of the course to steer to windward by an amount equal to the leeway you expect to make.

The amount of leeway depends on the point of sailing, the wind strength, the state of the sea, and the design of the boat. If you look astern and see that your wake is not directly in line with the boat, you are making leeway. You can roughly measure the leeway angle by using your hand bearing compass. Take a bearing on your wake and then compare it with the reciprocal (opposite) of your heading. To get the reciprocal, add or subtract 180° to your heading. The difference is the leeway angle. Typically, the leeway angle will be about 3–6° in a modern design, sailing close-hauled in moderate conditions.

When allowing for leeway, if you work with a 5° leeway angle in moderate conditions you will not be far off in most circumstances. In stronger winds, be prepared to allow more for leeway.

Adjusting the course

You can make the allowance for leeway in your head before you give the helmsman the course to steer. However, to avoid confusion, you may wish to pencil in the wind direction on the chart and adjust your track toward it. After applying the leeway angle to get the course to steer, correct the resulting course for deviation before giving it to the helmsman.

Here's a useful rule that will help you when applying leeway: Wind from the port side – subtract the leeway angle to get the course to steer; wind from the starboard side – add the leeway angle to get the course to steer.

Allowing for tidal current

IF YOU ARE SAILING IN TIDAL WATERS or in current, you will have to make allowance for the effect on your course and speed. If the stream or current is parallel to your track, it will not affect the course to steer but it will have an impact on your speed over the ground.

For instance, if your boat is sailing at 5 kn and there is a 2-kn tide against you, your speed over the ground will be reduced to 3 kn. On the other hand, a 2-kn tide running in the direction of your course will result in a speed over the ground of 7 kn – more than twice the ground speed achieved in the foul tide.

Symbols

Navigators use symbols on a chart, in order to save space and avoid confusion. Standard symbols are shown below but you can devise your own. Just ensure that everyone else doing chart work understands your symbols and uses them consistently. Time is usually written using the 24-hour notation (e.g. 2115) and should include the relevant time zone, for example, 2115 GMT.

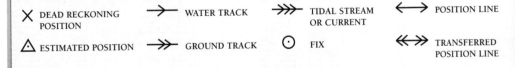

X DEAD RECKONING POSITION	→ WATER TRACK	⇉ TIDAL STREAM OR CURRENT	↔ POSITION LINE
△ ESTIMATED POSITION	⇶ GROUND TRACK	⊙ FIX	⇇⇉ TRANSFERRED POSITION LINE

Often, the tidal stream or current will not be parallel to your desired track but will push you to one side or the other. In this case, you must plot the effect of the current on the chart to find the course you should steer.

DEFINITION

The direction in which the tide flows is known as the set and its speed is called the drift. Set and drift usually vary on an hourly basis and can be obtained from the chart, almanac, or tidal current atlas. Remember that set is given in °T while drift is given in knots.

To accommodate the effect of the tidal current, you need to know the *set* and *drift* of the tide; you can find this from the chart or your almanac. For both you need to find out the time of high water at the local standard port, because tidal current information on the chart and in the almanac is presented according to the time before or after high water.

Tidal adjustments

Work out the time difference before or after high water for the time you are interested in and use the tidal atlas or the chart to find the set and drift of the tidal current at that time. Now draw the set and drift of the tide for the next hour on the chart. Draw the set from the point at the start of your ground track, and use the dividers to measure the length equal to the drift of the tide.

Open your dividers to the distance you expect to sail in the next hour and, with one point on the end of the tide line, scribe an arc to cut through the line representing your ground track. Join the end of the tide line to the point on the ground track and measure its direction. In the absence of leeway, this is the course you should steer to allow for the tide.

Remember that although you will steer this course, the boat will actually follow the direction of the ground track. If leeway is a factor on the course you will be steering, you must adjust the course to allow for leeway, as described earlier. Finally, allow for compass deviation before giving the helmsman the course to steer.

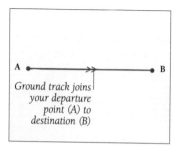

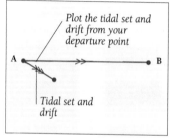

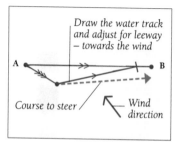

■ **Draw the ground track** *between your departure point and destination.*

■ **For the tidal vector,** *draw the tidal set and drift for the next hour from your departure point.*

■ **Make allowance for leeway,** *if necessary, once you have plotted your water track.*

Tides on long passages

On a long passage, you will have to allow for the tidal current changing hourly. If there are hazards near the track, you must plot the tidal set and drift, and plot a course to steer for each hour of the passage to follow the desired ground track. If there are no hazards it does not matter if you deviate from the track, so you can lay off several hours' worth of set and drift, one after the other, and plot a single course to steer.

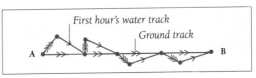

■ **Hazards close to the track** *mean that you must plot each hour's set and drift individually, and create a water track for each hour of the passage.*

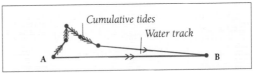

■ **With no hazards**, *you can plot several hours' worth of tide in one go to shape a single water track.*

Plotting a position

ALTHOUGH GPS ALLOWS YOU to fix your position at any time, the prudent navigator should still use the traditional practice of plotting an estimated position based on the direction and distance the boat has sailed since the last fix. This is necessary because it is only by comparing an estimated position (EP) with a fix that you can discover and assess any possible errors.

On any passage outside of local waters, you should keep an accurate record in your logbook of the course steered, distance run, times of course alterations, and the leeway experienced. From this information, you should plot your estimated position on the chart at regular intervals – every hour or so unless well offshore. When you do this, you will make allowance for all the factors that have affected your course, such as leeway and any tidal stream or current.

There are two stages in working up an estimated position. First, you produce a position based on your course and speed, known as a dead reckoning position (DR), then you allow for the effects of any tide or current to produce the estimated position.

Dead reckoning

The term dead reckoning is often used to describe the general business of plotting a position. However, in its correct sense it refers to the position created by drawing the course steered on the chart from the last known position and measuring off the distance sailed along it according to the log.

Plotting a DR position

Before you plot the course steered on the chart, you must allow for deviation to correct the course from °C to °M. If you prefer to do your chart work in °T, you must also allow for variation.

Once you have converted the course to a magnetic or true bearing, you can plot it on the chart, starting from your last position. Strictly speaking, the DR position should be plotted before applying leeway but, in practice, it is much easier to make an allowance for leeway after converting to °M or °T but before plotting the course on the chart.

Remember to apply the leeway correction to leeward of the course steered.

Plot your wake course from the last known position and mark it with one arrowhead. Use your dividers to measure off the distance sailed along the wake course. In the absence of any tidal stream or current, this is the dead reckoning position at that time. Mark the DR position with a cross and record the time and the log reading alongside it.

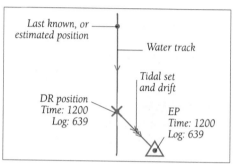

■ **Plot the wake course** and the distance sailed to get the DR position then plot the tide effect to find the estimated position.

Estimated position

If you are sailing in a tidal stream or current, the dead reckoning position you have just produced will not be your actual position. To find your estimated position (EP) you must now allow for the set and drift effects of the tide. Use the chart or tidal atlas to work out the set and drift of the tide in the time since the last known position. Starting at your DR position, plot the set on the chart.

Remember that tidal set is given in °T so you must apply variation before plotting it if you do your chart work in °M.

Use your dividers to measure along this line a distance equal to the drift of the tide. Mark this point with a dot in the middle of a triangle together with the time and log reading. This is your estimated position at that time allowing for predicted tidal effects.

Trivia...

Predictions for tidal set and drift are derived from a large amount of historical data but they are not infallible. Circumstances can cause variations from predictions. For instance, a strong wind blowing for some time will cause its own surface drift.

Now that you have plotted your EP on the chart, you can use it to confirm your position given by GPS, radar, or any other fixing method. If there are any discrepancies between the two, double-check your workings and look for a third way to confirm your position.

If you use a chart plotter connected to a GPS set, you will have the facility for a continuous visual display of your track on the plotter's screen. This is reassuring and convenient but you should still keep accurate entries in your logbook and periodically fix your position on a paper chart so that you can immediately revert to manual navigation methods if your electronic aids fail. For this reason, you should continue to use your plotting skills alongside the electronic aids so that you are able to revert to manual methods if the need arises.

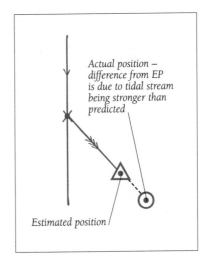

Actual position – difference from EP is due to tidal stream being stronger than predicted

Estimated position

■ **Comparing an EP to a fix** *provides a double-check and shows up discrepancies. Tidal effects may differ from predictions and this will result in a difference between the EP and the fix.*

A simple summary

✓ GPS and radar can provide an accurate fix, but they are not infallible. The traditional methods are still vitally important and you should practice using as many as possible so that you can cope with all eventualities.

✓ All methods of fixing position are based on creating two or more lines of position. The point where the position lines intersect is your position.

✓ Plotting a course is the process by which you identify the course to steer to reach your destination, after allowing for leeway and the effects of a tidal stream or current.

✓ A navigator produces an estimated position using the course steered and distance sailed since the last known position, and the tidal effects during the same time. An EP is used to double-check a fix.

PART SIX

Chapter 24
Crew Welfare

Chapter 25
Dealing With Emergencies

Chapter 26
Distress Procedures

LARGE BOATS NEED LARGE CREWS

LOOKING AFTER BOAT AND CREW

THE SIGN OF A GOOD SKIPPER is his or her ability to run a happy ship. When you sail your own cruising yacht, you will learn the importance of looking after your boat and crew. A *happy crew* will be eager to sail with you and will perform at their best when the need arises. They will have *confidence* in your abilities and will *trust* your decisions, secure in the knowledge that you are well prepared to handle any awkward situations that may develop.

In this section, you will learn how to deal with common mishaps, such as running aground or fouling your propeller, and *how to cope* if they develop into emergency situations. If a situation worsens to the point where you need to call for outside assistance, you must know when and how to summon aid and, in the worst case, how to prepare to abandon ship.

Chapter 24

Crew Welfare

WHEN YOU PROGRESS to being the skipper of your own boat, you take on the responsibility for the safety and comfort of your crew. If your crew members are experienced they will contribute considerably to the running of the boat and will be prepared for sailing on a passage. It is quite likely, though, that you will sail with a less experienced crew at times. You may sail with members of your family and, if they have not sailed much before, it is important for you to help them learn sufficient skills for them to enjoy the occasion.

In this chapter...

✓ Running a happy ship

✓ Well fed and rested

✓ Sailing with children

✓ Man overboard – prevention and recovery in cruisers

✓ First aid at sea

SAILING IS MEANT TO BE FUN – MAKE SURE YOUR CREW STAY SAFE AND HAPPY

Running a happy ship

LET'S FACE IT, WE GO SAILING FOR FUN, *and none of us likes to be shouted at or made to feel stupid. Unfortunately, it is all too common for an inexperienced skipper to allow his or her own uncertainties to create a nervous tension on the boat and this is not conducive to a relaxed sailing trip.*

The first rule for running a happy ship is to avoid shouting at your crew. Most sailors who have crewed on a number of boats will be able to tell you stories of sailing with a "Captain Bligh" figure who makes up for his own shortcomings by blaming his crew for his errors or lack of foresight. Do not become this type of skipper and remember that your crew come sailing with you because they want to enjoy themselves.

Sometimes it is necessary to turn up the volume to be heard over a strong wind or the sound of flapping sails, but this is the only time that you should need to raise your voice on the boat.

Knowing your limits

The next thing to ensure is that you do not overextend yourself and that you undertake passages that are within your abilities, especially if your crew are not very experienced. Start off with short passages, preferably of only a few hours duration, and try to pick weather conditions that allow you to have a pleasant sail without fighting the elements.

When you want to extend your experience by trying longer or more difficult passages, arrange for some experienced crew members to come with you. You will enjoy the trip and learn more than if you are worrying about inexperienced crew, especially if they are members of your family.

Briefing the crew

When you do sail with inexperienced crew, spend some time showing them over the boat and explaining the basic items of equipment. Make sure that they are properly equipped with clothing and safety gear before you sail and, if the weather is likely to be rough, suggest that they take an anti-seasickness remedy before the trip. Show your crew where to sit or stand during maneuvers like tacking, jibing, and coming alongside, and avoid giving them difficult or important jobs until they have gotten used to the basics of sailing.

Trivia...
Do not be fooled by the sophisticated systems and equipment aboard modern cruising boats – the realities of offshore cruising mean that the experience, attitude, and skills of the skipper and crew are the factors that help ensure a cruise is successful and enjoyable for all on board.

Always brief your crew before every trip and before any tricky maneuver such as getting in and out of a berth. This is important even when you are sailing with experienced crew, but it is key to ensuring that inexperienced crew members feel safe and relaxed on board.

Do not assume that everyone is as keen on sailing as you are. Many people just want to have a nice trip afloat on a sunny day with a minimum of hassle and not too much excitement.

■ **Keeping your crew** *involved in boat and sail handling helps them improve their skills, builds teamwork, and ensures that your crew enjoy the fun of sailing.*

Make sure that inexperienced crew members dress for the conditions so that they stay as dry, warm, and comfortable as possible. Advise them not to sleep in their waterproof outer wear or heavy clothing. If they undress at least partially before turning in, they will sleep better and feel more comfortable when waking.

While you may dream of rounding Cape Horn, most people are less keen on getting cold or wet, or generally being uncomfortable for too long. Be conscious of your crew's level of interest and do not try to push them further or harder than they want to go.

Avoiding the battle of the sexes

If you are sailing with your wife or husband, beware of standing on your rights as skipper or you may find your beautiful relationship turning sour. While the skipper must be in charge and take responsibility for the boat, it is not necessary to run your boat like a dictatorship. It is perfectly proper and normal to consult with your crew, and for the sake of continuing family harmony, you should ensure that your crew have an active part in decision making.

One of the most common sights in any harbor is a boat approaching its berth with the husband at the helm and his wife on the bow ready to handle the lines during the berthing operation. All too often, the maneuver is accompanied by shouted orders, increasingly irritated replies, much struggling, and perhaps a collision or two before the boat is secured and the unhappy couple retreat below to continue the argument!

Please do not allow yourself to get into this situation. I am directing this comment toward other guys because it seems to be a male tendency to insist on taking the helm during every maneuver. This is crazy! Steering the boat is the physically easy part during berthing or anchoring maneuvers, while handling the sails, lines, and anchor takes more strength.

In contrast to the above scenario, you will occasionally see a husband-and-wife-team handling the boat in a sensible way. With the female at the helm while the male handles the heavy work, the balance of abilities is sensibly arranged.

Many men respond to this suggestion by saying that their wife or girlfriend cannot steer the boat in tight situations. This is a poor excuse because there is absolutely no reason why anyone who wants to cannot learn to handle a boat safely.

The best solution to this problem is for both partners to take sailing courses and to learn the handling skills so that either of them is able to steer the boat in all situations. So guys, put your prejudices to one side and encourage your partners to learn as much as you. Share the tasks appropriately according to the physical demands of each job and each person's capabilities.

INTERNET

www.boatsafe.com
www.csbc.ca

These sites specialize in information about safe and responsible boating, training courses, and links to other safety-related boating sites.

■ **Sharing tasks** *as you approach a berth is a matter of common sense. Here, the woman is steering while the man is preparing to take the lines ashore.*

Well fed and rested

ONE OF THE MOST IMPORTANT REQUIREMENTS *for a crew on passage is to stay well fed and rested. If you ignore this essential need, your crew will quickly become tired and possibly seasick, especially if the weather becomes less favorable. Inevitably, everyone on board will weaken at about the same time, and as the crew's strength and well-being deteriorates, your task as skipper becomes harder and the chance of mishaps increases.*

Before starting a passage, or even a day sail in a dinghy, make sure that you have sufficient provisions aboard for your trip, plus an extra allowance to cater for any delays. In a dinghy this may simply mean that you should carry a bottle of water and a couple of chocolate bars, but if you are setting out on a long passage in a cruiser, you may have to spend some time planning, purchasing, and stowing your provisions. Hot soup can be made in advance and stored in thermoses to be consumed later if cooking becomes difficult.

■ **When wind and sea** *increase, it is important to find a comfortable position – whether in the cockpit, or below, where you are braced against the motion.*

It makes sense to organize mealtimes to coincide with the changes of watch so that all the crew can eat together. Try and share the cooking and washing up among the crew and make sure that you prepare at least one hot meal every day. It is common for the on-watch crew to prepare the meal and for the new watch to tidy away afterward, but you can arrange any system that suits you and your crew.

If rough weather is forecast, it helps tremendously if you can ensure that everyone is well rested before the weather deteriorates. A rough sea makes it difficult to cook, so it is sensible to prepare a hot meal that can be eaten before the bad weather arrives.

Sailing with children

TEACH YOUR CHILDREN TO SWIM BEFORE introducing them to sailing. It is not essential for all adult sailors to be able to swim and some very good sailors cannot do so (personally, I only enjoy being on the water, not in it), but you will never have any piece of mind when your children are sailing unless they have learned to swim first and are confident in the water.

You need to help your children to feel confident and comfortable on a boat and you will not be able to do so if you do not feel confident yourself. Your children will quickly pick up on your fears and will become frightened to go sailing. If you are not sufficiently confident in your ability, take some lessons to improve your skills before taking your children afloat.

Before you go afloat, make sure that your children understand the safety rules. Young children should always wear lifejackets in a dinghy or small boat; older ones who can swim well can wear a PFD. On a cruiser, a safety harness should be worn and clipped on whenever the child is on deck or in the cockpit.

Child safety

The age of your children will influence when and how you take them sailing. If you sail on a cruiser and are an experienced sailor, there is no reason why you cannot take a child with you from the time that he or she is born. In fact, sailing with a baby is a lot easier than taking a toddler afloat. While the baby will happily sleep for much of the time, a toddler will inevitably try and explore every inch of the boat. In this situation, one parent must always be with the child when he or she is on deck or in the cockpit. You should also make it a rule that a young child cannot go on deck without permission from a parent.

Sailing in a dinghy with a young child is trickier than on a cruiser. The ease with which the dinghy will heel can make it a frightening experience for some children, although others will enjoy the ride. Only take a young child in a dinghy once you have good experience of dinghy sailing and, even then, only in moderate conditions in a fairly stable boat. Explain beforehand how the boat heels over, and show your child how to move around. If possible, capsize the boat very close to the shore in shallow water, show the child how easy it is to right, and get him or her comfortable floating next to the boat in a lifejacket. Build confidence in easy stages and avoid frightening experiences.

If your child shows an interest in sailing, you should consider sending them on a children's dinghy-sailing course. Once they have learned the basics of sailing by themselves in a dinghy, they will be much safer and happier sailing with you on a larger boat.

Teaching children to sail

Children as young as 5 years old can safely be taught to sail very small dinghies in sheltered waters, and many sailing schools organize special children's courses during the school vacations.

If you are planning to take your children cruising, plan your cruise as a series of very short trips. Children will enjoy the experience much more if you plan to spend plenty of time in harbor or anchored off a sandy beach rather than on long passages. Make sure that you prepare the boat to suit the age of your children. If you have toddlers or young children on board, you should tie netting to the lifelines so that there is no danger of them slipping under or between the rails. Take a look around the boat from a child's perspective to identify any sharp corners or edges that could cause injury.

Make sure that you take your child's favorite foods and toys with you, and pack some games to keep them amused if the weather turns foul. Older children can be encouraged to help you with many of the chores of navigation and boat handling. Start by teaching them the simple tasks, such as coiling ropes and stowing fenders, and they will soon become an invaluable part of the crew.

■ **Children on board a cruiser** *should preferably wear safety harnesses to prevent them falling overboard, but they should always wear lifejackets (or PFDs if they can swim well).*

Man overboard – prevention and recovery in cruisers

HAVING A PERSON FALL OVERBOARD is one of the worst nightmares for any skipper. As soon as a person falls overboard, he or she is in grave danger and only your prompt and efficient action can prevent a fatality. Prevention is far better – and easier – than cure in this case, and it is your responsibility to ensure that safety harnesses are worn when necessary.

If a man-overboard situation occurs, it is vital to keep the person in sight and get the boat back to them as quickly as possible. How you do this will depend on the number of crew left aboard, the type of boat, and the conditions. Don't wait for the emergency to happen before trying out recovery techniques. Experiment using a fender attached to a bucket as a dummy, and see what works best for your boat and crew. Make sure that your crew practices without your interference just in case it is you that falls overboard!

Prevention

By far the best way of dealing with this emergency is to prevent it occurring in the first place. Every cruiser should have sufficient safety harnesses aboard for all the crew and each crew member should adjust theirs for a comfortable fit and ensure it is always accessible when needed.

You must set the rules for wearing a harness depending on the type of boat, strength of crew, and the conditions. There are no hard and fast rules but, in general, harnesses should always be worn and clipped on when:

- Sailing at night
- Sailing in areas of rough water
- The boat is reefed or a reef may be needed
- A person is working alone on deck

First actions

The immediate priority when a person falls overboard is to notify the rest of the crew with a cry of "Man Overboard." Keep the casualty in sight and immediately throw a lifebuoy and man overboard pole.

Any delay will result in the boat sailing farther away from the casualty and this will reduce the chance of them reaching the lifebuoy. On a fully crewed boat, one person should be designated to keep a continuous watch on the man overboard.

This may not be possible on a short-handed cruiser but it is imperative to keep the person in sight to have a hope of successful recovery. The next step is for the skipper to decide on a recovery procedure and to brief the crew quickly so that they know what to expect. If there are enough crew, someone should note the time and position in the logbook and activate the MoB (man overboard) position function on the GPS, if fitted. This information will be needed to conduct a search if the casualty is lost from sight.

Recovery under sail

There are no hard and fast rules as to whether you should recover the casualty under sail or power, or what particular method you should use if you choose to do it under sail. All that matters is that you stay within sight of the casualty and return to them under full control without hitting them with the boat.

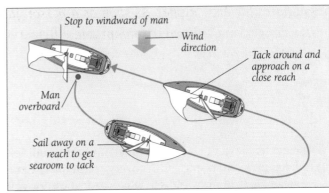

Stop to windward of man

Wind direction

Tack around and approach on a close reach

Man overboard

Sail away on a reach to get searoom to tack

■ **If you return under sail,** *position the boat to approach on a close reach, letting out the sails to slow down and stop alongside.*

The size of boat, number and experience of its crew, and the weather conditions will dictate the best course of action for recovering a man overboard. Even if you decide to maneuver under sail, you could start the engine, leaving it in neutral, so that it is ready if needed.

The recovery method for dinghies is often taught for cruisers and can work well, especially with a full crew. However, because it requires you to sail away from the casualty to gain searoom, it does mean that you risk losing sight of the person. In very rough conditions or at night, it will be difficult to keep the casualty in sight.

Using the crash-stop method

Another method to consider is the crash stop. This has the advantage of keeping the boat close to the casualty. The helmsman should push the tiller hard to leeward as soon as the person goes over the side. Whatever the point of sailing you were on, this will usually end up with the boat tacking or at least stopping head-to-wind.

Leave the jib sheet cleated if the boat tacks and the boat will end up hove-to. Push the tiller to the new leeward side to keep the boat stopped. There will be much flapping of sails and temporary disorder but the boat will stop and lie relatively steadily, giving you time to assess the situation and sort things out without sailing away from the casualty.

This method can work even if you are sailing with a spinnaker, although the boat probably won't tack and the situation will be chaotic until you can lower the spinnaker. However, the boat will still be relatively close to the man overboard. After a crash stop, you may be close enough to the casualty to throw a line. If not, you may be able to work the boat closer by adjusting sheets and tiller, or you could lower the headsail, sheet the mainsail in tight, and use the engine to approach the man overboard.

Whichever method you use to return to the casualty under sail, aim to make the final approach on a close reach so that you can adjust your speed by easing or trimming the mainsail. If possible, lower or roll up the jib to keep the foredeck clear of jib sheets, which can cause injury. In moderate conditions, aim to stop the boat alongside and to windward of the casualty so that it drifts to leeward as it slows down, allowing the casualty to be grabbed and brought aft to just behind the leeward shrouds.

Have a rope ready to throw in case you can't get alongside the person in the water, and have another ready to tie them to the boat.

Under power

If you are motoring when a person falls overboard, immediately turn the boat toward him. This will swing the stern away from the person as he passes down the side and prevent him getting caught by the propeller. As soon as the person has cleared the stern, put the tiller hard over in the opposite direction and turn the boat back toward the casualty. Keep the person in sight and approach slowly upwind, aiming to stop the boat with the person just forward of the shrouds to keep him away from the propeller. Secure them to the boat with a line tied under the armpits using a bowline and stop the engine while they are brought aboard.

Getting the person aboard

How you get the person aboard will depend on whether they can help themselves, the height of the boat out of the water, and the crew strength on board. It is much easier to do this on the leeward side, where the boat's heel reduces the freeboard. It is nearly impossible to pull a wet, heavy, and unconscious person out of the water, so some form of lifting tackle should be used. Make up a sling and tackle ready for this purpose, or buy a ready-made system, and stow it where it can be reached quickly. The tackle can be attached to a spare halyard or to the end of the main boom.

Use the most appropriate recovery arrangement for your boat and practice using the system before it is needed for real.

First aid at sea

THE CREW'S WELFARE AFLOAT is your responsibility and you should ensure that you know if any of your crew has an existing medical condition that requires specific medicines or treatment.

Make sure that you discuss this with your crew and that they know that they are responsible for informing you of any condition that may affect their performance and their ability to contribute fully in the sailing of the yacht.

It is then up to you to decide if a crew member's medical condition prevents them sailing on the boat and, if they are to sail, to ensure that they bring whatever medical supplies are required. You must also make sure that you have a suitable first-aid kit on board and that you or another member of the crew has some first-aid expertise. Many sailing schools run first-aid courses specifically designed for sailing. You should also carry a good first-aid manual on board and study it before an incident arises.

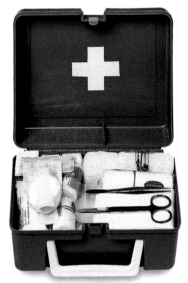

■ **Pick a first-aid kit** *that is suitable for the size of your crew and the type of cruising you do.*

A simple summary

✔ Sailing is meant to be fun so you should aim to run a happy ship – avoid shouting at your crew and ensure that everyone feels involved in decisions.

✔ When you sail with your partner, arrange the jobs to suit the physical abilities of each person rather than taking on stereotypical roles.

✔ If you are sailing on a passage, make sure that your crew is kept well fed, warm, and rested so that they can continue operating at maximum efficiency.

✔ Teach young children to swim before taking them sailing and make sure that you are confident in your abilities so that they do not pick up on your fears.

Chapter 25

Dealing With Emergencies

Whether or not an incident develops into an emergency is often decided by your readiness to tackle a problem quickly before it escalates into a more serious situation. Advance planning and practice can make all the difference between handling the situation or having to call on outside assistance. It doesn't matter if you sail a dinghy, a small keelboat, or a cruiser – there are various situations that you should be prepared to handle.

In this chapter...

✓ Be prepared

✓ Fouled propeller

✓ Running aground

✓ Hull damage

✓ Rig damage

✓ Fire fighting

THE LARGE CREW OF A RACING YACHT COMES IN HANDY WHEN THE MAST BREAKS

Be prepared

AS YOU DEVELOP YOUR SKILLS, you will inevitably encounter situations that you haven't had to deal with before. Experience is certainly a good teacher but there is a safer way of learning. Many sailing schools and other organizations run courses on a range of safety and emergency subjects.

Broadening your knowledge

Reading is an excellent way of finding out more. Practical books can explain the situations you may face and suggest solutions, while cruising stories and articles give you an insight into how other people deal with problems afloat.

Use your imagination to prepare for dealing with an emergency. Imagine the potential situations you could encounter in the sort of sailing you do, and work through them in your mind, thinking of all the ways that you might deal with the problem.

As well as preparing yourself to deal with emergencies, you should equip your boat with the appropriate repair and safety gear to deal with a range of situations. Look at your safety equipment and make sure it is in good condition and not out of date.

A CRUISER'S TOOLKIT

Buy the best tools you can afford and, where possible, pick materials, such as stainless steel, for maximum durability. Poor-quality tools will quickly deteriorate in the damp conditions on board. Tools should be kept lightly oiled and stored securely. Plastic toolboxes are useful, and a comprehensive tool kit could be split among several boxes. This makes it quicker to find the tool you need and makes storage easier. Some toolboxes have built-in compartments for small items and these can be useful for frequently used spares, such as tape, split rings, shackles, or fasteners.

A basic toolkit should contain:

- Selection of screwdrivers
- Electrical screwdrivers
- Assortment of wrenches
- Socket set
- Crescent wrench
- Mole wrench
- Wire terminal crimper
- Wire cutter
- Hacksaw and blades
- Power drill and bits
- Hand drill and bits
- Brace and bits
- Pliers/electrical pliers

Fouled propeller

CLEARING A FOULED PROPELLER *can be extremely difficult so preventing the problem from occurring is preferable to attempting a cure. Check that there are no ropes hanging over the side when you start the engine, and be alert to any ropes falling over the side when under power. It is bad enough to pick up a discarded, floating rope but it is even more annoying to be disabled by one of your own ropes.*

Trivia...

Although you should carry sufficient spares and tools to deal with breakdowns and emergencies, avoid turning your boat into a floating chandlery, especially if you rarely sail on long offshore passages.

Even if you are careful with your ropes there are many other floating pitfalls waiting to snag the unwary. Moorings, fishing lines, floating ropes, and plastic bags lie in wait for a passing propeller. Most ropes and debris are made from synthetic materials that typically melt and fuse from the friction of the propeller, creating a solid mass around it and stopping the engine.

Always be alert to the possibility of debris or discarded ropes in the water and, if possible, try to avoid them.

Go through your boat and examine every piece of equipment. Check the sizes and types of fasteners and ensure you have the right screwdrivers, wrenches, or sockets for the job.

Check the engine manufacturer's recommendations to ensure that you have all the necessary spanners, sockets, and allen keys to work on the engine. Also make sure that you have spanners and wrenches to service seacocks.

- Hammers
- Wood saw
- Files
- Small flashlight
- Underwater flashlight
- Wire cutters
- Mallet
- Selection of emery paper and sandpaper

UNDERWATER FLASHLIGHT

Cutting free

If a rope does foul the propeller, you may have a difficult task in freeing it. You may be able to release it, however, if you can reach an end of the rope. Turn the engine slowly, by hand, in the opposite direction to the way in which the propeller was turning. Pull on the end and the rope may, if you are very lucky, unwind and fall clear.

If you cannot release the rope from the deck, you have few options. Crucially, you must first make the boat safe by anchoring, or hoisting sail and making for harbor if possible before you attempt any further remedies. If the rope you have fouled is anchored to the bottom, find a way to cut it free so that you are able to sail away.

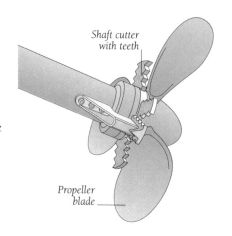

Shaft cutter with teeth

Propeller blade

■ **A shaft cutter** *cuts any ropes or floating pieces of plastic that are interfering with the propeller.*

A solution to the problem of a fouled propeller is a shaft cutter. This is a unit with sharp, serrated teeth mounted ahead of the propeller to catch and cut pieces of rope or plastic.

If you cannot reach the rope, try lashing a sharp knife to the end of a boathook to extend your range. If the weather is calm, you may be able to launch your dinghy and reach the rope from that. The last resort is for one of the crew to go over the side with a knife. This should only be attempted in calm weather with the person wearing a wet suit and a safety line.

Staying anchored by your propeller shaft can cause severe damage if there is any sea running. You must regain control of the boat as soon as possible.

If you can sail to harbor, you may be able to dry out alongside a quay, or heel the boat or trim it down by the bow sufficiently to reach the prop from the dinghy. Alternatively, you could hire a diver or use a boatlift to haul the boat out of the water.

Running aground

WE TALKED ABOUT CLOSE ENCOUNTERS *of the hard kind and how to avoid them when learning about navigation but let's be realistic and accept that at one time or another you may run aground. If you are sailing a dinghy and your centerboard hits the bottom, you can pull the board up a bit and head for deeper water. On board a cruiser, when it comes to a shuddering halt as the keel hits the bottom, the situation is more complex. Most groundings result in little more than wounded pride but the situation can be dangerous.*

Quick and effective action is required to refloat a grounded boat, or to minimize the danger and potential damage if you are stuck fast.

If you are in tidal waters, the state of the tide will be very important. If the tide is rising, the situation is not serious – unless you have been holed – because the tide will soon float you off as long as you can prevent the boat from being driven further into shallow water. If the tide is falling, however, you may have only a very few moments to get off before you are stuck until the tide rises again.

Refloating the boat

If you go aground under sail, decide if you can use the sails to help you get off. If not, drop them immediately and try to use the engine. In a small boat with a shallow draft, you may be able to send a crew member over the side to push the bow around, or you could try pushing with a spinnaker pole or boathook from the deck. If someone does go over the side, check the depth of water around the boat with the spinnaker pole or boathook first, and then tie a line to them so that they can't be separated from the boat.

Do not run the engine, even in neutral, if someone is in the water near the stern of the boat.

In a deep-keeled boat, you may be able to reduce your draft to sail or motor clear. If the wind is blowing off the shallows, sheet the sails in tightly to increase the heeling force. Alternatively, the crew can sit on the end of the boom and swing it over the side. Make sure that the topping lift is strong enough before you do this though! If the crew is reluctant to sit on the boom, hang a heavy weight, such as an anchor, from its end and swing it out over the side. Many boats have their deepest draft at the aft end of the keel and draft can be reduced by putting all the crew on the bow to lift the stern. A bilge-keel boat draws more when heeled, so you should bring it upright to minimize its draft.

Stuck fast

The amount of danger your boat is in depends on the type of bottom on which you ground and the sea state. If you are lucky and have grounded on sand or mud in settled conditions there should be no immediate danger, but if you have hit rocks you could be in great danger.

Check the chart to determine the nature of the bottom and test around the boat with the spinnaker pole or boathook to get an idea about the bottom close to the boat. Consider the weather forecast, and if you expect conditions to deteriorate, try everything possible to get the boat off quickly.

If you are definitely stuck fast until the tide returns, try and make sure that the boat lays over with the mast pointing toward shallow water. If you have grounded on a slope and the boat lays over toward deep water, there is a danger that she will flood through deck openings before she can rise on the returning tide.

If the boat has already settled heeling the wrong way, try shifting weight to the side you want her to heel toward or see if you can push the bow or stern round (or pull it with an anchor line) to get her pointing in the right direction.

If you are stuck, you must act quickly or the boat will settle too far and will be impossible to move.

If the bottom is rocky or very uneven, consider padding the outside of the hull before the boat lies on her side. Use bunk cushions, sail bags, or a partly inflated dinghy to provide padding, and remember to tie it to the boat so it can't float away when the tide returns. Padding the hull will help protect it from crashing on the seabed as it rises and falls on the returning tide. If the boat has been holed in the grounding, use sailbags, cushions, or other soft gear to block the hole and reduce the inflow as much as possible.

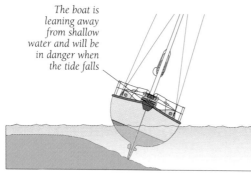

The boat is leaning away from shallow water and will be in danger when the tide falls

■ **If the boat settles** *on her side toward deeper water when the tide is falling, it may flood with water when the tide returns, rather than floating.*

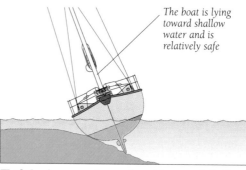

The boat is lying toward shallow water and is relatively safe

■ **If the boat settles** *on her side toward shallow water, it will not lie over too far as the tide falls, and will float when the tide returns, without flooding.*

Using a kedge anchor

If the tide is not falling very fast, you may have time to launch the *tender* and row out the kedge anchor toward deep water. Lay the anchor on as long a line as possible. Back aboard, take the line to the bow or stern depending on which end you want to pull toward deep water. Lead the line through a fairlead and then to an anchor windlass or sheet winch. If necessary, lead the line around two winches and wind on both of them. If you are lucky and your gear is strong enough, you may be able to winch the boat into deep water, recover the anchor, and motor or sail away.

If the keel is trapped in mud, the crew should try to heel the boat or rock it from side to side to break the suction. This will help free the boat from the bottom.

If you are stuck fast, lay the anchor as far as possible toward deep water to prevent the boat being pushed farther into the shallows by breaking seas, and to assist you in getting off when the tide returns.

> **DEFINITION**
>
> A tender *is the name for a small dinghy carried aboard a cruiser. It is used as a means of getting to and from the shore when the boat is on a mooring or at anchor.*

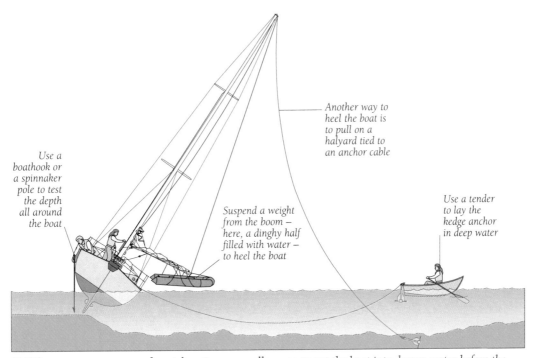

Another way to heel the boat is to pull on a halyard tied to an anchor cable

Use a boathook or a spinnaker pole to test the depth all around the boat

Suspend a weight from the boom – here, a dinghy half filled with water – to heel the boat

Use a tender to lay the kedge anchor in deep water

■ **When you run aground,** *quick actions may allow you to get the boat into deeper water before the tide drops. Work out where the deeper water is and try to heel the boat (if it has a fin keel) to reduce its draft. Lay an anchor in deep water and use it to winch the boat clear of the shallows.*

Hull damage

A HOLE IN THE HULL *is one of the most frightening potential accidents you can have if you sail a ballasted monohull. Most dinghies and multihulls will stay afloat even when holed, but a boat with a weighted keel will head for the bottom as soon as sufficient water has flooded through the hole.*

If the boat is holed above the waterline, you have some time to assess the situation and take action. If the hole is near the waterline, you may be able to heel the boat to raise it out of the water or at least reduce the pressure. If the hole is below the waterline, immediate action is required to prevent the boat from sinking. Your first actions must be to minimize the inrush of water and to start pumping to keep the boat afloat.

You have only seconds to take action if a hole is below the waterline, and the deeper it is, the worse the inrush will be.

Turn on all electric bilge pumps and the damage control pump if you have one, while a crew member works the manual pump. If the water is already over the cabin sole, use buckets to scoop water through the companionway into the cockpit. Sometimes the source of the water is not obvious, in which case you should suspect a broken engine cooling water, or toilet hose, or a failed seacock or through-hull fitting. Check all possible sources and, if the leak is from a hose, turn off the seacock. All seacocks should have a wooden plug tied to them for this eventuality. If a seacock fails you can quickly use the tapered plug to block the hole.

Blocking the hole

If the inrush of water is from a hole in the hull, block the hole in any way you can. It is possible to buy an umbrella-like piece of equipment that can be pushed through the hole and opened on the outside. Water pressure seals it against the hull and stops the leak.

Once you have blocked the hole from the inside, you may be able to lower a sail or a collision mat over the hole on the outside, using lines led under the hull to hold it down. This will help seal the hole from the outside. Assess the situation quickly and if it is clear that you will not be able to keep the yacht afloat, prepare to abandon ship. If you are near shallow water and the tide is falling, another option may be to deliberately ground the vessel. This may give you a chance to patch the damage before the tide rises again.

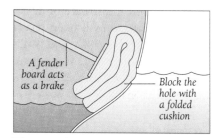

A fender board acts as a brake

Block the hole with a folded cushion

■ **Use soft materials** *such as bunk cushions or sail bags to push into the hole and stem the flow of water.*

Rig damage

SERIOUS DAMAGE TO THE RIG *does not occur often, at least not unless you race a lot, but if a piece of rigging does fail, it can result in you losing your mast entirely.*

It is important to inspect every part of your rig regularly, and to conduct a thorough check of all your equipment before you set off on a long offshore passage.

Long-distance cruising yachts often carry a long length of wire of sufficient diameter to be able to make temporary repairs should a shroud or stay fail on passage. If a shroud, forestay, or backstay does fail, you will have to react very quickly to save the mast. If you see a shroud on the windward side break or come loose, you must tack the boat as quickly as possible to get the damaged wire to leeward, where it will not be under load. If a leeward shroud comes loose, heave to on the same tack while you repair the damage. If the forestay fails, the headsail luff may hold the mast up for long enough for you to turn downwind to take the load off and save the mast. Similarly, if the backstay fails, try turning upwind and sheeting in the mainsail to provide temporary support.

Coping without the mast

If you lose the mast, the boat's motion will be jerky and this will make it difficult to work on deck, so make sure that all crew members wear and use their safety harnesses.

A mast will fall roughly downwind as the sails pull it over the side of the boat. As soon as the mast goes over the side, the motion of the boat will change dramatically as it loses the inertia of the rig high above the hull.

Your immediate priority is to prevent any damage to the hull or deck that could be caused by broken pieces of mast, which will still be attached to the boat by rigging, halyards, and control lines. Ideally, you want to recover as much of the mast as possible so that you can construct a jury rig (temporary rig), but this is often impossible in rough weather when it is usually necessary to cut away the rig to prevent it holing the hull.

You will need a large pair of wire cutters to cut the standing rigging. Otherwise, you will have to disconnect all the standing rigging at the chainplates, which can be a difficult task.

Once you have cut away or recovered the gear, you must assess the situation. You may be able to reach port under power if you have sufficient fuel, but don't start the engine until you have checked and rechecked that there are no ropes in the water that could foul the propeller. If motoring is not an option then you may be able to rig a jury rig, perhaps using the spinnaker pole and a storm jib, that will allow you to sail at least downwind, albeit slowly. Assess all your options and decide whether you are in danger or just temporarily disabled before you call for outside assistance.

■ **Dismasting** *happens more frequently to racing boats who use lightweight rigs, but cruisers can suffer this fate if their rigs are not well maintained.*

Fire fighting

PERSONALLY, THE THOUGHT OF FIRE *on board scares me more than just about any other emergency afloat, with the possible exception of a holing or collision, because of the speed with which it can destroy a boat.*

Fire is most likely to be the result of an explosion in the gas or fuel supply, or may be caused by a cooking accident or electrical fault. There is little to be done in the event of an explosion on board because it is likely to destroy the boat. However, the chances of this happening can be minimized by fitting and maintaining the gas and fuel supply properly, and by fitting a gas detector with a loud audible warning.

Do not run the engine or other machinery and avoid naked flames during any refuelling operations or when you are working on the engine or gas installation.

Fire-fighting equipment

Fire must be combated very quickly if you are to have any chance of getting it under control with a minimum of damage. To be successful you must have sufficient fire extinguishers of the appropriate type located in all the main areas of the boat. Foam extinguishers are effective against fuel or cooking fires but these should not be used on an electrical fire. Dry powder extinguishers can be used on all types of fire.

As a general guide, it is a good idea to mount extinguishers close to the galley and engine compartment and locate others in the forecabin and a cockpit locker. Aim to be able to reach an extinguisher easily from anywhere in the boat so that you cannot be trapped by fire.

Mount a fire blanket in the galley where it can be reached without going near a blazing stove. The blanket can be used to smother a cooking fire but should be left over the fire until it has cooled or the fire may restart. Remember to have all extinguishers pressure tested periodically and invert dry powder extinguishers each month to prevent the powder from compacting in the bottom of the container.

Learn how to use your extinguishers from an organized fire-fighting course and make sure that your crew know where they are stored and how to use them.

A simple summary

✔ Take all the necessary precautions to prepare yourself for dealing with emergencies.

✔ Take safety courses, read books and magazines, and imagine how you would handle potential situations on your own boat.

✔ Fit a cutter to your propeller shaft to reduce the risk of a fouled propeller.

✔ Act quickly when you run aground and use any method you can to move the boat to deeper water, especially if the tide is dropping.

✔ Carry the appropriate safety equipment for the type of sailing you do and make sure that it is not out of date, works efficiently, is easily accessible, and your crew know how to use it.

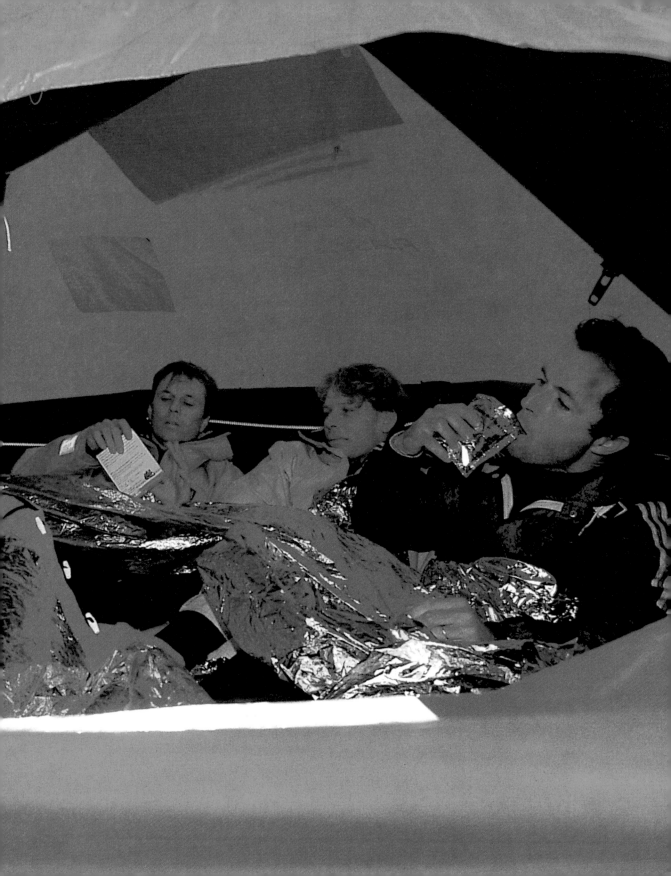

Chapter 26

Distress Procedures

MOST OF US LIKE TO IMAGINE that accidents will not happen to us. It helps us to avoid thinking about the sort of life-threatening emergencies we would rather not contemplate. Much better to dream of sailing in warm winds and sparkling seas on a boat that never breaks down! Unfortunately, emergencies do occur occasionally and some of these situations may be beyond your ability to handle without outside assistance. Alternatively, you may be called upon to help another boat in distress. In either case you will stand the best chance of success if you understand how to seek or give assistance and have thought through how you could handle various situations on your own boat.

In this chapter...

✓ Distress signals

✓ Being towed and towing

✓ Abandoning ship

BEING PREPARED TO DEAL WITH EMERGENCIES GIVES YOU THE BEST CHANCE OF SURVIVAL

Distress signals

BEFORE YOU DECLARE AN EMERGENCY and use distress procedures to summon outside assistance, be absolutely sure that you really are in distress. This can sometimes be uncertain when you are inexperienced and you encounter a situation you have not dealt with before.

Learn to identify a real emergency situation. It is not a sufficient reason to call on the rescue services just because you cannot get home on schedule or when you could call for a tow from a boatyard and pay the commercial bill. Always ask yourself if your boat or your crew are in any immediate danger.

An engine failure in an otherwise functioning sailing boat with enough wind to sail should not be interpreted as an emergency.

Think through emergency procedures so that you are well prepared should you ever be in a pressurized situation. Make sure that you brief the crew on your plans and, where possible, practice using emergency and safety gear in controlled conditions. If an emergency develops that you realize is beyond your ability to handle on your own, then the time has come to ask for assistance by using a distress or emergency signal. It is important that you understand the signals used in different situations and which ones are most appropriate for the type of boat you sail. Remember that if you see or hear a distress signal when you are sailing, you are legally obliged to give all possible assistance.

Radio

Sending a distress call by radio is usually the most practical way of seeking assistance, provided that the electricity supply is functioning or you have a battery-operated, hand-held unit. Most yachts carry a VHF radio (very high frequency) and some also use MF radio (medium frequency). The latest sets are designed to use a global safety system called GMDSS (Global Maritime Distress and Safety System). They are fitted with Digital Selective Calling and can be triggered to send an automatic distress signal that identifies the vessel in distress. Usually, a single button that is protected against accidental triggering allows the user to send an automatic distress message immediately, which, if the radio is connected to a GPS set, will also transmit your position to any ships or land stations within range.

If you have an older VHF radio, then you should transmit distress, emergency, and safety signals on VHF Channel 16 (or 2182 kHz on an MF transmitter). The recognized radio telephony distress signal is the word MAYDAY and it is used to indicate that a vessel is in grave and immediate danger. Any use of the distress signal imposes general radio silence on all vessels not involved in the emergency. Radio silence must be maintained until the emergency is over and the distress signal is cancelled by the authority controlling the emergency response.

Mayday

If you have to send a distress signal on a non-GMDSS set, check that the radio is switched on, the distress channel is selected, and the radio is set to high power to transmit. The form the message takes is very important. Fix a notice alongside the radio so that any crew member can send the message correctly in an emergency.

HAND-HELD VHF RADIO

Trivia...

There is a large range of safety and emergency equipment on the market but remember that you cannot buy safety – it is an attitude of mind. Pick the gear you need for the type of sailing you do and make sure you know how and when to use the equipment you have.

MAYDAY MAYDAY MAYDAY
THIS IS (name of yacht, repeated three times)
MAYDAY (name of yacht spoken once)
MY POSITION IS (give position in latitude and longitude or bearing and distance from a known point)
State the nature of the emergency
Explain what assistance is required
Give any other information that can help the rescuers
OVER

Listen for a reply, which, if you are sailing in coastal waters, should come at once. If you don't hear a reply, check that the set has power and try again. Once you have made contact, make sure that your position is repeated because this is of vital importance.

Other distress signals

Urgency signals are used in situations where you need to transmit an urgent message, but when you are not yet in grave and imminent danger. This may apply if a crew member needs medical assistance, or if your boat has been rendered helpless but is not in danger of sinking. In such cases, the PAN PAN signal is used (or PAN PAN MEDICO for a medical emergency) – repeated three times. It is usually broadcast initially on Channel 16, but you can normally switch to a working channel once contact has been made with a coastal radio station, coastguard, or other vessel. The PAN PAN signal takes priority over all but a MAYDAY message. The third type of safety signal consists of the word SÉCURITÉ spoken three times. This indicates that the transmitting station is about to transmit an important safety, navigational, or weather warning.

Another radio aid increasingly found aboard yachts is an EPIRB (emergency-position-indicating radio beacon). This transmits a distress signal to GMDSS satellites.

The satellites locate the EPIRB's position and then relay the signal and the position to an earth station and rescue co-ordination center. When you purchase an EPIRB, you must register it and give the details of the vessel to which it belongs so that search and rescue services have this information in the event of the EPIRB being activated. Larger offshore yachts are increasingly fitted with satellite communications systems for email, fax, and sometimes telephone connections. These systems are also able to transmit distress signals to the GMDSS system at the touch of a button.

Receiving a distress signal

If you hear a radio distress or emergency signal, wait to see if a rescue center responds. Meanwhile, note the position of the vessel in distress and plot it on your chart to see how close you are to the other boat. If you do not hear a reply, then you should reply to the call yourself before transmitting a further call – called a MAYDAY RELAY. Use the same format as for a MAYDAY signal but repeat MAYDAY RELAY three times and give the details of the other boat's distress situation together with your position details.

It may be that you are closer to a shore station than the other boat and your transmission will be heard whereas they are too far away to make contact. In this case you will have to relay details between the boat in distress and the rescue services. You should follow the instructions of the rescue controller throughout the emergency. If you cannot make contact with the rescue services or a larger ship, you will have to respond as best you can to reach the other boat and offer whatever assistance you can.

Flares

All boats that sail on the sea or large stretches of inland water should carry flares as a primary means of signalling distress. Ensure you have more flares than the minimum needed – flares may fail to ignite and you may not be seen immediately. All flares have limited life spans and should be replaced when necessary: they can be returned to a chandler for safe destruction. Store them where they are readily accessible but kept dry.

When using any flare, ignite it according to the directions on the flare, hold it high, and point it downwind. Rocket flares turn into the wind when launched so point them downwind, about 15° off vertical in strong winds, or near vertical in light winds.

■ **A red parachute** *fires a bright red flare up to 1,000 ft (300 m) and burns for about 40 seconds. They are not effective in low cloud, when they should be fired at 45° downwind to keep them under the cloud.*

The hand-held white flare is not a distress signal but it is an effective warning of a collision risk. The hand-held red flare is for use when you are within sight of assistance, to indicate your exact position. The hand-held orange smoke flare is for use in daylight and offers good visibility, particularly in light winds.

The buoyant orange smoke is used for signalling position to searching aircraft. Once ignited, it is dropped into water to leeward of the boat and it emits a dense orange smoke. To attract attention when you are some distance from help, use a red parachute flare. Mini-flares are for personal use and are either hand-held, or rocket type.

Ensure your crew members understand how to use flares and where they are stored, as well as the importance of not using them unless instructed to do so by the skipper.

■ **For a simple** *distress signal, slowly raise and lower your arms.*

Other signals

If you are sailing a dinghy and are in sight of the shore or another boat, you can signal for help by standing in the boat and slowly and repeatedly raising and lowering your outstretched arms from down by your sides to above your shoulders. Do not simply wave your arms, as this is likely to be misinterpreted as a friendly wave!

In a cruiser, radio, flares, and EPIRBs are the main methods for signalling distress, but there are other methods that can be used when in sight of another vessel or the shore. Code flag V signals "I require assistance," code flag W signals "I require medical assistance," and code flags N flown over C indicate "I am in distress and require assistance." A black square shape flown above or below a black ball shape also indicates distress, as does the Morse code distress signal SOS (...---...), which can be signalled by a flashlight or a proper signalling lamp, or with a foghorn.

■ **Code flag N is flown** *above Code flag C, to indicate distress. It is a good idea to carry the flags that are used to summon help in case you are unable to use an EPIRB, radio, or flares.*

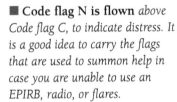

■ **Code flag V** *indicates that you require assistance, such as a tow, but are not in distress.*

■ **Use the code flag W** *to signal that you are in need of medical assistance.*

■ **Even if you have no** *flags, you can hoist a black square shape over a round black shape to indicate distress.*

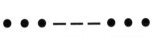

SOS SIGNAL – SIGNALS DISTRESS

Being towed and towing

WHEN A BOAT has been disabled, it may be necessary to tow it to sheltered waters to effect repairs. Towing may appear easy to the uninitiated, but it is difficult, and serious damage can be caused if the sea state is at all rough.

Being towed

If your boat has been disabled, you may have to accept a tow. Towing at sea is difficult and has to be handled correctly if there is to be any chance of success. You must also be aware that a tow may make you liable for a salvage claim by the towing vessel – try and negotiate an agreed fee at the outset. Also note that a yacht or cruising power boat is not well equipped for serious towing because it places high loads on both craft. The towed yacht is particularly vulnerable if a much larger vessel is towing it. Don't take a tow from a large ship unless there is no alternative, and always rig a suitable towing bridle to distribute the loads among all the yacht's strongest points.

Rig long lines to form a towing loop (bridle) at the bow, with the lines leading from the bow cleats back to the cockpit winches, stern cleats, and mast. Attach the towing line or chain to the towing loop and use plenty of chafe protection on the towing line where it passes through the bow roller or fairlead. It is best to use a springy nylon line or chain for towing to help absorb the high shock loads.

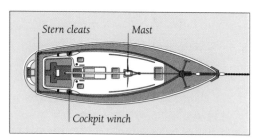

Stern cleats   Mast

Cockpit winch

■ **When you are being towed**, *distribute the load over as many strong points as possible.*

Towing

The boat to be towed should rig a bridle, while you rig a stern bridle so that the loads are distributed over strong points, such as at the stern cleats and on your sheet winches.

Do not simply attach a tow rope to a single stern cleat because this will make it difficult for you to steer the boat.

Attach a stern bridle by fastening one end of a line to a sheet winch and then to the stern cleat on the same side. Lead the other end out through a fairlead. Take the bridle out around the stern and back inboard through the fairlead on the opposite side. Fasten that end to the stern cleat and winch on that side. You now have a loop around the stern to which you can attach the towrope with a bowline. Better still, put a large shackle on the bridle and tie the towrope to the shackle.

Pass slowly close by the other boat's bow and pass or throw the end of the towrope across. Motor slowly ahead of the other boat, keeping the tow rope clear of your propeller. Keep paying out the towrope and, once it is made fast on the other boat, motor gently forwards until the strain comes on the rope and then set a suitably slow speed for the tow.

As a rough guide, the towrope should be at least three times the length of the longest boat, but as long as possible if you are towing in waves or if the line keeps jerking taut. In rough weather, you may need to add a weight, such as an anchor, to the middle of the line to prevent or reduce jerking. Another solution is to attach the towrope to the towed boat's anchor chain to add weight.

INTERNET

www.uscg.mil/
www.ccg-gcc.gc.ca

The US and Canadian Coastguard sites have safety and services information.

Abandoning ship

IN EXTREME CASES, *a situation may develop to the point where you have no choice but to abandon ship. The decision to do so must be very carefully considered. Unless the yacht is in imminent danger of sinking, it is usually safer to stay with the yacht. There are many cases where crews have taken to the apparent safety of a liferaft only to perish while the yacht survived. Sometimes the yacht may be badly damaged and the presence of a ship or helicopter may offer the chance to abandon the yacht in relative safety. The pressure then is on the skipper to abandon ship to protect the crew in case the situation deteriorates.*

Preparing to abandon ship

Speed is vital if you are faced with the need to abandon a sinking yacht, and your liferaft is the only option open to you. Prepare the liferaft for launching and get the crew to dress in their warmest clothing with full foul-weather gear, harnesses, and lifejackets. Watertight containers should be filled with extra water, and cans of food and a can opener should be collected. A chart, compass, and plotting equipment will be useful, as will a hand-held GPS set, a portable VHF unit, extra flares, and a flashlight. An offshore yacht should have a ready-prepared panic bag containing such items ready to grab in an emergency.

With everything prepared, don't rush to launch the raft. The best advice is not to step off the boat until it is about to sink under you.

Using the liferaft

A liferaft should be of a type approved by your national authority and should be big enough to accommodate the whole crew. Familiarize yourself with how the inflation mechanism works, and attend a survival course to learn how to board and use a raft.

When you are ready to launch the raft, cut or untie its lashings but leave its painter tied on the vessel. Launch the raft by throwing its container over the leeward side. After a sharp tug on the painter, the raft will take about 30 seconds to inflate. As soon as it is inflated, the first crew member boards the raft. In rough seas this will be difficult, but try and stay dry, because this will help your survival chances. Once the first person is in the raft, an additional painter should be rigged. The raft's painter is designed to break to prevent the raft being dragged down by a sinking vessel but in rough seas there is a danger that it will break before everyone is aboard. Once all the crew are aboard, both painters are released.

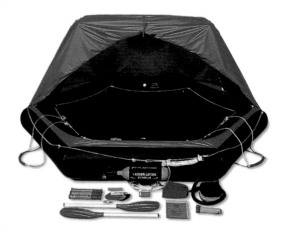

■ **Liferafts** *are available in different sizes and types. Pick one to suit the sort of sailing you do and make sure it has appropriate survival equipment.*

Bail out any water in the raft and try to keep it dry because it will help you stay warm.

Shut all openings in the canopy and stream the drogue – a parachute-shaped piece of material that can be attached to the bow or stern to reduce drift and stabilize the liferaft in severe weather.

Rescue by helicopter

Helicopters are often used for search and rescue operations when the casualty is within flying range of the coast. The helicopter's crew will communicate with you directly, usually using marine VHF. Always follow their orders and help them complete the rescue as quickly as possible, because the time they will be able to spend hovering will be limited. The helicopter will be unable to hover directly over the yacht because of the danger of becoming entangled in the rig. The helicopter's crew may decide to pick up the yacht's crew from a dinghy streamed on a line behind the yacht or from the water. All the crew should don lifejackets and if they have to use the dinghy they should connect it to the yacht with a long line of about 100 ft (30 m). The helicopter will either lower one or two lifting strops, or send a winchman down to assist the survivors. In rough conditions, you may have to be picked up from the water.

In this case, each crew member in turn should be tied to a long line before entering the water to drift astern of the yacht, ready to be retrieved by the helicopter.

Alternatively, the helicopter may use a Hi-Line method. A long nylon line, with a weight on the lower end and with the upper end attached to the recovery hook, is lowered across the yacht. Once the yacht's crew have the line, the helicopter will move off to one side of the yacht. The line must not be made fast on board but should be pulled in as the helicopter lowers the winchman or lifting strop. The line is attached to the lifting hook by a weak link designed to break if the line snags.

Be careful not to touch the winch wire until its end has been grounded by the sea, because static electricity can give a fatal shock.

Once the winchman is on board, follow his instructions. When the winchman and the first survivor are being lifted off the yacht, the nylon line is fed out. Keep hold of the end if further casualties are to be lifted.

Rescue by ship

If a ship or lifeboat comes to your assistance, follow her skipper's instructions. A lifeboat will normally come alongside and your crew should be ready to board it. A large ship may lower a boat if the size of the seas permit, but in rough seas it may stop to windward of the yacht to create a smoother area in her lee. Be aware that the ship will drift downwind rapidly and the yacht and her crew could be vulnerable to a collision. The ship's crew will lower a ladder or net over the side for you to climb up. If you have to jump for a ladder or net, wait until the yacht is on the top of a wave to avoid being crushed between the ship and the yacht.

A simple summary

✔ Do not call for emergency assistance in a situation that is inconvenient but not dangerous.

✔ Make sure you understand how to use and interpret all the necessary distress signals.

✔ Plan in advance how you will arrange the tow rope if you have to be taken under tow or if you have to tow another boat.

✔ Unless a ship, lifeboat, or helicopter is standing by to rescue you, do not abandon your boat until it is about to sink.

Ropes and Knots

Handling ropes

When you are tying knots, you need to be familiar with a few basic terms used to identify the parts of a rope and some simple techniques that are particular to sailing.

Loop   Crossing turn

Standing part

Working end

Round turn   Simple turn

■ **A loop** is an uncrossed circle. For a crossing turn, one part of the rope crosses another.

■ **The rope goes** one and a half times around an object for a round turn and once around for a simple turn.

Cleating

A common way of securing a rope on a sailing boat is to fasten it to a horned cleat. The rope is attached to the two horns of the cleat by a series of figure-eight turns.

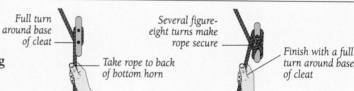

Full turn around base of cleat

Take rope to back of bottom horn

Several figure-eight turns make rope secure

Finish with a full turn around base of cleat

1 **A full turn**

Start at the back and bring the working end once around the cleat to make a full turn.

2 **Figure-eight turns**

Take the rope up behind the top horn, then across the front of the cleat, and back behind the bottom horn to form a figure-eight.

Figure-eight

A figure-eight is a stopper knot used in sailing to prevent a rope end from running out through a block or fairlead. It is a simple knot to tie, does not jam, and is easily undone even when it has been under load.

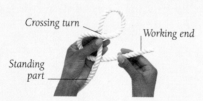

Crossing turn

Working end

Standing part

Standing part

Crossing turn

1 **The crossing turn**

Make a crossing turn, and bring the working end of the rope around and behind the standing part of the rope.

2 **Tying the knot**

Bring the working end up to the top of the knot and then pass it through the center of the crossing turn. Pull both ends to tighten.

Bowline

If you learn only one knot before you go sailing, make it the bowline (pronounced "bowlin"). This knot is used to make a loop in the end of a rope or to tie to a ring or post. The bowline cannot be untied under load.

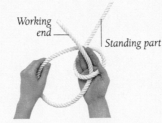

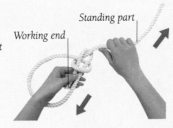

1 The working end

Hold the working end over the standing part. Bend your fingers down to push the working end under the standing part.

2 A crossing turn

Turn the hand and the working end clockwise so that a crossing turn is created around the hand and the working end.

3 Pull to tighten

Pass the working end behind the standing part and down through the crossing turn. Tighten by pulling on the two ends.

Reef or square knot

This knot is used for tying the ends of rope of equal diameter and is named after its most common use, which is tying the ends of a sail's reef lines when putting in a reef. Remember: left over right, then right over left.

1 Left over right

Take the rope under the object and cross the left end over the right end.

2 Two working ends

Bring the left working end up, over, and behind the right working end.

3 Right over left

Bring both ends up and tuck the now right working end over the left and through the middle.

4 Tighten the knot

Pull on both working ends to create and tighten this distinctive square-shaped knot.

Clove hitch

The clove hitch is used for mooring a boat temporarily to a ring or post, or for hitching fenders to a rail. If you wish to make the clove hitch more secure, keep a long working end.

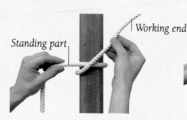

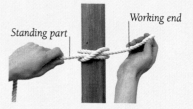

1 Make a turn

Take the rope around the post, bringing the working end up over the standing part.

2 One more turn

Make another turn in the same direction, taking the working end behind and bring it to the front.

3 Make the knot

Tuck the working end under the second turn. Pull on both ends of the rope together to tighten the knot.

Sheet bend

A sheet bend is one of the best ways of joining two ropes together. If the two ropes are of different diameter, make the loop in the thicker rope. For more security, tie a double sheet bend by taking an additional turn around the loop (repeat steps 2 and 3).

1 Make a loop

Start with a loop in the first rope. Pass the working end of the other rope through it.

2 Pass the working end behind

The working end of the second rope goes over the short part of the loop, then up, behind the loop.

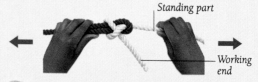

3 Back to the front

Bring the working end of the second rope over the long part of the loop and under itself.

4 Tighten the knot

Pull on the loop and the standing part of the second rope to tighten the sheet bend.

Sailing on the Web

THE INTERNET is an excellent resource for sailors, with many sailing-related sites covering all aspects of racing and cruising in large boats or small.

www.american-sailing.com

Check out this site of the American Sailing Association for their wide range of sail courses and locations.

www.apparent-wind.com/sailing-page.html

This is Mark Rosenstein's sailing page – one of the oldest sailing-related sites on the Web. It contains a large number of links to other Web-based sailing resources.

www.boats.com
www.boatforsale.org
www.ancasta.co.uk

Visit brokerage sites like these for used boats and to compare specifications and prices.

www.boatsafe.com
www.csbc.ca

These sites specialize in information about safe and responsible boating, training courses, and links to other safety-related boating sites.

www.bostonsailingcenter.com

The Boston Sailing Center is one of the leading sailing schools in the United States.

www.capjack.com/
www.powercruising.com/macnaut.html

Many sites such as these offer software navigation tools.

www.fijiyachting.com/nav.html

There are many resources on the Web that can help with passage planning, such as this site on navigation in Fiji.

www.gosailing.com
www.sailnet.com
www.uksail.com

These US and UK sites offer lots of useful sailing content.

www.laserinternational.org
www.lasersailing.com

The International Laser Class Association's site and the Laser Center's site will tell you all you need to know about the popular Olympic singlehander class.

www.marlowropes.co.uk/yachting

Visit Marlow Ropes' web site for comprehensive information on rope for halyards, sheets, and lines.

weather.noaa.gov/
www.weather.ec.gc.ca
www.meto.gov.uk
www.meteo.fr

The national weather centers of many countries are good starting points for online weather information.

www.musto.co.uk

Musto makes a wide selection of outer and under garments for all types of sailing and is a leading manufacturer in the sailing clothing market.

www.racingrules.org

This is a useful site for learning about the rules that govern all types of sailboat racing.

www.raymarine.com
www.greenham-regis.com

These sites are good starting points when looking for electronic instruments.

www.realknots.com/knots/index.htm

If ropes and tying knots capture your imagination, this site will tell you all you need to know.

www.rival-bowman.co.uk

This UK company, Rival Bowman Yachts, makes the Starlight and Bowman range of cruising yachts, including the Starlight 35.

www.sailing.ca

The Canadian Yachting Association's site provides news and information about recreational sailing and racing.

www.sailing.org

This is the site of the International Sailing Federation (ISAF). It has information on the organization of world sailing (mostly racing) and has links to national authorities for sailing.

www.sailingsource.com
www.madforsailing.com

These are useful sites for news and articles on sailing.

www.sailing-tv.com

This site has video coverage of top-class racing events. You can view sailors in action to see how performing the basic skills well is crucial to good boat handling.

www.sailmakers.com
www.yourguide.net/boating/

Check out these sites for information on sail manufacturers.

www.sailsail.com

Visit this UK site for links to dinghy and keelboat classes and for a good summary of the latest racing news.

www.seldenmast.com

Seldén Masts supply rigs and all the ancillary parts for most yachts, from dinghies to cruisers. They also offer a useful guide to handling a spinnaker on a cruising boat.

www.setsail.com

This is a great site for anyone interested in long-distance cruising. It has lots of practical advice on boat handling, cruising matters, and weather forecasting.

www.silverpetrel.com

This site follows the progress of the rebuild of my own boat, an Ohlson 38 called Silver Petrel.

www.sonar.org

This Sonar Class site features the popular 23 ft (7 m) International Sonar keelboat, which is popular for training and offers high-quality racing.

www.uscg.mil
www.ccg-gcc.gc.ca

The US and Canadian Coastguard sites have safety and services information.

www.ussailing.org
www.american-sailing.com
www.rya.org.uk

Check out these sites for recognized sailing schools and courses in the US and UK.

www.westmarine.com
www.on-line-marine.com

These two online chandlery sites are useful for purchasing equipment or researching alternatives and prices.

www.yachtpaint.com
www.brava.it
www.epifanes.com
www.hempel.com

If you need to find out about any aspect of painting, varnishing, or antifouling a boat, you can find the information you need on one of these paint manufacturers' sites.

www.yourguide.net/boating/

This site provides information about sailing schools, boat sales, yacht clubs, and sailmakers in Ontario.

A simple glossary

Abaft Behind or toward the stern of a boat.

Abeam At right angles to the fore-and-aft line of a boat.

Aft Toward, at, or near the stern of a boat.

Anchor A heavy device used to secure a boat to the sea- or riverbed and attached via a rope or chain.

Anchorage A safe place to drop anchor.

Anchor windlass The crank mechanism, sometimes motorized, that raises the anchor on some cruisers by winding the rope or chain around a drum.

Angle of attack The angle between the front part of the sail and the wind.

Astern Backward, behind the boat.

Backstay The wire that leads from the mast to the stern.

Balance A dinghy is balanced when it is kept upright – fore and aft and side to side – by the crew's weight.

Balanced helm When a boat has a balanced helm, it has neither weather nor lee helm and will tend to follow a straight line if the tiller is released.

Batten A wooden or plastic strip that slots into a pocket in the leech of a sail to support the roach.

Beam reach Sailing with the wind blowing directly over the side of the boat.

Bearing The direction of an object from your boat, or between two objects.

Bearing away Turning away from the wind.

Beating Sailing close-hauled to windward and zigzagging to reach an objective to windward.

Beaufort scale A scale for measuring wind strength.

Bermudan mainsail A three-sided mainsail.

Bermudan sloop A rig with a triangular mainsail and a single headsail.

Berth A place to park alongside a quay or dock.

Bilge The parts of the hull where the sides curve in to form the bottom of the boat.

Bilge keel A twin keel.

Bilge pump A pump that removes water from the bilge.

Binnacle The pedestal on which the steering wheel is mounted.

Block A pulley through which a rope may be passed.

Boltrope A reinforcing rope along a sail edge.

Boom A horizontal pole along the foot of a sail used to control the sail's position in the wind.

Boom vang A line to stop the boom from rising while the mainsail is set.

Bow The front end of a boat.

Bow line A mooring rope that runs from the bow to a point ashore. Also known as the head rope.

Bowline (pronounced "bowlin") A knot that makes a loop in the end of a rope for tying to a ring or post.

Broach When a boat turns broadside to the waves. This can happen in moderate to strong winds if the sails are not balanced adequately.

Broad reach Sailing with the wind coming over the port or starboard quarter of the boat.

Buoyage The system of navigation marks used to identify hazards and safe channels.

Cabin The accommodation below deck.

Cabin sole The floor of the living quarters.

Capsize A boat tipping over to 90° or 180°.

Cardinal marks Buoys used to indicate hazards.

Catamaran A twin-hulled boat.

Centerboard A plate that pivots up and down below the hull to resist leeway.

Centerline The centre of a boat fore–aft.

Chart A nautical map.

Chart datum Level from which soundings and drying heights are measured.

Cleat A fitting used to secure a rope.

Clew The lower aft corner of a sail.

Close-hauled Sailing as close to the wind as possible.

Close reach A course between close-hauled and a beam reach.

Coach roof The raised part of the cabin in the middle of a boat.

Cockpit The working area from where a boat is steered.

Col Regs The official regulations aimed at preventing collisions at sea.

Compass north The direction to which a compass points.

Crew All those aboard. The crew may be a single person on a dinghy.

Cruiser Usually refers to a boat with built-in accommodation.

Cruising Traveling under sail to visit a number of destinations.

Daggerboard A plate that can be lowered through its case out of the hull to resist leeway.

Dinghy A small boat that can be powered by oars, sails, or an outboard engine.

Dismasting The occurrence of a broken mast.

Displacement A term to describe the weight of a boat.

Downhaul A rope for hauling down sails or controlling a spinnaker pole.

Downwind A course that is further away from the wind than a beam reach is known as a downwind, or offwind, course.

DR Dead reckoning position plotted by drawing the course steered from the last known position.

Drift The strength of a tidal stream.

Drogue A parachute-like device towed behind a boat to reduce speed.

EPIRB Emergency-position-indicating radio beacon. This transmits distress signals to satellites that are part of the GMDSS.

Fairlead Any bolt, ring, or loop that guides a rope.

Fender An oblong or oval cushion used to prevent damage to the hull while moored alongside.

Figure-eight A knot used to prevent a rope from running out through a fairlead.

Flying sail When a headsail is attached only at the tack, clew, and head, and not to the forestay, it is said to be a flying sail.

Foils The rudder and centerboard.

Foot The bottom edge of a sail.

Fore Toward the front of the boat.

Foredeck The deck that is nearest to the bow.

Forestay A stay that runs from the mast to the bow and holds the mast upright.

Freeboard The height of the topsides out of the water.

Galley The boat's kitchen.

Gennaker A cross between a genoa and a spinnaker.

Genoa A large headsail.

Gooseneck A fitting that attaches the boom to the mast.

GMDSS Global Maritime Distress and Safety System. This produces an automated distress signal identifying the vessel and transmitting its position (if fitted with a GPS set).

GPS The Global Positioning System receives information from a network of satellites to plot a boat's position accurately.

Groundtrack The course followed relative to the seabed.

Guardrails Safety rails fitted to the edge of the deck.

Gunwale (pronounced "gunnel") The top edge of the hull.

Guy A rope that controls the spinnaker pole.

Halyard A rope used to hoist a sail.

Hand bearing compass A portable compass.

Hanks The clips used to attach a sail to the forestay.

Head The top corner or edge of a sail.

Head Usually refers to the toilet on board a boat but can also mean the compartment containing toilet, washbasin, and shower.

Headrope *See* Bow line.

Headsail A sail set in front of the mast.

Heaving-to Bringing a boat to a halt by sheeting the headsail to windward.

Heel When a boat tilts to one side as it sails.

Helmsman The person steering the boat.

Hiking straps Webbing straps under which the crew can secure their feet when leaning out.

Hove-to A boat at a standstill, after the headsail has been sheeted to windward.

Hull The outer shell of the boat; the part that sits in the water.

Hull speed The maximum speed at which a boat can be pushed through the water and is a function of the boat's length.

IALA International Association of Lighthouse Authorities – the association responsible for the organization of buoys.

Impeller pump A pump with a propeller-like rotator.

Inboard engine An engine located in the hull.

Jib A triangular headsail.

Jibing Turning the stern of the boat through the wind.

Jib sheets Ropes used to trim the jib.

Jury rig A temporary rig constructed in the event of a dismasting situation.

Kedge anchor A small anchor in addition to the main anchor.

Keelboat A boat with a weighted keel under the hull.

Knot A unit of speed – 1 nautical mile per hour.

Latitude Grid lines on a map or chart that run from east to west, parallel to the equator.

Leech The aft edge of a sail.

Lee helm A boat has lee helm if it turns to leeward when you release the tiller.

Lee shore A shore is a lee shore when the wind blows onto the land.

Leeward (pronounced "loo'ard") Downwind, away from the wind – the opposite of windward.

Leeway The difference between the course steered and the course actually sailed through the water.

Lifejacket A flotation device that provides full support to a person in the water.

Lifelines Coated wires surrounding the boat, supported by stanchions.

Logbook A written record of the boat's position, course, and distance run.

Longitude Grid lines on a chart or map that run from north to south, between the poles.

Long keel A traditional style of keel that runs along half to three-quarters of the length of a vessel.

Luff The forward edge of the sail.

Luffing up Turning toward the wind.

Magnetic north The direction of the magnetic north pole.

Magnetic variation The angular difference between magnetic north and true north.

Mainsail (pronounced "mains'l") The principal sail.

Mainsheet A rope attached to the boom and used to adjust (trim) the mainsail.

Man overboard pole A floating marker pole attached to a float.

Mast The vertical pole to which the sails are attached.

Mast step A wooden block or metal frame, which holds the bottom of the mast in place.

MAYDAY The international distress signal to be repeated three times when you are in serious danger.

Monohull A single-hulled boat.

Mooring A system of cables and anchors to which a boat can be moored.

Mooring line A rope used to secure a boat.

Nautical almanac A source of tidal and navigational information for a given area.

Nautical mile A unit of distance defined as 1 minute of latitude. It is slightly longer than a land mile.

Neap tides The opposite of spring tides, these tides have the smallest range between high and low water.

Oarlocks Fittings on each gunwale that support the oars and enable them to be pivoted to row the boat.

Onshore Directly or at an angle to the shoreline.

Outboard engine An engine that is mounted on the exterior of the hull – usually on the transom.

PAN PAN The international urgency call that takes priority over all other calls, except MAYDAY.

Passage A single sailing journey between two ports.

Personal flotation device A device that provides support in the water but is not as supportive as a full lifejacket.

Pilotage Navigation when in sight of land.

Plotter A device used to plot a course on a chart.

Point of sail The direction in which a boat is sailed relative to its angle to the wind.

Port The left side of the boat when you look forward.

Position line Used in navigation to enable you to plot a fix on a chart.

Pre-bend The amount of bend set in the mast.

Prop walk The movement produced by the propeller.

Pulpit The metal rail around the bow of a boat.

Reaching Sailing with the wind on the beam.

Reef To reduce sail area.

Reef points Lines that are sewn into a sail to tie up the loose fold when the sail is reefed.

Rig The system of sails and mast.

Roach The curved part of a sail on the leech, that is outside the straight line from the head to the clew.

Rode The rope between boat and anchor.

Rudder An underwater blade controlled by a tiller or wheel to steer a boat.

Safetrack A course followed in constricted water.

Seacock A valve in the hull.

SÉCURITÉ A safety signal, indicating that a transmitting station is about to send a safety, navigational, or weather warning.

Set The direction in which the tide flows.

Sheaves The pulley wheels in a block.

Sheet A rope attached to a sail or boom used to adjust (trim) the sail's angle to the wind.

Shroud Wire ropes either side of the mast.

Skeg A projection from the hull that supports the rudder.

Slipway A launching ramp.

Spar Pole-shaped nautical equipment.

Spinnaker A large downwind sail.

Sport boat A small, fast, day-racing keelboat.

Spring tides Tides that have the largest range between high and low tides.

Stanchion A post that supports the lifelines.

Starboard The right-hand side of the boat when you look forward.

Stern The rear part of a boat.

Stern pulpit The metal rail around the stern of a boat.

Tack Front, lower corner of a sail.

Tacking Turning the bow through the wind.

Telltales Strips of fabric that blow in the wind to indicate the best trim for the sail.

Tender A small boat carried aboard a larger boat for transportation of people and provisions.

Thwart A seat fixed across a dinghy or tender.

Tidal current The horizontal flow of water caused by the rise and fall of the tide.

Tidal drift The strength of a tidal stream.

Tiller A handle used to direct the rudder.

Transit Two objects in transit are in line with each other and the observer.

Transom A surface forming the stern of a boat.

Trapeze Supporting wire on high-performance dinghies. Enables crew to stand out from the boat.

Trim Adjustment of the sails.

Trimaran A three-hulled boat.

True north The direction of the true north pole.

Turnbuckle A fitting that adjusts the tension of the shrouds and forestay.

Twist The difference between the angle of a sail at its foot and the angle at its head.

Uphaul or topping lift A rope for adjusting the spinnaker pole; opposite to downhaul.

Water track The course to steer through water in order to achieve the required groundtrack after allowing for tidal stream or current.

Weather helm A boat has weather helm if it turns to windward when you release the tiller.

Weather shore On a weather shore, the wind blows off the land.

Winch A device to pull in a sheet or halyard.

Windage The amount of surface area above the water.

Windlass The winch used to raise the anchor.

Windward Toward the wind.

Windward shore When the wind is blowing away from the shore, it is a windward shore.

Yacht Usually refers to a larger sailing boat with accommodation.

Yachting The sport of sailing was originally more commonly known as yachting.

Index

Acknowledgments

Author's Acknowledgments

My thanks are due to the team of editors and designers at Studio Cactus and at DK who have worked with me on this book, and to all my friends and family who have given me their understanding, yet again, as I immersed myself in writing. Thanks are also due to the United Kingdom Sailing Academy, Rival Bowman Yachts Ltd., Raytheon Marine, Plastimo, Musto, Seldén Masts, and all the other individuals and organizations who provided valuable assistance with the production of this book.

Publisher's Acknowledgments

Dorling Kindersley would like to thank the following people for their contributions to this project: Neal Cobourne for designing the jacket and Melanie Simmonds for picture library research.

Packager's Acknowledgments

Studio Cactus would like to thank Kate Grant for editorial assistance and picture coordination, Sharon Rudd for styling the text, and Barry Robson for the dog illustrations. Thanks also to Polly Boyd for proofreading and to Chris Bernstein for compiling the index.

Picture Credits
t = top, b = bottom, c = center, r = right, l = left

Denise Cronin: 29, 32, 65, 78, 80, 83, 92, 147, 231, 310
Dubarry Footwear: 10
Patrick Eden (www.patrickeden.co.uk): 22, 28, 31, 36, 39, 46, 76, 100, 114, 166, 189, 215, 249, 252, 270, 282, 289, 292, 304, 306, 309, 311, 313, 318, 328
Kingfisher Challenge 2000: 14–15, 16–17, 30, 44, 244
Musto Limited: 6, 7, 8, 49tl, 49cr, 49bl, 50cl, 50cr, 50br, 51, 52tr, 52bl, 53
Plastimo: 12, 13, 102, 206, 259, 272, 280, 330, 334, 338
Raytheon Marine Company: 9, 11, 258, 279, 333
Steve Sleight: 226, 281
Studio Cactus: 37, 42, 52br, 64, 70, 71, 72, 194, 246
Turtle Photography (www.turtlephotography.co.uk): 34, 66, 98, 116, 126, 136, 142tr, 142cr, 148, 159, 160, 162, 165, 169, 170, 172, 177, 179. 181
Alan Williams/Dorling Kindersley: 186

Jacket
Christel Clear Marine Photography: Front bl
Patrick Eden: Back tl, cl
Musto Limited: Back bl
Turtle Photography: Jacket flap

All other images © Dorling Kindersley.
For further information see: www.dkimages.com